BREAD, JAM AND A BORROWED PRAM

A nurse's story from the streets

BREAD, JAM AND A BORROWED PRAM

A nurse's story from the streets

DOT MAY DUNN

ISIS

LARGE PRINT

Oxford

First published in Great Britain 2011
by
Orion Books
An imprint of The Orion Publishing Group Ltd.

Published in Large Print 2012 by ISIS Publishing Ltd.,
7 Centremead, Osney Mead, Oxford OX2 0ES
by arrangement with
The Orion Publishing Group Ltd.
An Hachette UK Company

British Library Cataloguing in Publication Data
Dunn, D. M. (Dot M.)
    Bread, jam and a borrowed pram.
    1. Dunn, D. M. (Dot M.) - - Diaries.
    2. Visiting nurses - - England - - Birmingham - -
    Diaries.
    3. Birmingham (England) - - Social conditions - -
    20th century.
    4. Large type books.
    I. Title
    610.7'3'092–dc23

        ISBN 978–0–7531–5308–6 (hb)
        ISBN 978–0–7531–5309–3 (pb)

Printed and bound in Great Britain by
T. J. International Ltd., Padstow, Cornwall

To the indomitable spirit of Birmingham people

Prologue

It is 1958 and Dot, a young nurse recently qualified as a midwife, has a new adventure ahead. With few Community Midwife posts available, Dot has trained as a Health Visitor and been posted to an inner-city clinic. Now Dot is preparing to set out on the streets, visiting the children and parents who need her most. With just her case-notes and her black bag in hand, Dot's work will take her into family homes of all kinds and into a fascinating world, all recorded by her diaries.

CHAPTER
ONE

Monday, 8th September 1958

9.00a.m.

With a roar, and a belch of diesel fumes, the bus pulls away from the pavement's edge and my friends are gone. I know they will climb to the top deck; Janet will have to have "a quick puff" and Joyce, moaning about smokers, will be behind her. I search the bus windows for them but already they seem to have vanished inside. I peer down the road but the bus has gone and with it my student days.

I had trained as a midwife and, during my training, had been attracted to Community Midwifery but it was already on the wane and no posts were being filled. Midwifery on the ward at the Burlington General Hospital had not been for me and, keen to get out and about, I had applied to Burlington Council for a place on their Health Visitor's Course, and had been accepted.

Janet and Joyce had been my constant companions on the course; through all trials, tribulations and the impossibly hard subject matter, they had been there. But the year has ended; we three have passed the examinations, and have celebrated to the fullest extent.

Now we are trained to work in preventive medicine and this morning, one by one, we stood before the Director of Health Visitors and signed contracts to work as Health Visitors. I will be working in Maternity and Child Health, based in one of the city's Child Health Clinics. As well as running clinics for both children and antenatal women, I will be expected to visit, on a regular basis, all homes where a woman is pregnant or where there are children under the age of five years old. I have been told that my patch will be in the centre of the city; Lancaster Street Clinic to be exact. Janet and Joyce are to work in the suburbs. I can't quite believe our time together is over, but at the same time I am eager to start my new job.

A small, oval, pewter-coloured badge now resides on the lapel of my jacket and announces, to anyone who would wish to enquire, that I work for the city of Burlington. I think of the lessons drilled into me. We have been informed many times that we visit not just the child but the whole family, that we take with us nothing but our black bag and our professional knowledge, and that we offer a non-judgemental ear and advice to suit every need. We have no right of entry to any person's property; we must, by our professional behaviour, seek, and if possible obtain, such permission. Should entry be denied and we deem it essential, we may seek the support of the Medical Officer.

As I run my thumb across my badge to reassure myself that it's there, I think with relief how glad I am that I have been reimbursed for the money spent on "suitable clothing to be worn at work." During the last couple of weeks of the course, the Senior Tutor had said with a stern face, "It is your professional knowledge and behaviour which is up for judgement and not your dress. But remember, you are a professional and must appear so — these aren't parties you'll be attending. A yearly allowance will be given, from which a navy-blue suit, three blouses, white, cream or light blue, two pairs of black or navy shoes, a navy raincoat, a navy top coat and a navy hat, must be purchased. Do not spend great amounts of money on your first suit; in time you will need a warm winter coat, believe me."

This morning receipts have been presented, and the suitability of our purchases examined. I am pleased to say that my new clothes have been deemed acceptable and I have been reimbursed.

Janet and Joyce are gone, and the whirl of the city encompasses me. I have walked away from the bus stop and, as I turn, my reflection in a shop window looks at me. The neat dark suit with its fitted jacket and calf-length skirt, and the low-heeled shoes, makes my slim, five-foot figure look almost frail, and the light auburn hair, which refuses not to curl, almost hides the navy cap, which sits on the crown of my head. Brushing the hair back under the cap I turn and, with a racing heart and a proud stretch of the mouth, a habit inherited from my four feet ten inches of fiercely determined mother, I head for my own stop, from which I know the bus to Lancaster Street Child Health Clinic leaves and my new life beckons.

10.00a.m.

"This is your box."

The hand, with its age marks and manicured nails, lies on the top of a brown wooden box. Eighteen inches wide and extending the width of the desk, the brown varnished box looks unimpressive. The voice continues: "As far as I know, the caseload is about a thousand; no one has worked it for the last six months, except for new deliveries, of course."

I look across at her face; grey hair closely surrounds an equally grey face, and small eyes, behind their rimmed glasses, hold little sparkle. Her mouth, whose lipstick has almost disappeared, attempts to widen into a smile and the hand, which she places on my shoulder, I take as an attempt at comradeship.

"I'll leave you to get acquainted with your caseload; you might start with a quick look at your patch." So saying she taps the varnished nail of her forefinger on a piece of cardboard, which resides on the desk against which we both stand. "If you want any help, you know where my office is."

Before I can say that I have no idea where she hides, she has turned and on silent feet has left the room. The door remains open, and although the day outside is sunny and bright, this room is dull and stuffy. The large hall, through which we had just passed, had been equally dull, but because it was large and had no ceiling, only rafters, it felt airy — that is, if you can call that distinct smell of a medical establishment airy.

6

10.15a.m.

I take off my suit jacket, anxious not to crease it on its first outing, and hang it on the back of the upright chair which stands by the desk. I need to still my anxiety by doing something, so taking a deep breath I look around the room. Another desk stands under a high window whose leaded lights let in little illumination. Dominating the ledge of the window, and acting as a screen against sunshine entering to lighten our darkness, the face of the Virgin Mary looks down on a neat and tidy desk. I tell myself, "No doubt about *her* point of view."

Having been brought up during the Second World War, under the influence of the Presbyterian Church but by a Jewish mother, I have long doubted the authenticity of any one brand of religious doctoring. I have also learned not to waste my time in argument with the confirmed so I hold my own council, unless asked for an opinion.

A third desk faces the far wall. Piled high with clinic notes and various pieces of paper, it gives little information about its owner other than that he or she is disorganised.

The ring of a phone fills the room and I almost jump out of my skin. A table stands by the door and a blotting pad with a curled and torn edge, covered many times over with numbers, names and doodles, supports a black Bakelite phone. The ringing continues and no one comes to answer it.

I remind myself that I am now a qualified Health Visitor and that it is my responsibility to deal with cases, so taking a deep breath I answer the phone.

"Lancaster Street Clinic, Miss Compton speaking, may I help you?"

For a moment there is silence then a distinctly Irish, and educated, voice asks, "Is Mrs Burns there please?"

Since entering the building I had seen no one but the superintendent, who had just left me, and whose name I knew to be Miss Hampton, and a clinic clerk, whose name I did not remember, but whom, I recalled, had been introduced as "miss", so I make the assumption that Mrs Burns is a fellow Health Visitor. The voice speaks in my ear again. "Hello, is that the health clinic?"

Now I jump to attention,

"Yes, I'm very sorry for keeping you, but is Mrs Burns a Health Visitor?"

The voice half laughs as it replies. "Yes indeed she is, and you must be Miss Compton the new Health Visitor. I have heard much about you and can I say that you are very welcome."

The voice stops and I wonder if the speaker has gone, but then the voice speaks again. "By the way, I am Father Michael from the presbytery; tell her I will ring later."

The click sounds and the phone goes dead, so assuming that the Virgin Mary looks down on Mrs Burn's desk, I place a note in a suitable position before heading out to explore.

4.00p.m.

I made an attempt to take a look at my patch on foot but the dark factories, the incessant traffic, the invasion

8

of schoolchildren and finally the rain, had sent me searching for the bus.

It is crowded; in fact, it is so crowded that I am unable to put both my feet on the floor. I stand with one foot on top of the other, my face very close to the back of a woman whose toilet has been less than adequate. In these crowded and damp conditions her odour is overpowering. But still the voice of the conductor calls out: "Pass down the bus please; move down the bus as far as you can go."

I can go no further: the large lady blocks my way and almost blocks my airways. Beyond the lady stands a man; his back is broad and bent, and in the grey jacket it stands steadfast, like granite that has stood for millennia. Virgin, untouched, bus space extends before him. Like open range in the cowboy films, it offers space and fresh air. With a jolt I am thrown even deeper into the odorous body and we are both pressed against the granite mass, which moves not an inch. Another man, in a jacket and flat cap, rises from one of the seats off to my right and he fights to gain control of his body as the bus jerks. He leans back against the fogged and wet window, then with much kicking of booted feet he makes it to the central aisle of the bus. Every standing passenger leans to their right as he fights his way down the narrow passageway provided and my odorous companion now sinks into the newly vacated seat with a grunting sigh.

A brawl ensues by the entrance to the bus as schoolchildren in shirt sleeves, workmen in overalls, and women with children in their arms fight to escape the sudden torrential downpour of rain that has swamped us in the past hour. Again the voice shouts, "Only the first three please, get off the bus, sir, only the first three. Two seats upstairs, one passenger inside, get off the platform, sir; I won't start the bus until you do."

The voice continues, but the words are lost. Now I can breathe, and if I lean sideways I can see out of the window. Well, at least I think that I can see out, because the dull grey, damp, silent mass inside the bus seems to be repeated on the other side of the glass as the bus moves, and dark grey walls, with black iron-clad windows, crawl across my vision. They continue to fill the whole of my view for such a length of time that I begin to feel that I am on the wrong bus. I had seen a canal marked on the map of my area, and in my mind I had envisaged the green and pleasant walks of my childhood which I had taken by the Cromford Canal with my father. My father is a coal miner, but much of the time he does have above ground has always been spent in long walks in the Derbyshire countryside. Throughout my childhood I had walked up green hills and down steep dales beside this strong and silent man, pausing only occasionally to examine a hedgerow flower, a shy violet found for Mothering Sunday or a wild orchid in high summer.

But here only wet and bedraggled figures crawl past grey walls, heads drawn into jackets, flat caps pulled low against the rain. Two small shops stand open by the pavement's edge, their insides dark and forbidding, and their windows, made opaque by time and traffic dust, show few wares. The bus passes slowly and a man with

10

hands cupped stands by a shop door; he strikes a match, lowers his head over his hands, and then with head back he watches me crawl past as smoke pours from his nose and mouth.

"Canal! Anyone for the canal?"

As the conductor's voice calls out again, it rises to a higher note to sound above the grinding of the bus's gears, and again I am thrown forward, this time into the smell of engine oil, as the man of granite finally turns, mumbles "sorry," and makes his way off the bus, his lighted cigarette held high. There is much coming and going and several of the windows are wiped; now I know that I am on the right bus and I try again to look for the canal. But from my present vantage point I can see no green, only grey, in all its differing shades.

"Lancaster Street and the Health Clinic, Health Clinic here, miss." The voice rings out and brings me back with a start. All eyes watch me as, with my black leather bag held close to my chest, my face burning red and my once neat jacket steaming, I descend on to the now sunlit pavement.

5.30p.m.
That night, my landlady, Mrs Ramshaw, opens the sitting room door as I close the front door; I had seen the lace curtain move as the gate clicked open, and I knew that she would be waiting for me. It is a well-established house standing in a long row of similar houses in the Moseley area, in what is locally known as a respectable part of town.

11

"Mr Ramshaw, God rest his soul, was an engineer, worked all through the war . . ."

Although I knew that she was not of the Catholic religion, as she had a Methodist chapel prayer book resting on the hall table, she had crossed herself before dabbing the corner of her eye with a small handkerchief. Throughout this well-practised exercise she had not taken her eyes from me.

". . . but there we are, times are now hard and I must let a few rooms."

She had given me this information on my first visit, when I answered her advertisement in the *Burlington Times*.

My boyfriend, Alan, had been delighted when I'd taken a place on Burlington Council's Health Visitor course. It had meant that I would be staying in the city where he was completing, or trying to complete, his doctorate. So when these lodgings, not too far from the university, came on the market I had eagerly snapped them up. But after a year under Mrs Ramshaw's watchful eye, the digs have started to lose their appeal.

"Hah, Miss Compton." She emphasises the double S at the end of my prefix with an outlet of air that sounds like a viper. "I had many applicants for the rooms in my premises; I selected you because you informed me that you were of a sound Presbyterian background."

Without moving her eyes from me she places her hand on the prayer book that continues to remain in its particular, and as far as I know, unmoved, position on

12

the hall table. "Now I hear from your neighbour, Mr Betts, that when I was away last weekend, a gentleman was in your rooms until late into the night, and possibly all night, as he was seen going to the bathroom at an early hour."

The word "rooms" makes me laugh as I have one room for bed and sitting, a small partitioned section as a kitchen, and the toilet facilities are shared with Mr Betts, who is a biology teacher at the local grammar school and who looks and behaves like one of his own bottled specimens. I have no doubt that he had been spying on me until late and that he was up early on the same job. He had, on many occasions, visited my room on the most ridiculous pretences, and I had had difficulty in getting him out before bedtime.

Her voice continues on as I try to head for the stairs and the safety of a closed door.

"This is not the first time that I have had to remind you of the ten-thirty rule. My dear Charles, I know, would not put up with such behaviour in his house, nor would he allow such a laggard, as your gentleman friend appears to be, to enter his estate."

I back towards the stairs mumbling my apologies and saying that it won't happen again. I had known this was coming because Mr Betts had given me the hint when he passed me on the way from the bathroom this morning.

"When the cat's away, hey, Miss Compton?"

He had looked me up and down as I tried to pass him, and had squeezed against me as I entered the steamy bathroom, which still smelt of his keen aftershave.

Now I feel near to tears. My first day as a Health Visitor has been, to say the least, a shock, and now I feel exhausted. I want to take a bath and to change my clothes. And I want to ring Alan. We have known each other for a long time, from our schooldays, in fact. At school he had always been a pleasant boy, tall and slim, with dark blond hair and a ready and infectious smile. We had shared much of our knowledge, our joint delight in mathematics always pulling us together. But I was not to continue on to university because my father had felt that studying would addle my brains. We were reunited when we met at a "hop" at the University Students' Union. I was doing my part two midwifery and Alan was just starting to write his doctoral thesis in mathematics. We have become what they now call "a unit". Alan still has another eighteen months left in which to complete his thesis.

"Maybe another two years," he moans.

When I had given up my midwifery job and taken a Student Health Visitor's wages, money had been short. Alan had lodged with other students and I had taken this room. After my results had come through we had talked about taking a larger flat and moving in together. These arrangements had been discussed two weeks ago at the celebration held for my passing but things at the party had got a bit out of hand, so the arrangements were rather tentative. However, after Mr Betts and Mrs Ramshaw's comment, I decide that they must be put into action, if Alan agrees, that is.

14

CHAPTER
TWO

Tuesday, 9th September

9.00a.m.

As I approach the office on my second day, the large brown doors stand open. Well, at least one side of the door is open; a large bolt, which disappears into a stone slab holds the rest of the heavy door firmly closed. I push on the partly open door; it scrapes across the floor and opens wide enough to let me pass through. The hall is as large as I remembered it to be, but today there is a distinct smell of lavender polish and the wooden upright chairs have been placed in neat rows in the centre of the hall. A woman, dressed in a pink dress and white cap, scurries across the hall, the cloth in her hand busily seeking out grains of dirt that might still reside on any part of the newly arranged chairs. I recognise the maid's uniform and draw breath to speak, but without letting me get out one word she turns partly towards me, drops half a curtsy, and is gone.

Now I realise my mistake. The half-spoken word had sounded the alarm and, like a cat jumping out on a mouse, Miss Hampton appears. Her glasses rest in her hands and the chain which supports them around her neck manages to find a flicker of light, which it reflects across me like a pointing finger. The clock above our heads gives a resounding clunk. Probably it had once chimed, but so much noise is no longer allowed. Her eyes rise, mine follow, and the finger of the clock tells us that it is nine o'clock. Pursing her lips forward and dropping her eyes to mine she speaks.

"Hum! Miss Compton, I know that the working hours are from 9.00a.m. to 5.00p.m., but we do try to be at our desks and ready for work before the appointed hour."

Taking another look at the face of the large round clock, which resides high on a wall between two doors on my right hand side, I start to make my excuses, but changing my mind, instead I say, "Yes, Miss Hampton," and attempt to smile.

I had left my flat quite early; in fact, I had been up early enough to make it to the bathroom before my neighbour. I had walked quickly down to the main road and the bus into town had been on time. However, I had jumped on a different bus than yesterday, and the connecting bus from town to the clinic had been hard to find. The journey had been quite short, in fact short enough to be walked and, had I done so, I would have arrived early.

The hall is now empty. Miss Hampton, having honoured me with a few belligerent stares, has returned to her lair. Not wanting to risk any further contact, I hasten down the hall and head into the office. Today it is not empty, although it is still silent. The back view of a woman, who wears a long-sleeved white blouse and a mid-calf, dark navy-blue skirt, hides much of the desk which stands under the eye of the Virgin Mary. At the far side of the room, a mop of red hair, touching navy-blue clad shoulders, hangs over the other desk. The red mop stirs, the chair pushes back with a scrape, and the tall, well-built body rises. Turning with a cup to her lips the redhead looks at me over its rim, grunts what I hope is an "Hello", picks up a navy beret, crams some of the red mop into it, and, with black bag in her arms, squeezes past me, and is gone. Breathless silence, broken only by the intermittent rustle of paper, fills the room and the Virgin Mary, with impassive stare, looks on. The woman in the white blouse does not move.

My box, carrying my caseload, stands where I had left it, on the table in the middle of the room. Unopened, unexplored, awful but exhilarating, it stands, and with trepidation I approach it. A voice makes me jump. The woman in the white blouse.

"Compton, is it?"

I had expected her to be old and dour, but I am pleasantly surprised. The face is small and round, and the brown hair, neatly waved and curled around it, looks rather like that on the advertisements for the permanent waves, which are in fashion at the moment. The voice, with just the slightest of Irish accents, is lively and bright and the hand, which she extends to me, is manicured, and cared for.

"Miss Compton, how good it is to see you. Father Michael said that he had spoken to you. Always in first is he — I think he does more of my work than I do. By the way, I'm Burns, Mrs Burns."

With a smile extending from one ear to the other I step towards her.

We stand in the kitchen and wait for the kettle to boil.

"Always have a cup before we set off; I've had one, but I can always manage another."

Again the warm smile. She is not a young woman, but her manner is that of a woman younger than her years. I am later to discover that she has recently been married to a rediscovered childhood sweetheart. I have already noted the bright gold band on her left hand which is flashed with great regularity and obvious pride.

"Don't worry about our redheaded colleague — Miss Winthrop seems to be hardly here. She dashes in and out, has her dinner at home, never here with us. By the way, have you brought food for dinner time?"

I shake my head and, passing me a steaming cup and the biscuit tin, she continues without waiting for further comment.

"I've to go almost into town, so I'll try to get something for you, but in future you'd better bring food in with you because you won't be able to buy much on your patch."

Now Mrs Burns has explained the layout of the box on my desk, whose double-sided lids now lie open, I can make more sense of my caseload, and a load it is. The one-year course at the Health Department and the university, which followed nursing and midwifery training, making altogether five-and-a-half-years study, has done little to prepare me for such a titanic enterprise. On the last count, six months ago, there were one thousand and two hundred families under my care; three hundred of these have need of special care and of these, thirty have been designated by my predecessor as being in need of special attention. Mrs Burns has tried to visit some of these families, but has not been able to give them the care which she feels they require as she carries a caseload of equal size and problems of her own.

"Hope that clears thing up a bit! Sorry I can't tell you much more now."

She speaks as she pulls on her coat, and with her black-leather bag, which is bursting with worn cream-coloured envelopes stuffed full of children's case-notes, she is gone.

10.00a.m.
Today the bus is not quite so crowded; I am travelling in the opposite direction and it is mid-morning. On Mrs Burns' advice I have decided to visit those families in my boxes who are designated as needing special care. She had felt that it would be a good way to reconnoitre my area, and my mother had always taught me "if you've got a big job to do you'd better just get started somewhere." I have also found a blue card filed in the new-birth section. This records a prematurely born infant, and although the infant is now almost three weeks old, it has not yet been visited. I had noted that several attempts to visit the family had been made but to no avail. So with the black bag sitting upright on my

lap, and selected cream-coloured envelopes and their contents filling it, along with the blue card, with resolve I once again set out in search of pastures green.

Again we traverse the canal, but I see neither water nor any sign of the green plants that might grow near to water. Today I know that the sky is light, but at this point along my journey the grey walls rise so high that it becomes impossible to see the sky at all; however, if I screw my head sideways against the bus window I can see occasional straggly green plants that fight to rise above the grey chasm. The conductor's voice calls me from my reverie and I struggle to stand whilst controlling my bag.

"Park Lane, anybody for Park Lane?"

Swinging from side to side I head down the bus. As I reach the back of the bus the large West Indian conductor offers me his arm and, swinging off the platform before the bus stops, he helps me to alight.

"Mind the step there, miss. Have a good day."

His smiling face disappears behind bodies as he swings himself back on to the bus.

My predecessor had drawn a rough map of the area, but as I stand beside the dusty, dirty road, whose grey walls seem to continue on into the far distance, once again it seems of little help to me. I had looked at the blue card several times and now know that Baby Broses and his family live at Number 8, Court 7, Upper Thomas Street, and I also know that Upper Thomas Street runs off Park Lane. My expectations had risen when I had seen the name Park Lane; there must be a park with green space and trees within the vicinity, but now hope starts to fail me as I look along the grey vista. A lorry crashes past, barrels rattle loudly in its open back, and suddenly I realise that, far from being overcome by the pollen of overhanging trees, I am being overwhelmed by the sour smell of brewing beer. Hastily I set off up the road. I must get away from this nauseating stench and Park Lane beckons.

There are few road signs to follow but after some searching I see "Park" written on what remains of a sign, which hangs high and precariously over the doorway to a corner shop. A large lady stands in the shop doorway counting money in her hand and I hope that the sign does not choose this moment to fall, though it does look as if it has hung as it is for a good length of time. Park Lane offers no better prospect than the road which I have just left. The flat grey walls have disappeared, but these have been replaced, on both sides of the road, by rows of grey, narrow-fronted houses. Doors, firmly closed and unpainted, face on to the dusty, broken pavement and single windows, heavily curtained, can let in no light, if there was light to be let in.

I check the sign again. Park Lane it is.

"Maybe the park is at the other end of the lane," I tell myself.

The map says that Upper Thomas Street is off to my right, and so it is. Now I need to find Court 7, which must run off Upper Thomas Street. I had, several years ago, been with my father to what remained of a large country house in Derbyshire. Stables had stood behind the house, and from the stables had run a cluster of small cottages; an elderly relative of ours had lived in one of these cottages, in what was called Stable Court. For me, houses in a court are neat and tidy, have small gardens, and plenty of flowers. I look again at the address; yes, I must find a court. But no flowers appear and certainly the smell that invades the air is not of roses or lavender, but of sharp, boiling vinegar. I walk along the row of houses, their fronts grey and still, like a fortress under attack. A woman appears around a corner; I had not noticed an opening. She hobbles towards me, her swollen legs making hard work of the short journey. I step towards her, my hand raised to attract her attention. When she sees me she makes to cross the road, but my speed is greater than hers and I waylay her before she can leave the pavement.

"Excuse me, madam, I wonder if you could help me? I'm looking for Number 8, Court 7."

I look down at the front of the notes in my bag to make sure of the number and her eyes follow mine. Without speaking she raises her finger and points towards the upper part of the grey house against which we stand, and without a word sets off across the road.

I look at the house which stands grey and unmoved. How can this be a court? I walk past two more houses and then, attached high on the front of a house, I see it. A small wooden plaque, with the sign Court 7 burnt into it, directs me to a narrow alleyway.

I step tentatively into the narrow space which runs between two houses. There is no light; it feels damp, cold and inhospitable, and I withdraw.

"Surely this can't lead to homes." It must lead to some factory or works," I tell myself.

I recheck the sign; it has not changed, and no flowering gardens have appeared, so to defend myself with the authority of my position, I draw the black bag up before me and step tentatively into the dismal and narrow space.

After a short distance the alleyway widens and I realise that I have walked past the gable end of a house. Now a step, green with moss, leads down into a small concrete square. The square is almost in darkness and looks so damp that for a moment I think that I am looking down into water. Then I see a door, drab and broken, and beside it a small window, whose panes can not be readily discerned, only its shape giving expression to its function, stands sightless. I check the notes again and with my pulse quickening I step on to the wet black concrete and stand before the door. The number 8 is fastened at an angle and for some stupid reason I try to straighten it. It does not move. Taking a final check of the address I knock at the door. The sound is soft, the door is not hard or heavy, and the sound does not travel. I try again, only this time I bang harder. The door seems to rattle in its frame, but no one replies, no sound comes from within, or from anywhere around. For a moment I am quite pleased; I have no idea what I will find if the door does open, or even if I can handle whatever presents itself. Willing to relinquish my responsibility and to write "no answer at the address" I turn to walk away. But then I see the blue card, and I know that a small infant, weighing no more than five pounds three ounces at birth, should be living somewhere behind that door, and that this is the address that I was given.

Above the step the passageway continues on. Within a few steps it widens to accommodate another door with the number 9 decorating it. Now doors present themselves at both sides of the alleyway, but still little light shows from above. The smell of boiling vinegar makes me retch and in haste I turn to retrace my steps along the alleyway.

"There's little chance of there being a back entrance," I tell myself.

As I pass the side of house number 8, I hear the sound of water running out of a pipe and into a drain. Some of the water splashes onto my shoes, and as I look down at the water the fact dawns on me: if water is being run then someone is at home.

Standing close to the door, I call: "Mrs Broses, I have called to see how you and your baby are getting along. My name is Miss Compton and I work at the Health Centre."

The water stops but no other sound replaces it. My mind tells me, "You have got this far, you must keep trying."

"It is Mrs Broses, isn't it? Only if I've got the wrong address written down I will have to go and check it again, because Baby Broses is quite small and he might need some special food, or some vitamins. I can get these for him from the clinic if I know where he and his mother live."

I stop talking and, holding my breath, I wait to see what happens. The door opens just two inches and an eye looks at me. We seem to watch each other for an age; the eye rests on my face and seems not to move. And then, without another sound, it disappears and the door closes. For a moment I am lost. What I thought I had gained, I have lost. I step forward and, as I reach the door, it opens again. For a moment I see no one, just a black and empty space, and then a hand appears tentatively around the door. The hand moves, beckoning me to enter, and as I pass through it, the door is closed behind me.

I can see little, but I feel her move behind me, and now, from the little light that comes through the window, I can make out a room. A small wooden table, with green painted legs, stands on a woven straw mat in the centre of a small space and a young woman, at first impression no more that seventeen years of age, stands behind it, wringing her hands. An empty fireplace stands on the far wall and a dark and rather ragged curtain hangs beside it. Feeling that I am being rude in staring around her home, I turn my attention towards her, but I feel that for some reason, my presence makes her feel afraid. So, taking my eyes from her, I return to my old friends, the notes. Looking up from them again and smiling, I ask, "Am I speaking to Mrs Broses?"

She clears her throat but no words come. I smile and look down at the notes again, and now it is my turn to fight to find a voice.

"Hum, I see that you had a little boy on 20th August and I've called to see how you are both doing."

The room is silent. There is no sound, or sign, of a baby, and the lack of clothing or equipment around the room leads me to feel that no baby is being cared for here. The cold is absolute, and I shudder. She had been standing as if made of stone, but now she comes to life and, with the minimum of movement and without a word, her emaciated body disappears into the alcove at the far side of the fireplace. I stand in the middle of the room; the sound of footsteps on wooden stairs has faded. Out in the alleyway a woman's voice shouts and a child cries, another woman shouts and all goes quiet. The stairs creak again and the young woman reappears, carrying a wooden apple box. Without speaking to me she places the box on the table. With tender emotion, face close to the box, she speaks for the first time, her voice almost inaudible.

"He's asleep, takes a lot of getting off, but he's asleep now."

The eyes continue to look into the box with a gentle light and her long thin hands hover over it. I speak as I move towards the table.

"May I see him?"

She raises her hand as if to protect the baby.

"Yes, but don't you wake him."

I look down on the tiny head. No larger than a tangerine orange, it lies against grey-white material and a minute hand rises above the edge of the piece of grey towelling that covers his body; the rest of the box seems to be filled with a piece of pink blanket. Putting out my hand instinctively I touch his anterior fontanel; it feels full and the head is warm.

26

"Don't wake him."

The voice is the loudest that I have heard, and now I gather courage as I ask, "How are you feeding him?"

For the first time she looks in my direction and I see that the eye, the one which did not look at me through the door, is very bruised.

"Doing it myself," she murmurs.

Now she suddenly stands to attention and lifts the box in her arm, and her voice shows alarm as she nods her head towards the door.

"Go! Get out now."

Men's voices sound, muted in the distance. Her face now has colour, red cheeks are bright against the colourless face as, with her elbow, she directs me towards the door.

"I'll call tomorrow and bring you some vitamins."

I manage to shout the words as the door closes in my face. Men walk along the alleyway their voices loud, but they don't look down on me in the yard and I hurry away unnoticed.

12.30p.m.

I have walked until my feet ache and now stand where I had stood yesterday, at the bus stop. The street seems to be full of men, most of them in overalls; the day has warmed up considerably and the smell of beer is almost overpowering. For the length of Park Lane I have been unable to detect even a sign of parkland; in fact, the only green to be seen was growing around some rubble on a small open space. This grass was long and straggly, and not even the smallest scrubby tree had made an effort to grow.

The family I had attempted to visit after Mrs Broses lived at the far end of Park Lane, the end furthest from the brewery. I had taken a rather old and worn cream envelope from the black bag; so worn that it had to be supported by a good deal of Sellotape along its edge. A new and much cleaner envelope had been pushed into the old one, and when I had first looked at it I had assumed that the newer envelope was there to eventually take over from the old one. But when I stood on the corner of the street, and attempted to refresh my memory on the size of the family, I had become confused. In the old envelope there were four cards, one for a child of just less than a year, one for a child of three years, one for a child of four and one for a child who should now be at school. In the newer envelope there were two cards, one for a child of two years of age, and again, one for a child almost a year old; all the children had the same surname, and two of the boys had the same Christian name. I had been standing by the roadside considering the cards when a skinny, pale-faced girl with mousey-coloured hair, a thin colourless dress, shoes and no socks, pushed past me. Without speaking, but treading on my foot, she entered the house in front of me. I looked at the door as it shook in its frame.

"Well, at least I know there is someone in," I told myself.

So, taking a deep breath, I tapped on the door before it finished shaking. The girl who had closed the door

28

opened it. Well, she opened it just a crack and with dreary eyes viewed me without speaking.

Silenced by her silence, I gazed back at her and then, gathering my bag in front of me and looking down at the notes, I asked, "Does Mrs Watts live here?"

I was about to add "is she in?" but she had gone.

A girl, just a little older than the one who had just left me, but equally as pale and thin, came to the door. "Could this be Mrs Watts?" I asked myself.

The girl spoke.

"Yes?"

"Um! I'm looking for Mrs Watts. Does she live here?"

Without further comment the girl stepped back, opened the door wide, and disappeared into the black void which lay behind her. I looked at the open space for a moment and then, deciding that there was nothing else to do, entered. The distinct smell of human habitation had filled the air and it took time for my eyes to adjust, as the only light offering any help had come from the open door behind me. Being able to smell their presence, but as yet unable to discern anyone, I stepped forward. Off to my right some meagre light entered at what seemed to be almost ground level; it came from a doorway and I approached with caution. Two concrete steps dropped down and, from my vantage point on the top step, I looked across those assembled in the small, but lit, room. Eyes watched me from colourless faces; all were silent, a baby cried, and no one moved. For that moment I had the distinct feeling I was looking down on a Lowry painting waiting to be hung in the Tate Gallery. Then the picture moved. A young woman, with baby in arms, stepped towards me. Shouting loudly up towards me she had proclaimed, "Mam's not here."

"Oh! I've called from the clinic, the one on Lancaster Street," I explained, just in case there might be several more in the vicinity. "I've called to see your mother, and all of you." I added this just in case one of the gathered throng might feel left out. No one spoke and I seemed to run out of words.

"Mam's not here," the girl repeated.

"Will she be back this afternoon?"

The words had sounded silly as I asked them, and the girl raised an eyebrow and one shoulder. Eyes continued to watch in silence and I had the distinct feeling that I had outstayed my welcome so, lifting my black bag a little higher, as though it were a weapon of defence, against what I wasn't sure, I stepped backwards.

"Well, thank you for seeing me, and please tell your mother, should she come back home, that I will call later this afternoon. Oh! My name is Miss Compton and I'll see you all again."

Having cast what I hoped had been a benevolent smile across the assembled throng; I headed for the outer door and fresh, well, nearly fresh air.

The next visit I had tried to pay, to a family on Park Lane, had produced little more of value. The home of this family had been situated a good way up Park Lane, on the opposite side of the road and just a little further along from that of the Watts family. This address, I had been told by the set of yellow cards, was lived in by the Tate family. I knocked on a dilapidated brown door which opened directly on to the pavement. There had been no reply, but I had seen a rather dirty curtain move in the small bay window beside the door. The house stood on the corner of an entrance to one of the courts and so had a side door. I decided to try an approach through this door, but an unshaven, rough-looking man had blocked my way and had more growled than said, "Bugger off! We don't want no nosey sods here."

Intent on kicking me, he had swung out a leg. I stepped back and landed on something I wasn't able to see, but I had been able to see that the bottom of the man's trousers were tied around with string. From the quantity and condition of the debris underfoot, I made the assumption that the trousers had been tied to prevent rats from his yard climbing up his leg and not just those from wherever he worked.

Park Lane, dusty, broken and silent, was overlooked by shabby houses for its full length. No park could be found and nor had I found any hospitality or shady tree. I once again stood dejected and waiting for the bus to bear me back to the clinic's neat world of polished floors and chairs in ordered rows.

1.15p.m.
Double doors stand open and another small door, beside the clinic's red-brick front, hangs ajar; to where

it leads I am not sure. The large hall now seems to be lighter, a few electric lights, surrounded by opaque globes, hang from the ceiling on long cables and, lit, add some brightness to the environment. The chairs still stand in rows, but they have been turned ninety degrees and now face a table on which stands a blotting pad and an overstuffed paper holder. Filing cabinets, which stand under the wall clock, have now been unlocked, and the top drawer of the nearest one to the table stands half open. A tall, thin lady of middle years walks into the hall, from the direction of the Health Visitors' office. She is dressed in a green smock and does not see me at first as she is looking down into a small box file which she carries in her arms. She must be the clinic clerk and I realise that I had seen her yesterday, but had not spoken to her. She is almost upon me before I speak.

"Hello there, don't let me knock that box out of your hands."

She jumps back with a start.

"Oh! I do apologise, I didn't see you there. May I help you? The clinic is not open until two."

Having placed the box file on the table she turns, and directing her brown eyes and long thin pale face towards me, she smiles. I had not wished to distract her from her task, but at least she has told me one thing: today is clinic day. In all the pandemonium and chaos my mind has been in, I have forgotten to ask about the clinics. Now I panic — am I to run this clinic?

"Can I help you?" Again the face is looking into mine.

"Oh! My apologies, I am Miss Compton, the new Health Visitor."

Her face lights up and her hand shoots out.

"How pleased I am to meet you! I am the clerk and my name is Miss Haines."

Footsteps echo on the polished wooden floor, they sound loud; Miss Haines turns abruptly towards the open filing cabinet, and seems almost to disappear into it.

Miss Hampton enters and looks up at the clock.

"You are rather late returning, Miss Compton."

I start to make my excuse — the buses can always be blamed — but she stops me, and with a raised finger and body half turned towards the desk, continues, "We all have a considerable amount of work to do. However, we work as a team and so manage our cases so that we can be where we should be at required times. Taking meals is essential, so unless you have notified someone that you will be eating elsewhere, you will be expected back at the clinic by twelve thirty. It is also essential that outside bodies can contact you, so we must know when you will be in to take calls."

She turns and gives Miss Haines her full attention, and from past experience I know that I am dismissed. So, deciding that discretion might be the better part of valour, I head back towards the kitchen.

The mention of eating has rung bells. Mrs Burns had been correct and during my travels I had found no place that had enticed me through its doors to buy some food. My stomach is rumbling and I have nothing to eat. Mrs Burns, who is talking on the phone when I walk into the office, smiles up at me and then returns to her conversation. The clock says that the time is 1.15p.m., and, after my unsuccessful visits this morning, I am hungry, thirsty and dejected, and hope against hope that I do not have to take this clinic. Mrs Burns stops talking on the phone and walks back to her desk, making a note on a child's card as she goes, and without looking at me speaks.

"Had the lecture, have you? Don't worry, we all get it, but then we probably all need it."

She turns and smiles and says, almost as an afterthought, "I got you a tin of soup, didn't know what you were doing, but I thought a tin of soup would stand if you didn't need it, and there is some bread in the bread bin, though it might be a bit old."

I don't wait for the words that follow, but shouting, "Thanks, I'll pay you for it," I am off.

For a moment the clinic is forgotten, but then, as I cross to the kitchen I see Miss Haines and hesitate. Have I got time to eat, or should I dash over and find out what my duties are? From behind the desk Miss Haines looks across at me and more mouths the words than says them, "When you have eaten I can tell you about the clinics."

In a whirl of black bag, navy-blue coat and perfume, Miss Winthrop passes and disappears into the office.

With a tin of vegetable soup and a lump of dry bread inside me I feel calmer as I approach the desk and Miss Haines. A young woman, much better dressed than the ones I had met this morning, is passing through one of the doors which stand open beneath the wall clock, a baby of about seven months of age upright in her arms. Miss Haines closes the filing cabinet drawer, places a manila file on the desk, opens it, writes on a piece of paper on her blotting pad and, picking up the manila envelope, follows the young woman and her child through the door. All is silent as I stand by the desk until I hear Miss Winthrop speak. At least, I think it is Miss Winthrop; she has not yet spoken to me. Returning, Miss Haines sits behind the desk.

"Right, let me give you all the paperwork first. These are the times and days of the clinics. You and Mrs Burns will do the Thursday clinic."

I sigh in relief. I don't have to dash into the clinic now and, thank goodness, I will be working with Mrs Burns.

The list goes on: immunisation clinics; visits to the Health Department; child health clinics. Park Lane with all its rows and courtyards comes into my mind. How am I going to visit all of these families with so many other duties? Then I remember: I have said that I will visit Mrs Watts this afternoon. I can't miss the first appointment that I have made.

3.00p.m.
Having made my apologies to Miss Haines and having grabbed my jacket, hat and black bag, I board a bus. Schoolchildren are sauntering towards the bus as I alight; the afternoon has almost passed. I half run and half walk down Park Lane and I am a little out of breath as I approach Sutton Street. The door stands

35

open behind him as a boy I recognise from this morning leans on the door frame. I smile as I approach and ask, "Is Mrs Watts in, please?"

Filling his mouth with bread, the boy pushes himself upright. He wears long trousers that are considerably too large for him, and a jumper which seems to almost envelop his thin upper body. The gaunt face is level with mine but the eyes register no interest in me. Without utterance he turns and walks into the house. As I have as yet received only six words from anyone in this house, I make an assumption that they are a family of few words so, straightening my jacket and lifting my bag, once again I step across the threshold.

This morning I had thought the house to be full, but I had been wrong — this afternoon it is full. Silently, in half light, children of all ages move around each other. They fill the room with a slow and constant movement, passing before me and now behind me, in silent concentration on what I can now see is eating. Each child bears a slice of bread balanced on their hand. Small children, aged down to what I would guess to be as young as two years of age, mill amongst some of teenage years. A wedge of bread, about two inches in thickness and piled high with jam, passes before my face. It is born forward on the palm of a young man's hand; it passes onwards silently and disappears down into the throng. The voice that I had heard this morning calls out, "Has everybody had one?"

There is no reply, just the mumble of overstuffed mouths, so the voice continues, "There's some more coming if anybody wants another."

The thin doorman, who had slumped against the wall beside me, rises to his full height again and, leaning forward, holds out his hand.

Now the mumbling voices are still again and my eyes are drawn to those of the young woman who had addressed me this morning. Taking her eyes from me, and returning them to her task, she calls out, "Mam, there's the Welfare here again."

A little space is cleared around me; taller children retreat to the sides of the room and a loud and deep voice speaks.

"Well, tell her to come in; we don't stand on ceremony here."

Hoping that I have at last found Mrs Watts I step forward into the space that has been cleared before me, and although I can not yet see her I speak.

"Good afternoon, Mrs Watts, I'm sorry to come when you are busy, but I had told your, um . . . um, *daughter* that I would call back this afternoon."

No one speaks and now I stand on the top concrete step and look down into what I had assumed this morning to be the kitchen. Still I can not see her, and then her head rises as she lifts a baby of nine or ten months old. She is short and, from where I stand, and from what portion of her I can see, she is round; she is probably as far around as she is high. The voice booms out again — the body is small, the voice is large.

"Come in, miss. Thought you were one of the children. Move over will you and let the Welfare through."

At last I am standing beside her and yes, she is short; I would say about four feet nine inches tall. Trying to break the ice I say, "Looks like you are having a busy day."

"Yes," she replies, as she reaches up to a line, which crosses the ceiling of the room, and pulls down a rather grey and worn piece of towelling.

Three small children hang on to her full skirt and their eyes watch me from beneath tousled, but reasonably clean hair; their clothes seem to have been put on their bodies to cover them rather than to fit them, and none wear shoes. The two older girls stand by a wooden-topped table, whose main support appears to be the darkly stained wall, and whose upper reaches show that it was once painted pale blue. This table is the only piece of furniture I have seen in the house, apart from a rickety pram, which stands in the doorway to another room. The crumbling remains of bread are being coated with jam and eager fingers await them.

"Right, miss."

She speaks as she presents me with the child, who is now encased from under his arms to his knees in pale-grey terry towelling, which I am pleased to say is dry. The child leans back and surveys me; he has obviously taken part in the feast, as his face is covered with jam, and what hair he has is stuck to his head. He puts out a jammy hand and grabs my nose, and when he tries to throw himself back into Mrs Watts' arms I realise that he is quite a heavy and strong boy. Mrs Watts doesn't want him, but one of the girls, having wiped her jammy hand down her dress, takes him. He looks back at me with a belligerent stare.

When I turn back, Mrs Watts has disappeared. Then the voice booms out from the space behind the pram.

"Sissy, make the Welfare and me a cup of tea — you'd like a cup wouldn't you, miss?"

I am about to say no, but the clink of pot already sounds, and I almost lose my hearing, as she bellows over her shoulder, "Sissy, get the proper cups, the ones from the top shelf."

She turns back and smiles at me as she waves her arm towards the crumb-covered table.

"Would you like some refreshment? There is plenty, got an extra loaf last night, he did."

I thank her profusely, but refuse, although the crusty bread does look appetising. The tea arrives, and as she walks to meet it I realise that she limps rather badly.

We stand facing each other as we drink tea in the small featureless room while tiny children hang onto her skirt, and figures move around as numerous children enter and leave with murmuring voices. Each "thanks" is acknowledged with a nod by Mrs Watts. I have placed my bag on the floor between my feet, and cannot review the size of her family, so speak as young people leave us.

"Quite a family you've got here, Mrs Watts."

For a moment there is silence and then she throws her head back and roars with laughter.

"Lord love us, miss, you don't think all these are mine, do you?"

Now the two girls laugh and, although most of them have no idea why they laugh, the remaining children join in. I would think they have few reasons to laugh, so when the opportunity arises they take it. The laughter is infectious and now I join in. Wiping her eyes on her apron, Mrs Watts pulls herself together and manages to gasp.

"Wait till I tell our Jimmy that. No, miss, he works at the bakery and when he comes home in the morning he brings us yesterday's broken bread. The posh people don't like their bread broke, so a few get broken."

She gives me a long and meaningful wink.

"I get jam or stuff from the pickle factory; and the kids drop in after school."

She nods her head towards the table and smiles.

"Come to see what we've managed to get. Some of the poor buggers would have nothing; have to go to bed hungry if they didn't stop off here."

Now, shuffling off with the two best china cups firmly held, she calls over her shoulder, "Must go, miss, my shift starts in five minutes."

4.45p.m.

I stand on the pavement, which is now empty. I am confused and bemused; this family is in my "in need of special care" file yet Mrs Watts gives to others. She asks for no payment or reward, and I should think that she *is* in need of my special care but not in the way I had expected. I shrug my shoulders and look back at the closed door. Still, I had better come back on another day, I have not yet found out to whom all the children

40

under school age belong. I look down at the cards, which I have again removed from the leather bag, and in pencil make a note on the cream envelope just to remind me of the visit.

The next card in the bag belongs to the family I had tried unsuccessfully to visit this morning. I can see the house just a little way along the road. I mumble to myself as I start to cross the road, "I wonder if the man is still there."

I had forgotten how late it had been when I left the clinic and as I glance at my watch I freeze on the spot; my watch tells me that it is a quarter to five. I know that I should finish work at 5.30p.m., and I have no idea if the door of the clinic is locked at night. What I do know is that I don't have my purse with me and I have brought just enough money for two short bus journeys on my patch, not enough for the journey all the way back to my home.

Now I panic. I know that I am a good way down Park Lane, and if I walk as fast as I can it will probably take me twenty minutes to get back to the bus stop. I think to myself, "I will probably have to wait for a bus for hours; I'll never get back before half past five."

Then I remember the map. I search in my bag; it's only a drawing to give me general directions, but it might help. It is not there, I have not brought it with me. I look back across the road to the house I have just left. I am sure that on the map the end of Park Lane joins Lancaster Street and I tell myself that if I walk down Sutton Street it should bring me out part way down Lancaster Street and I might get back in half an hour.

Feeling reassured, I set off down Sutton Street with a bright and confident step. The street is long and straight, two-storied houses front on to small, unkempt gardens and, to fit in with the general decor of the area, doors are unpainted and windows are dusty. On the opposite side of the street sizable houses bear evidence of better times. But today all vestige of grandeur is gone. Large, unpainted doors stand open above soiled and broken stone steps. Small gardens, onto which the lady of the house had once looked through curtained bay windows, now support weeds tall enough to cover any windows, and the flowering plants that remain have grown well past their flowering stage of life. Several women sit on the steps of one of the houses, their flowery aprons and turbans the only colour in sight. Silence falls and all eyes watch me as I pass; the children on the pavement cease their play and two boys in short grey trousers and wrinkled socks start to follow me. A loud and raucous voice calls out, "Our Bert, yo gets back here!"

With the final kick of a stone, which hits me on the back of my leg, my followers leave.

Sutton Street lies before me, straight and unbending. To my left, a terrace of small mean houses runs off the street, and I am once again joined by a number of children who seem to find my unexpected presence very entertaining. They follow me along the road, calling loudly to each other as we go. I try to ignore them, but they are becoming quite numerous. Thomas

42

Street crosses before me, and a corner shop stands where the two streets meet. Two older women step out of the shop, one leaning on her companion for support. She wears a dirty white bandage around the lower part of her leg, and almost falls over one of my followers. The woman with the bandage swings her arm out towards the child, and the woman supporting her hits him on the back of his head with a sizable handbag. The shouts are loud enough for anyone to hear.

"Get home, yo noisy little devils, afore I box your ears!"

I am ignored by the two women, who, reorganising their legs, arms and bags, slowly depart up Sutton Street.

The children scatter and I make my escape down Thomas Street. The street soon becomes darker. High, grey-painted, corrugated iron walls rise off to my left; I think that I will cross the road as houses still front on to the other side of the road. But as I look along I realise that even higher grey walls rise from that side of the road. Some of the smaller children have retired at what could well be their grandma's command, but half a dozen older boys still dance around me. One calls out as he moves backwards before me and makes a grab for my bag.

"What yo got in there, missus, why yo hanging on so close?"

I begin to feel a little frightened, and I ask myself whether waiting for the bus might not have been a better option. I am halfway along the grey corrugated wall when a door opens; well, not really a door, just a piece of the corrugated iron bends outwards. The boys have melted away like snow in summer as a man in soiled overalls and heavy boots steps over the iron bar at the bottom of the gate. He almost bumps into me and steps to one side as two more men, similarly dressed, pass through the gate. They are followed by the bitter smell of galvanised iron.

"Sorry, hen," the first man says as he steps back.

He looks me over and then enquires:

"What are yo doing here? Place's closed now, boss has gone home."

The other two men, having replaced the corrugated iron gate, glance at me, walk around me, and set off up the road.

Taking in a deep breath I let my shoulders drop.

"Yo all right, miss?" he asks and I look at him for the first time; he is quite young.

"Yes, thank you, but I'm afraid I've got rather lost."

I am now feeling quite disorientated as I turn and look back up the road.

"Them lot don't help anybody . . ." He nods his head towards the retreating youths. "Should get um into work, never mind stopping at school until they're fifteen. Where you heading for, miss?"

My voice sounds a little shaky as I try to recover my equilibrium. "I'm trying to find Lancaster Street; I'm trying to get to the clinic, thought this might be a short cut."

I stop speaking as he purses his lips and sucks breath through them.

44

"Oh! Yo've got quite a way to go yet, miss, now how can I explain it to you? Do you know where the canal bridge is?"

I have no idea where any canal bridge is, except for the one on the bus route, and now I realise that I am completely lost.

"Come on miss, I tell yo what, I'll walk part of the way with you, till we find Lancaster Street, anyway."

I thank him profusely and find out that he is called Bill White. He is married and lives in one of the closes; he has one child, a boy of three.

"On the housing list we are. Don't know if we will ever get a house, but we can try. Our mam told me we won't stand a chance until we have another kid. Said it must be a girl so that we can say that we will need another bedroom, but I don't know how we can g'rantee getting a girl."

He looks at me sideway and smiles. I am getting quite an education; I had not thought that getting a council house could depend on such issues of gender.

I told him that I would look out for a card appearing for Baby White, and if it did I would do all I could to get him re-housed, whatever the sex of the child.

"Here we are then, miss."

We had passed long factory walls, turned left and then right and we had crossed over the canal, which had no water in it. Now I see the road sign Lancaster Street and I feel quite elated.

"I think yo need to go that way, miss."

He smiles as he points off to my left and, turning back from my right, I shake his hand and, thanking him profusely again, I set off with brisk step, buoyed by Bill White's unexpected kindness.

Lancaster Street is longer than I had expected it to be and in parts it is pretty dark as windowless grey walls rise high enough to block out the sky. I glance at my watch; it is a quarter to six. To reassure myself that I am going to make it I reprimand myself out loud.

"I know I would have been better on the bus, I would have been at the clinic by now."

I decide that I had better get a move on, so half walking, half running, I turn a corner and, with great relief, see the clinic before me.

One of the doors stands open and with caution I step through. I had expected to see the cleaners polishing the floor and straightening the chairs, but instead I see two women sitting on chairs which face the table under the wall clock. A box file stands on the table and a small filing cabinet, which stands away from the two clinic filing cabinets, stands open. Both women look at me as I step through the inner door and their dress and general demeanour claims my attention. The first lady seems to be quite young; she has very rosy cheeks, round black eyes and long blonde hair. The second lady seems rather familiar, and then I realise that she looks rather like the "Madam" that I had met at a brothel when I was doing my midwifery training. I smile at them and wish them a "Good evening". The Madam, with her high-piled hair and bright red lips, responds but the other remains silent.

I can hear voices coming from the kitchen, so head in that direction.

A middle-aged man of medium size, with a balding head, leans against one of the kitchen cabinets. I assume that he is middle-aged; I am twenty-five and anyone who has passed my age I think of as being of either middle or old age. Mrs Burns stands by the sink and both she and the man are drinking tea. As she sees me, her face brightens and she calls out: "Ha! Miss Compton, we wondered if you had got lost; we were just going to send out scouts, weren't we, Doctor?"

The man turns and looks at me. Finishing the last swallow of tea he puts his cup down. Clicking his heels together he salutes smartly and, in a clipped voice, says, "Indeed we were. By the way, I'm Dr West, on midnight duty at the VD Clinic."

Mrs Burns swishes her cup under the tap and puts it in the sink. She speaks, her voice edged with laughter.

"Ignore him; he still thinks that he's in the desert with Monty. Must fly or I'll get shot — tea in the pot if you want it."

I do need a cuppa, so as Mrs Burns passes me, I head for the teapot. The doctor walks with me, cup in hand.

"Have I got any customers yet?" he asks as he reaches the sink.

"There are two ladies in the hall," I reply.

"Oh, well, I'd better go and give them their injections."

He walks back across the kitchen, singing as he goes, "I painted her, I painted her."

At the door he stops, turns around, and pulling a mocking face says, "Not as bad as it was in the old days — then we gave the ladies cyanide and painted their bits with Gentian Violet. Thank the Lord for the antibiotic, hey!"

Still singing, he is gone.

It takes me some moments to realise what he is going to do. Venereal disease had not entered my mind when, two years ago, I had delivered a woman called Mary. She had worked in a brothel, and my then level of innocence and ignorance now astounds me.

After finishing my tea, I drop my black bag on my desk and leave. The two ladies have gone, but another one passes me as I depart. I smile at her; she is the same age as Mary had been.

7.00p.m.

I don't arrive home until 7.00p.m. The chip shop had beckoned me, and now I push a plate of cod and chips into the oven to warm and look at the pickled onion I had also purchased. "Should I eat you now or save you?" I ask the shiny onion.

The knock startles me. Mrs Ramshaw stands at the door, her nose twitching. I don't know which offends her, the onion, which I still hold between my fingers, or the chips, which are now warming nicely in the oven. I don't enquire.

Turning her face away from me and pouting her lip, she speaks.

"A young man called to see you this evening, asked if you would ring him."

"Was it Alan?" I ask as I make the decision to put the onion in my mouth.

She replies from halfway down the stairs.

"I'm sure I don't know."

A short while later, the chips are eaten and I stand in the phone box dialling Alan.

A woman answers.

"Is Alan Bunting there?" I ask

The voice calls out, "Alan!"

After a short wait he speaks.

"I called round, Dot. You were out late."

I don't reply.

"You there?" he asks.

"Yes, hurry up, I've only got two pence left."

"Right, a chap in the rooms here says that there is a flat to let in a house just down the road from me, so I wondered if you wanted to go and have a look at it?"

"I can't go tonight, I'm too whacked. Can we go at the weekend?"

"Don't get too enthusiastic, will you. I'll have a look at it and see what it's like and why don't you meet me at the university? Tomorrow, say six o'clock in the bar."

I am just going to reply when the bleeps go.

"OK," I reply to the dead phone, too tired to care.

CHAPTER
THREE

Wednesday, 10th September

7.30a.m.
It had been raining when I headed for the bus at 7.30a.m., and there had been a queue, so I hadn't been able to get under the shelter at the bus stop. I had asked if this mac was waterproof when I bought it and the woman in the shop had assured me that it was; she had lied.

I sat on the bus on the way into town, damp and squashed and not feeling very happy. Was Alan asking me to live with him? Was last night's phone call a roundabout way of doing it, or was he just fed up with living in university digs, but couldn't afford to move out on his own? We had not talked about love, marriage or any of those things that suddenly seemed so bourgeois to our generation. I had moaned to myself as I fought my way through town centre traffic and passed dirty factory entrances, "Anyway, I don't know how to get to the clinic from the university. It's all right for him to live close to work, but what about me?"

9.30a.m.
When I head back out from the Health Centre to make

my morning calls, my mac is still wet, but I will have to manage, and at least it has stopped raining, so I won't get any wetter. The bus arrives; throwing up dirty water, it stops a couple of feet from the pavement. I have stepped back to avoid taking a shower, but now I must try to leap over the pond and make the running board. I make it with one foot; fortunately the conductor is there to pull me onboard. It might be a rough journey on this bus but, after last night's adventure, I am taking no more risks: it is the bus to Park Lane for me from now on.

"Park Lane!" the voice calls soon enough.

This morning it is the pungent aroma of hops that fills the air. I'm getting used to the smell now, or maybe I am becoming addicted, I tell myself.

Park Lane is no better than when I left it. Far from washing the road, the downpour has just soaked all the litter, and the old newspaper which has gathered by the factory gates now looks like a grey papier mâché dam. The reservoir which has formed behind it would make any of the engineers beyond the high gates proud.

My black bag is full and today I intend to start my visits at the far end of Park Lane. Whether the man with his trouser legs tied up is there or not, I have every intention of paying a visit on Mrs Tate and her family, so with a firm step and unshakable intent I walk along the road.

10.00a.m.
It is the third time that I have approached this house in as many days, and this time I will not waver. The

pathway which runs along the side of the house is damp and dark, but not too wet. Now I realise why it is not wet: the yard, from which the back door to the house opens, is lower than this path. As I step down into the yard I step into I know-not-what. I tap at what remains of the door and, with my black bag held tight in my arms, I wait for the man whom I presume to be Mr Tate to answer. No one comes to the door. My tap had sounded rather hollow and I am about to repeat the process with a little more determination when the door opens, a little way at least. Something stops it from opening any further. Putting one foot into what I assume is the kitchen I call out, "Mrs Tate, are you in?"

No reply. But now I realise that I am not alone; something moves in front of me. Putting my foot back in the yard I look down at whatever it is that has moved. My eyes become accustomed to the light, or lack of it, and now two small faces come into focus. They both look to be about the same size and from the fact that they both wear only short tops I can see that they are both boys.

"What you want?"

A girl's voice makes me jump and in haste I look up to see if the man is there, too. A girl of about thirteen appears behind the children and, putting her hand across them, she pushes them backwards. Neither makes a sound.

I must answer the question. "Ah! I have called to see Mrs Tate. Um . . . does Mrs Tate live here?"

52

"What you want?" The girl repeats the question and I realise that I have not yet answered it. What have I come for? Taking a breath I start again.

"I have come from Lancaster Street Health Centre to see how your mother and her children are."

She does not move, nor does she speak. I tell myself, "I've got this far so I had better make every effort to see somebody," so I continue.

"I'm the Health Visitor and my name is —"

I get no further. A voice, more cultivated than I had expected, calls out, "Is that the Welfare, Jenny? Tell her to come in."

I don't know what I had expected, but reality beats all expectations. In the dark kitchen it had been impossible to see, but the room I now enter is lighter. The connecting door to the next room has gone, and as the sun has now condescended to shine, light comes in through a bay window which overlooks the road, and illuminates both rooms. A woman comes towards me; she walks from the far room and, with the sun behind her, I can see just her outline. She is of medium height, has hair which sticks out like a halo around her head, wears clothes through which the sunlight passes and, as far as I can see, has no underwear beneath them. I walk towards her with my hand held out.

"Good morning, Mrs Tate, my name is Miss Compton; I am the new Health Visitor at your clinic."

She walks towards me but does not stop; instead, without a word, she skirts around me and disappears into the black abyss of the kitchen, I stand, hand still extended. Now three small children, one wearing only knickers, the other two wearing just shirts, stand and look up at me; the older girl has disappeared and I hear a baby cry. A long-legged, mangy puppy bounds from the other room and without making a sound the three young children pounce on it. The puppy yelps, but the children remain silent. A wooden table stands in the centre of the room on what must once have been coloured linoleum — a little orange colour still fringes the room. The children roll under the table, where pieces of faeces lie fresh and steaming. I am startled. Is it animal, or is it from one of the children?

I am about to make a comment, to draw someone's attention to the faeces, when the woman's cultured voice calls out, "You'll take a cup of tea, will you, miss?"

My eyes are fixed on the mess under the table, which no one else seems to have noticed. What do I do?

And then I hear myself saying, "Yes please, Mrs Tate, that will be very nice."

The china cup, with matching saucer, has been placed in my hand, and the woman stands before me with a similar cup in hand; a smile wreaths her face. She is a woman in her middle thirties and now that she smiles I can see that she must once have been a handsome woman. But not today. Today her face is soiled; her hair, which might once have been red, is now faded and unkempt and her dress, which appears to be the only clothing that she wears, is badly stained.

54

"I do apologise for not asking, it was very rude of me to make the assumption that you would take milk, but I'm afraid that I am fresh out of lemon."

The refined voice again startles me and I have to drag my eyes from her smiling face and the hand which holds a cup with finger raised. The cup in my hand holds milky-coloured water and when I raise it to my lips it is cold and very sweet — condensed milk and water, I am sure.

I hear my voice saying, "This is absolutely fine, thank you, Mrs Tate," as I raise the cup for a second sip.

The cry of the baby saves me. Turning to look for some place to safely deposit my precious cup, I ask, "Is that Simon I hear crying? May I see him?"

The smile has gone; a vacant stare has replaced it. The girl, who I assume is the Jenny of my notes, appears as if by magic and takes the cup from her mother's hand. Mrs Tate relinquishes it without comment, and all the pieces of china disappear into the black abyss. The baby's cry is thin and reedy, but now it is constant, and I realise that it is coming from the next room. Retrieving my bag, which is wedged precariously under my arm, I look at the top set of notes. According to my records Simon Tate should be just over six months of age, but his cry sounds like that of a much younger infant.

I repeat my request, "May I see the baby?"

She stands, the expression on her face asking "Who are you?" Again Jenny appears, moves her mother to one side and, without word, invites me to follow her across the room.

"He's in his pram, miss, does a lot of crying, he does." This voice too has cultured undertones, but here a hint of a Midlands accent rides with the culture.

The room which I have just left has the limp smell of unkempt children, but as I move past the broken room partition and into the second room the smell is of urine and it is almost overpowering. The only furniture, a pram without hood and with a broken handle, stands in the bay window at the far side of the room; the baby's cry comes from it. At first he is hard to see. A grey mass of urine-sodden material covers the bottom of the pram. I say the bottom, because there appears to be no mattress, or other support on which a child should lie, just the metal bottom. Now I see the thin, pale body lying flaccid among the rags. It does not move, and the eyes of a tired and frightened old man look up at me from an emaciated face. For a moment I am shocked and I almost turn from the sight. The girl stands motionless at the head of the pram, then she puts her hand out and touches the infant's head.

"I don't know what to do with him; he cries so much and he won't drink nothing." She removes the hand and looks down at the infant.

At last I find voice. "May I hold him?" I ask.

The frail, limp body is hard to separate from the sodden mass in which he lies. It rises naked in my hands, almost weightless. The nearly hairless head tries to raise itself and look at me, but it falls limp against my shoulder. I go to put my hand around the body and then realise, to my increasing horror, that there is little skin upon the back. Putting the child across my arm I look down on him. From the back of his hairless head to the rounds of his fleshless heels his skin is red and blistered and in parts it is raw.

The girl speaks. "He keeps wetting all the time."

Mrs Tate's voice sounds crisp and cultured behind me. "Growing, isn't he? Be a big boy like his father soon."

I turn to ask her why she leaves her son in this condition, but the face just smiles at me as she places one finger on her child and says, "Coochy coo." Now I realise that Jenny is my only hope. Passing the infant to her I take off my jacket and, putting it on the floor by the pram, remove my blouse and wrap the infant in it. Taking the infant back into my now bare arms I ask, "Does the baby have any clean clothes, Jenny?"

Silence pervades and Jenny stands unmoving before me.

"Is there anything clean, any cloth of any sort, a napkin or a sheet?"

I look up at her face and the cheeks are blushed and the dark brown eyes swim in tears as she shakes her head sideways to say no. Simon attempts to raise his head from my shoulder, but again he fails and only a murmur rises.

"Jenny, is there some place that I can bathe Simon?"

The dark kitchen reveals a cupboard, unopened for years. Kitchen towels, from a past life, are uncovered. Jenny has ventured to the far end of the kitchen, which as far as I can see, is just a mound of wet, rotting cloth and from the movement within it, when I step near, I appreciate Mr Tate's need to wear his trousers tied around at the bottoms. But kitchen towels and a small hand towel are successfully retrieved. I gently sponge Simon's body with cold water and my clean handkerchief and, still wearing my blouse and with a kitchen towel wrapped around his nether reaches, the baby rests, now too exhausted to cry. I hold the silent child in my arms: what to do with him now? I cannot put him in the pram and I cannot leave him with a raw and bleeding back. The eyes open and look at me; they ask for help, but what help? The skin on his back had reminded me of a child who had been admitted with burns when I worked on a children's ward. Vaseline gauze had been used to heal the child's skin that time and I wonder whether it would help Simon?

"Jenny, hold Simon while I go to the shop. I'll be back in a couple of minutes, just don't put him down."

With Vaseline on his back, and milk, which I had also obtained from the corner shop, inside him, Simon sleeps in the pram. Just a tea towel lies between him and the metal, but he is dry.

12.30p.m.
The bus journey back had seemed to take forever, but at last I am back in the office and my coat is thrown across a chair. During the journey I had time to calm down and think about what my next move should be. I had left Jenny with the jar of Vaseline and strict instructions not to leave Baby Simon in a wet state, because I knew that if infection set in he would not

58

survive. I also knew that at any moment Mrs Tate, who I could not make any sense of at all, could decide to take over and the baby would then be at her mercy. She had attempted to become part of the action when we were washing the baby, but she had got lost when I asked her to do a particular task, such as passing me the Vaseline. I also realised that I was asking a thirteen-year-old child to stay away from school in order to care for her brother. Another variable had also suddenly come to mind and had been added to the equation: Mr Tate. He had not been there at the visit I had just made, but I am well aware that he will be a force to be reckoned with. I had thumbed through the notes while sitting on the bus; the family had presented problems before, but they had only moved to Park Lane two years ago. The other children, who are now five, four and three years respectively, had not been born at this address and there was little information on how Mrs Tate had managed them. I had decided that I must seek help.

The clinic lies in silence; neither of my colleagues has returned and Miss Hampton's office is still and locked. I return to my desk and once again pull out the children's notes. I had missed it on my preliminary scan; the family were under the care of a Children's Officer. The phone number of the Children's Department and the name of the officer, Miss Jessup, is pencilled on a scrap of paper which had been pushed into the soiled and broken family envelope. In one step I am by the phone.

The phone rings twice, a clipped voice says, "Council House, may I help you?"

In my innocence I had expected Miss Jessup to answer and so take a moment to reply.

"Council House, may I help you?" The voice is even more clipped.

I have to be on the ball here, there is no time to gather thoughts. So, attempting the same clipped tone of voice, which I don't manage, I ask, "Could you put me through to the Children's Department?" I murmur a "please". Old habits die hard.

"Children's Department." The voice is less clipped, but it does not invite *entente cordiale*. "May I speak to Miss Jessup, please?" The please has sneaked out again, and I make up my mind that, if this is standard practice, I must try to control my Ps and Qs.

"Who is Miss Jessup?" The please has not helped, the voice once again hangs me on a peg.

"Umm, she is a Children's Officer."

"Who are you?" The voice continues, the tone remaining unchanged.

"I am a Health Visitor from Lancaster Street Clinic." I must learn to adopt the right tone of voice, too, I think.

"Putting you through." The click sounds and silence follows.

The phone rings for a considerable length of time; I am just about to hang up when a voice speaks. "Children's Officers."

Jumping to attention I ask, "May I speak to Miss Jessup?" This time, I manage to hold back the please.

"Umm, not here, must be out on a call."

In haste, before the breathless voice disappears, I ask, "When will she be back?"

"Don't know. What's your number? I'll leave it on her desk?"

I mumble what I think is our number and the phone goes dead.

For a moment I look at the Bakelite handpiece, Baby Simon almost forgotten, my inability to get any satisfaction, or even civility, dominating my thoughts and emotions. Sound comes from the large hall and I am reminded of the matter in hand.

Miss Haines stands by the desk; she still wears her outdoor clothes as she looks through the post that has arrived.

"Oh! I am glad to see you, Miss Haines!" I am aware that I am almost shouting as I approach her at full speed.

Still holding some of the post she turns and holds out her hands towards me.

"Miss Compton, Miss Compton, whatever has happened? Are you all right?"

I stand rather breathless before her. "Yes, I'm fine, but I have a family that needs a good deal of help and I'm not sure where to get it."

I start to explain about the Children's Department when she stops me.

"I think that you had better discuss that with one of the other Health Visitors, but I am just going to make a cup of tea, if that will help?"

★ ★ ★

The tea has been drunk, the office, from which she sells
baby food and vitamins during the clinic session, has
been opened and invaded. Samples of barrier cream,
which a travelling salesman had left, along with rusks
and a tin of baby milk now stand on my desk. The key
to the Aladdin's Cave, which occupies an attic above
the main hall, has been retrieved and I stand
mesmerised as I look at the mounds of excellent clothes
and baby equipment that lie hidden behind its door.

This treasure trove is a recent discovery for me. A
woman had arrived first thing this morning, carrying
with her a large brown-paper parcel, which she had left
with Miss Haines. My curiosity piqued, I'd asked Miss
Haines what it contained.

"Baby clothes, I should imagine," she answered.

"Who for?" I asked, instantly thinking of Baby
Broses.

"For Aladdin's Cave." Miss Haines looked at my
puzzled face and carried on. "Come on, I'll show you
quickly."

With the parcel in one hand, Miss Haines led me
through a door at the back of the hall and up a narrow
flight of stairs. At the top the stairs opened on to a long
room, which, though poorly lit by its small windows, I
could see was filled with assorted boxes, little piles of
baby clothes and a few larger items on hangers. But I
had little time to explore all the goodies. Miss Haines
had deposited the new parcel and was already ushering
me back out.

"Where do all those come from?" I asked.

"Not all our families live by the canal, Miss Compton. Some families beyond your patch have things they can pass on and we're always happy to find a home for them."

Steering me back into the hall, she tucked the key back in her pocket. All Aladdin's riches had remained untouched . . . until now.

3.00p.m.

I raise my hand to knock, but the door opens before it has time to reach the wood. In the half light I can just see the man's form; it is as I remember, large. I pause, but with my black bag held before me I am ready to defend my right to enter and to see the infant. To my surprise, the voice does not growl but speaks gently.

"Her said as how yo had bin to see the nipper."

As it speaks the form melts back into the gloom. For a moment I stand, then two small figures appear at the door, a large hand pulls them back and the voice grunts again, "Get back yo buggers, let the Welfare in."

As Mrs Tate floats towards me, still in the same flimsy dress, I notice that the faeces, now somewhat squashed, still rest beneath the table. Mr Tate, for that is who I assume him to be, walks past his wife without looking at her, and disappears into the next room. Smiling at Mrs Tate, I follow him.

There is little light in the next room; one small and dirty window opens into the enclosed yard. The floor is wet because it has rained, and when I walk around Mr Tate's large form I tread on something which disintegrates beneath my foot, and the smell that rises makes me gag.

Baby Simon lies sleeping in his pram. The smell of urine is not quite so great but the towel, which I had left, lies unchanged beneath him and the one he wears looks pretty wet. The man's voice beside me speaks.

"Not crying as much now, he's not." When the large, stained and soiled hand reaches out and touches the head, the child starts. "Given him the milk like yo said, likes that he does. I got him another bottle from the milkman." Again he touches the head.

Suddenly I realise that I have not seen Jenny.

"Is Jenny around?"

"No, her's at school this afternoon; always skiving off if she can."

For a moment I panic. I had wanted to teach her how to look after the baby. I had collected clothes, nappies and pram covers from Aladdin's Cave, and I had envisaged showing her how to care for Simon. Mrs Tate hovers in the background, but makes no attempt to care for the infant. Who will do it now? As the baby is lifted from the pram, the wet tea towel falls across large hands, and small frail arms and legs shoot out as Mr Tate holds him.

With little help from me Mr Tate has bathed his son. The water in the mixing bowl was cold, but at least it was clean, and my handkerchief makes a tolerable flannel. I never did like that hankie, I think to myself. The new barrier cream, carried down from the clinic, is applied to the back, and with much manoeuvring one of the recycled nappies from the clinic is put in place. I offer to hold the baby for Mr Tate while he pins on the nappy, but my offer is rejected, and I am amazed at how gentle these large, rough hands are. We have spoken little; he is a man of few words, but as my hand goes to offer help he speaks.

"I've done this bugger a few times before, miss."

He speaks through tight lips as he manipulates the napkin and applies the large pin to keep it in place. Baby Simon is dropped into the rubber pants and, wearing an infant's shirt, he starts to look like a little chap at last. My blouse is retrieved. At least, it's in a bag and is on top of my black bag, though what I'll do with it I don't yet know.

Throughout the whole procedure we have stood. The only furniture in the room is a very greasy, dirty gas cooker, which stands opposite the yellow sink with its cold tap. The three young children, who don't look undernourished — and I can see most of their bodies — hang on to their father's legs. They are silent; and make no attempt to speak. The figure of Mrs Tate floats into the kitchen and white arms appear around Mr Tate's neck.

"What are you doing, what are you doing in here? Come into the other room, I want to talk to you."

The cultured and demanding tones ring with great incongruence within this dark, degrading environment. He ignores her while he works, unwinding the arms and pushing her away when I take the baby. The extra nappies have been handed over along with another tube of barrier cream.

She takes the child from him and, sitting on a wooden fruit box which has been placed by the bay window, she lifts a feeding bottle from the floor, sucks the nipple and pushes it into the child's mouth. Her eyes are narrowed and her mouth is straight; she watches my every movement as I unpack a thin mattress, a sheet and blanket.

The pram now looks more comfortable. The samples of Cow and Gate baby milk, which I had liberated from Miss Haines' room, lie at the bottom of the bag in which they came.

"Did you say that you had some milk for him?" I speak to anyone who is listening.

"Yes, miss," Mr Tate answers.

I see him smile for the first time. He walks away from me, and returns holding a pint bottle of sterilized milk and he speaks as he walks towards me.

"I got this sort; I know as how babies need special sort of milk."

The tall, thin bottle, with its metal top pressed back in place, has had milk removed from it and I make the assumption that Baby Simon is now drinking it. I do not take out the Cow and Gate Milk samples; the look on Mrs Tate's face tells me that we can go no further today.

I retrieve my mac, resist brushing it down, and, gathering my bag from the mantelshelf, I head for the door, calling over my shoulder as I go,

"I will call to see Simon tomorrow, Mrs Tate."

I am startled by a sudden outburst. Mr Tate's voice roars louder than I had yet heard and I jump round to see if it is I who should set off at quick pace.

He stands upright before his wife and jabs a finger at her.

"Yo keep your hands off these things, do you hear me? They belong to the baby. If I see yo as much as touch them yo'll know about it."

"I saw you looking at her!" the cultured voice scream out.

"Never mind what yo thought yo saw, if yo take one of the baby's things yo'll know about it. Do you hear me?" The rafters of the ceiling are now shaking, and I stand rooted to the spot. But then, in a quiet voice and calm persona, and with his hand on a young child's head, he turns to me and speaks. "We will be pleased if yo could come again to see Simon, miss."

6.00p.m.

The university bar is full, and even though it is only just turned six o'clock, several of its internees are well down their pints of beer. I can't see Alan; last night we had arranged to meet here at six, but the money in the phone had run out before the arrangement had been finalised and I hope he comes. I am longing to get away from Mrs Ramshaw and Mr Betts.

I look along the bar. Do I want a drink? I'd better not because I'm rather hungry and it would go to my head. I almost missed lunch because I didn't want Miss Hampton to catch me eating at 1.30p.m., so a quick slice of bread and butter was all I had time for.

I hear Alan's voice before I see him. He is standing in the entrance to the bar, talking to an older man. He stands tall and straight, with his eyes cast to the floor, his bag hanging from his shoulder and papers clutched under his arm. He moves from one foot to the other, his head nodding occasionally. I think that I remember him saying he had a meeting with his supervisor this afternoon; I hadn't paid too much attention, my new work dominating all my thoughts. The man turns and starts to walk away but he changes his mind, returns, gives Alan a piece of paper and then, with briefcase swinging, disappears.

With his eyes on the paper Alan almost bumps into me as I walk towards him.

"Hello, thought you weren't coming."

I have gained his attention, and he looks down on me (he is, I should say quickly, about one foot taller than I). Then his eyes look lost for a moment, still full of numbers and formulae, I am sure.

"Oh, sorry, I got caught up with things. Am I late?"

We both look at the clock over the bar.

"Just quarter of an hour."

He speaks as he bends over to kiss my face. "Been here long? You want a drink?"

He asks both questions without waiting for an answer and is at the bar ordering a shandy and a beer before I can speak. He downs almost half of the pint in one gulp and then, putting down the glass, he lets out a long breath.

"How did it go with your supervisor?" I ask, although I think that I can guess already.

"He's a prat. I do wonder where some of these people studied maths — that is, if they have studied the subject at all." He picks up the beer but this time takes

68

just one swallow. "It's the first time that I have seen him, and I don't think that I should have bothered. Old Johnson broke his leg on holiday. His wife rang, said he should be back before term starts, and she made the arrangements for this bloke to do this session, but I should have waited, he's a right prat." He had been drinking while he spoke, but I had drunk little; now he downs the last swallow, looks up at the clock, gathers up his papers, and turns from the bar. "Come on, I told the landlady that we would be there by six thirty, don't want to make a bad first impression."

The shandy is down in two gulps.

6.30p.m.
Mrs Pointer stands behind us, holding her chin in her hand and looking rather like a female Falstaff.

"Probably about as bright and crafty as he was," I think.

She wears a turban and a tight, long-sleeved blouse, which disappears under the dark skirt around her corpulent middle. Small high-heeled shoes complete the outfit, so a couple of bells and a tassel on her turban and Falstaff will be complete.

She watches us in the mirror and when she catches my eye it is I who looks away.

"So do yo want it then, cause if yo don't I've got others that do?" She turns away. She has spent long enough following us through the one small bedroom, living room and room divide into long, slim kitchen, and even slimmer bathroom facilities.

69

"I've told your . . . um . . . chap, I don't want any rowdy parties. Don't usually take students, but he's not a proper student is he?" She smiles at Alan. Well, at least the mouth stretches and the eyes narrow.

"How much did you say you wanted?" I ask the question as I look into the narrow kitchen again.

"Told *him* how much — if you can't afford it, don't waste any more of my time." She is turning to leave.

"Excuse me." I get her back; there are domestic issues to discuss. "You advertise this as a furnished flat, but can we bring in our own furniture and fittings, and can we decorate and hang pictures on the walls?"

Without turning she replies. I can hardly hear her for Alan mumbling in my ear, "What furniture and fittings?"

I kick him on the shin.

"Yo can put in anything that yo can remove when yo leave, but if yo change anything ask me first. Make your mind up, I've got to go out."

Before I can draw breath Alan shouts over my shoulder while pressing his fist in my ribs, "We'll take it."

The voice echoes up the stairs, "Move in at the weekend?"

"Yes." The reply hits the front door as it closes with a firm thud.

So we are to move in together. We stand and look around. Suddenly I realise that this will be the first time that I have been in charge of my own home, that I am

70

now the woman of the house. I scuttle from room to room, and Alan follows me.

"What did you mean, bring in our own furniture? We haven't got any."

"Well, we can buy some; make the place more like our own." We have reached the bedroom in our travels; the bed lies with bare mattress and pillows. "We might want to buy a new mattress and certainly new pillows."

I stand and pock a pillow with fingertips. Alan is behind me; he puts his arms around my waist.

"We could try out the old one before we throw it away."

In wreaths of laughter we fall on to the bed. Without undressing fully — after all we don't start paying rent until Saturday — we make love. Later, as we pull the door closed behind us and head down the road, we see Mrs Pointer weaving her way towards 46 West Street, the address that will now be my own.

I have the pleasant, and at the same time unpleasant, task of telling Mrs Ramshaw that I will be leaving on Saturday. She accepts my notice on the understanding that I will pay her a week's rent.

CHAPTER
FOUR

Monday, 20th October

7.00a.m.
The weather has been beautiful; for the last three weeks the sun has shone.

"Like June isn't it," the woman next door had said as I hung washing on the line in the rather overgrown garden.

"Could put some veggies in here," Alan had said as he kicked the tops off some nettles and stung his leg. We have become quite domesticated; the sitting room has been decorated and bamboo paper now climbs up one wall while the other three are a pale green to match its shoots. The coke burner now works and we got it burning without filling our newly decorated room with smoke. The kitchen is daffodil yellow from wall to wall, and Alan's mate has hung a cupboard on the wall next to the cooker. Blue-and-white striped beakers dangle on hooks beneath it.

The park, which is just a short walk away, has been a blaze of colour, and we have played like kids in the fallen leaves, work forgotten for a brief moment. The park entrance is almost hidden by high hedges, but once inside you enter another world. A grassy slope is bordered by oaks, horse chestnuts and beech trees and the city seems to vanish. This is the kind of place I'd hoped to see when I first trod Park Lane and I wish some of its residents could swap their factory gates and colourless courts for this riot of autumn colour.

I had written to Mother to tell her that my address has changed and she had written back to say that, should I need them, she has curtains which she no longer uses. I have been home and now the torn drapes have been replaced, and almost-new velvet curtains hang to hide the broken woodwork. They might not be quite the right colour, but you can't have everything. I had tried to give my parents the impression that I lived alone, but Father was quick to note my use of the pronoun "we".

"So who's the we?" he had asked.

"You remember Alan, the Alan from school I told you about? He is reading for his doctorate at the university and he helped me with some of the decorating."

Both pairs of eyes watched me, but it was Father, as usual, who asked the question. "What else is he helping you with?"

I could never resist a challenge. "Oh, this and that, you know Dad." I had left the room as Mother tried to convince him that I am now twenty-five years of age.

But today the sun is not shining. A stiff north-east wind is whistling through the cracks around the sash window and Alan quickly draws the curtain.

"I think I'll work at home today," he mumbles to the window, his thick jumper covering most of his pyjamas.

"Don't keep the electric fire on all day; we'll have a bill on the moon."

My final word is spoken as I slam the front door in haste, knowing that if I miss the 7.30 a.m. bus Miss Hampton's telepathy will tell her.

9.30 a.m.

I made it to the clinic on time and now stand and wait for the bus to Park Lane. As ever it is full, but now the crush is just part of the day and my smart suit is no longer smart. The West Indian conductor, who now knows me well, helps me off the bus at Park Lane. I don't really need the help but smiling I thank him, because acts of civility are few. I stand by the dusty road, my thin summer mac feeling like a piece of paper around my legs. In the park at home the wind had been whirling the remaining leaves, but here there are never leaves for the wind to whirl; dirty paper is all that it can find. The smell of beer is less intense than it has been.

"Maybe they're not brewing today," I tell myself.

A lorry full of barrels crashes past and I realise that it is the direction of the wind that has changed and not the habits of man.

But at this moment I feel good because I have a pleasant task to perform. Last Thursday Mrs Burns and I had been running the usual Child Health Clinic. About a dozen mothers had arrived, most of them with small babies, but some with toddlers. It had been my duty to weigh the babies, record their weight and note the condition of the child as it lay, or stood, without clothes. Mrs Burns had been advising the mothers in the adjacent room. A smart and neatly dressed woman, not too young in years, walked in, and the two-year-old who came with her knew exactly where to find the toys.

"Is Mrs Burns in?" she had asked as the toddler, apparently called Arnold, selected a fire engine and held it head high.

Hearing the voice Mrs Burns had entered the weighing room, and before I had time to put down the piece of paper that I was holding, she had walked towards the woman, hand outstretched and voice conciliatory.

"Mrs Wilberforce."

They had disappeared back into the main hall, and after I had weighed the baby who was waiting in the scales, his naked body enjoying the chance to stretch, curl and to watch his urine rise two feet into the air, I followed them. A smart black pram, polished to perfection and with an immaculate hood and waterproof covering, stood between them. The well-articulated voice said, "If you can use it, I would be delighted. I have absolutely no intention of using it again. And if by God's Grace I should need another I have told my husband that he will have to buy a new one."

Everyone, including Miss Hampton, who had shot out of her office, and Miss Haines, who had hesitated in her filing, laughed.

I had joined in with the laughter but my thoughts were not with Mrs Wilberforce and Arnold, they were with Mrs Broses and her baby. I had talked everyone into letting me have the pram; in fact, I had been cheeky enough to suggest to Mrs Wilberforce herself that Baby Broses, who had now progressed from his apple box to a wooden drawer, might greatly welcome a warm pram to sleep in.

"It is a little torn inside and I can't get off all the crayon marks." Mrs Wilberforce had nodded towards Arnold, who was now zooming around our feet. Arnold's hair was ruffled, much to his chagrin, for Miss Hampton's hands are not light. Now I almost hum to myself as I head towards Number 8, Court 7.

Since my first visit I have called on Mrs Broses almost every week. Cream buns have been bought at the corner shop and we have eaten them together, although on the pretext of being allergic to cream, I have eaten little. Samples of vitamins, for both mother and baby have been supplied and, as far as I know, taken. Baby Broses, whose Christian name is Dean, is now nine weeks old and he smiles at me when I talk to him. He is being weaned on baby rice and now sits supported. I have every hope that when the pram is installed Mrs Broses will bring him to the clinic.

I swing into Court 7, which no longer represents horror and for me holds hope. But something is wrong, the small house looks different. I drop down the step on to the damp yard, my mind and body alert. The door is slightly open; I tap on it and call her name. The door swings open a little. I step through the gap, calling out as I go. The room is dark and empty, the smell of the

76

baby is just discernable, but now the stale smell of the damp room prevails. I stand bemused and look around.

"Maybe she has taken him out for a walk," I tell myself. But a cold shudder, which has little to do with my present environment, runs through my body.

The wooden drawer, so little time ago his bed, stands empty, thrown against the wall, its side broken. Many of the baby clothes have gone, but when I look upstairs some of the more recent acquisitions are strewn across the bare mattress.

"What has happened?" I cry out to myself.

The alleyway is now dark and the cold, north wind lifts wet paper, which glues itself to my shoe. An old woman, whom I have seen before, waddles towards me. She turns sideways to pass me and her overpowering odour secures her a clear passage as I step back into the yard. In my anxiety to find out what has happened to Mrs Broses I call out to her.

"Excuse me, have you any idea where the lady who lives in this house is?"

Without looking at me she nods no, then after a couple of steps she half turns and speaks. "Her went off somewhere last night."

I speak as I step up behind her, and in an attempt to stop her leaving before I get an answer, I rest my hand on her arm and call a little too loudly, "Did she take the baby?"

She waggles her head and, lifting one hand, removes my offending appendage and starts to walk away. Then she stops and, turning, faces me. "Yo the Welfare?"

It is my turn to nod, and to turn sideways, as in one step she has moved to just inches from me. Raising her fist she swings it towards the dark and damp entrance which I have just left.

"I hope yo's not going to try to put anyone in there. 'Cause my daughter is going to have first chance with that."

I nod my head to say that I have no intention of stealing the choice accommodation. I can utter no words of reassurance; my sorrow and her bouquet make speech difficult. She grunts again and is gone; Mrs Broses and Baby Dean have hardly impinged on her world.

I wait for her to make her ponderous way out on to Upper Thomas Street. I don't want to follow too closely; I can hear her still mumbling to herself, and as she turns and looks at me again I know that I am still the central figure in her thoughts. Not wanting to have the thoughts verbalised again I return to Number 8. Nothing has changed, no message as to where they have gone, no hint as to why they went. My black bag now weighs heavy as I look down at the name which tops the blue card that lies in front of all the other cards: Dean Broses. Behind lie cards that hold the details of children I have not yet seen. In fact, the card of an infant who was the same weight as Baby Dean at birth still lies unopened. This infant must be visited today. I close the door carefully on the damp little home as my sad thoughts speak.

"Maybe they were my hopes and not his mother's ambitions."

78

I peep out of the alley.

The large lady is waddling her way down the street, obviously on her way towards the corner shop. I had thought that I might call in at this shop to ask if Mrs Broses had been in, but I now think to myself, as I turn right and head up the street, "No I don't think that is a very good idea." The wind blows; a shower of grit hits the back of my legs and it makes me skip away from the good lady at a faster pace. "Maybe she called in at the shop on the corner of Tower Street," I tell myself as I run one, walk one, up the slope. "Do you know why she should have told anyone in a shop where she was going?" Now I am talking to myself, and I have no answer.

With five Woodbines in my pocket, and no more information in my hands, I leave the shop a few minutes later. The black bag is now gripped to my chest, partly to keep me warm, but mainly because I am now feeling useless and ineffective. I look down at the strong leather bag; I see it as a possible defence against many types of unexpected and unwanted intrusions, but at the moment I can find no shelter from the feelings of dejection that come from within.

"Maybe I'm in the wrong job." I tell myself as I look at Baby Dean's card, with only so little of it used.

And then, just a little rim of the new bright-blue card appears, a card as blue as Baby Dean's had been, or maybe it is the five-and-a-half-years' training, bright and new and not yet put to the test, that encourages me onwards. The wind whirls dirt up into my face as a lorry passes along Thomas Street, its empty back rattling over the potholes. I turn my back on the lorry and pull the new blue card a little higher. Brown, the card announces, a little further, just another left, 35 Sutton Street. I let out a sigh and with deflated lungs I take my last look at the shop and decide that I'll look for Mrs Broses and Baby Dean elsewhere after I've visited the Brown family.

11.00a.m.
The front door to 35 Sutton Street rises above two concrete steps. Like the Tate's house it has a bay window, and an alleyway runs along its long gable end. Here the similarity ends. The alleyway, as I pass it, looks clean and dry. Some paper rides the wind, borne high it travels towards the houses and the lavatories which lie behind number 35.

"I bet somebody dropped that on the way too make a call, I bet they were happy when they got there empty handed." I laugh to myself as I recall my father's remarks on such an occasion.

The door opens to my knock; a girl in her early teens looks down on me as I stand one step down. She turns back into the room and calls, "She's here, the Welfare's here, Mam."

Without my having to make any announcement she steps to one side and indicates for me to enter. The room looks smaller than that of the Tates', mainly, I realise, because it is furnished. A fire burns in the fireplace, a settee with cushions stands back from the fire, and an armchair, into which the girl throws herself, stands beside it. A low guard surrounds the fire

80

and terry towelling napkins hang over it. I have little time to observe more as the doorway between the two rooms is filled by a well-built woman in her middle thirties, who speaks as she arrives.

"Expected you yesterday, they let her out on Sunday."

I glance down at the notes which record the birth of a male infant.

"Sit yourself down then; Jeannie, you always take the best chair, get up and make sure that door is closed, there's a draught fit to cut your legs off."

With a grunt Jeannie rises, but ignoring the chair I sit on the edge of the settee. I don't want to get too comfortable. The woman turns the napkins over, and then gives me her attention.

"Mrs Brown is it?" I ask.

"Yes that's me," she says. "But I don't think that I'm the Mrs Brown you want." She throws her head back and laughs loudly.

I look back at the notes; have I got the wrong address?

I had not heard her enter, and I had not felt her sit down beside me, but now a voice makes me turn.

"Hello, miss, glad you came." An older woman sits down beside me. Her face looks tired and her body worn, her greying hair, newly washed, is drawn back from her face and the tired eyes work hard to smile at me. I smile back.

"This must be the baby's grandma," I think.

"How are you feeling, Mrs Brown?" I address the woman who still stands by the fire.

"Oh I'm fine, but then I haven't just had a baby, have I?"

I look up. Is it the girl — Jeannie — who has given birth? Oh, I hope not; she looks even younger than Mrs Broses. The girl sees the direction of my stare, and with a loud exclamation leaps out of the chair.

"Not me!" she shouts. "The new babby, he's my *uncle*. It's my gran that's gone and done it," she says, pointing at the older lady seated beside me.

The other woman, who I now assume to be Jeannie's mother, pushes her across the room.

"You go and make some tea, never mind being cheeky to your grandma."

The baby is carried downstairs by Jeannie's mother who is married to the baby's brother. My head is in a spin as I try to work out the complicated web of relations.

"Always wanted a brother, did my husband, but he got three sisters. He says it's a bit late now, he can't imagine going to a match with him. Or leaning on a bar down the pub," Mrs Brown junior says as she puts him in my arms and lifts the baby's tiny hand. "Look at him, isn't he lovely?"

It seems that her mother-in-law had been seven months pregnant and had gone into premature labour before anyone suspected a pregnancy. Mr Brown senior is denying all responsibility, but the family are blaming the break in Blackpool, which the family had given mum for her fiftieth birthday.

"Some birthday present," she sighs as I check her breasts.

The baby has been named by his niece; he is to be called Nat and I have written Nathan on the card.

"No, it's Nat," Jeannie says in anguish as she almost takes the card from me. Her mother takes her by the shoulders and pulls her backwards.

"We'll let him call himself Nat, but he has to have a proper name on his birth certificate."

The girl gives me a malignant stare.

"But he's mine! And I'm going to call him Nat."

Jeannie and her mother disappear into the next room, the girl being told that he is not a toy, and the daughter reminding her mother that she did not give birth to him either.

I leave, having given instructions on how they might get to the clinic, and the times and dates for attending. The three women watch me leave and I raise my hand to say goodbye, thinking how strange it is — so many infants have so little care, and some have so much.

CHAPTER
FIVE

Saturday, 8th November

5.00p.m.

Winter has arrived; a walk around the park is now more an ordeal than a pleasure. The wind blows in around the sash window as though there is no windowpane in place; the velvet curtain does its best, but it is not always good enough. Every evening, when I arrive home from work, Alan has the entire room covered with papers.

"Don't touch anything," he screams out as I enter.

The room is usually very warm, and the two-bar fire is usually blazing away. Most evenings are a repeat performance; I throw off my newly acquired heavy coat, leap across the papers, throw up the switch and extinguish one of the bars of the fire as I shout, "Alan, we are going to have a bill on the moon if you don't stop switching on both bars!"

He replies, "If you touch any of these papers I'll kill you. And what do you want me to do sit and freeze?"

He is starting to write up his dissertation and must have his introduction in a presentable form by the beginning of next term, just after New Year. He tells me almost every day that he must have the handwritten copy with the typist by the middle of November.

"Must have the corrections in, and sorted, before Christmas."

I mumble these dates, and times, to myself before he can finish telling me, and he becomes angry.

There had been two windows at the clinic through which a cold wind blew. Two men had arrived with a roll of polystyrene foam. They had opened one of the windows; one side of the thin strip of polystyrene was glued, and they had pressed this to the inside of the window frame and had closed the window on it. The effect had been instant and noticeable.

I now stand with the window open, and a large roll of the said material in my hand. Alan sits in front of the electric fire; only one bar burns and he wears a thick woollen jumper with the polo neck turned up. I shout as I hang out of the window, the glued side of the polystyrene stuck to my face,

"Alan come and help before we both freeze."

A woman who walks along the street looks up at me.

It takes three layers of the foam to block up the space around the sash window, and the middle sheet of the *Guardian* newspaper is used to finish off the job. Fighting with the window seems to have improved Alan's humour, or maybe it's just walking away from his papers. A bucket of coke is found at the back of the garden shed; it looks as though it has been there for some time, and so, as it is Saturday and the landlady is out, we nick it and light our coke burner. At last the room is warm and, after eating the pasties which I had bought at the corner shop, we now lie on our new rug in front of the fire and remind ourselves why we came together.

9.00p.m.
The bonfire flickers in the back garden of one of the student's accommodations; it is not burning well. Rockets and sparklers have been ignited, and hungry mouths have demolished all the food; I have just finished eating a half-cooked potato, and I know indigestion awaits. Through the haze, which the rough wine has produced, I half recognise a face. I can't think why I know her, but she seems to know Alan — very well. Everyone here is from the university, she must be a lecturer or a fellow student, I tell myself, to quieten the nagging voice at the back of my head.

It has started to rain, slowly at first, but now it is a downpour and the party ends abruptly. In the flat the coke burner still glows and the room is warm. After removing wet coats, restocking the burner and producing sandwiches, we return to the rug. Vaughan Williams completes the mood.

CHAPTER
SIX

Tuesday, 11th November

11.00 a.m.

I feel I have a cold coming because my throat aches and my nose keeps running. Things are not being helped by the present environment. It rained heavily last night; Park Lane has not been improved by the deluge and now an ice-cold wind, which contains spits of rain, blows. I have made a couple of visits and, on leaving one house, I had stood by the edge of the kerb and a lorry had thrown up a sheet of dirty iced water. I managed to avoid getting my new coat soiled, but my feet are now soaked. The only ray of light is that I will be doing the clinic this afternoon and will be in the warmth.

I have just visited a family in Upper Thomas Street; the house was just above cold, and the family reasonably organised, and so, as I am in the vicinity, I have called in to see if Mrs Broses has returned with Baby Dean. I have hardly stepped down on to the yard when the large lady, who I now know lives two doors down, is standing over me. I retreat rapidly, without even waiting to knock on the door. More Woodbine cigarettes now rest in my bag, but the man in the shop has not been able to give me any information about Mrs Broses.

I had spoken to Mrs Burns about the situation.

"You can't do much, just ask around, and keep your eyes open," she had said and returned to her work and then, as an afterthought asked, "Does she have relatives around the area?"

"It didn't look as though she had left to visit someone; it looked more like she had made a hasty retreat, and the lady two doors down doesn't seem to be expecting her to return. But I think that woman knows more than she is saying."

I had avoided answering Mrs Burn's question as I have to admit I had not gone into details on family support. Mrs Broses had said that she had come down from the north of England the year before the baby was born, but I had not checked if she had any family near her present home, a mistake I should not have made.

"Good to make a note of anyone near in case of emergencies, especially when the mother is young," Mrs Burns had said and left the office, black bag loaded.

The cold winds strikes again as the Tate house comes into view. Almost on instinct I have turned into the alleyway and now stand in sludge almost to my shoe tops. I have called in to see Baby Simon many times. During the week in which I had found the family, I had called every day. I had bought washing powder and had taught Jenny to wash nappies. Sterilizing bottles was more than I could ask for, but as Simon has made it to eight months of age and can now sit up in the pram and take food from any of his siblings, sterility is not paramount. Now that Simon's sores are healing and I can take my eyes from him, I have, over the weeks, got to know the other three children.

The elder of the three toddlers, a girl of five years of age named Patricia, should have already started school. Today I have every intention of discussing this issue with whomever is at home. I hope that it is Mr Tate, because I have another issue on which I need to speak. I had rung the Housing Department to have a "heated discussion" with someone about the state of the Tate's kitchen. I was going to start with the kitchen and try to move along, if the opportunity arose. However, the wind had been taken out of my wings when a sweetly spoken, polite woman informed me that the houses on Park Lane were privately owned by the brewery.

"That figures," I had thought.

Today no one answers the door, but I no longer wait, I just walk in. Jenny crouches over a few pieces of wood, which smoulder half-heartedly in the fireplace, the three small children, still half-dressed, sit almost on top of the flames. My first instinct is to pull them backwards, but, what the heck, this will probably be the only heat they feel today. I notice that, although the puppy is no longer in evidence, the faeces still remains. The pram still stands in the bay window; Baby Simon does not look over the side. The seat-cum-apple box no longer rests beside the pram and the word "fruit" is just being devoured, in the fireplace by a sudden flame.

"Not at school today then Jenny?"

She turns a red and swollen nose towards me as she wipes the sleeve of a grey jumper across the offending appendage.

"Got a cold, haven't I?"

I have to admit that it does look as though she is correct, but wonder whether she might not feel better in the warm school.

"Is your mother out?" I ask as I step across the room to take a peep at Baby Simon; his eyes watch me from below the thin blanket, but he smiles, so I am reassured.

"No, her's gone up to see Winnie."

She nods her head towards the kitchen, so I make the assumption that Mrs Tate is visiting her friend, a woman who lives in one of the houses in the close behind their house.

At that moment the cultured voice whirls into the room, closely followed by the figure of Mrs Tate wrapped in a heavy brown coat. Her shoes though are plimsolls and the dress, underneath the coat, is still the summer one. I smile as I mumble to myself, "She is the only member of the family with any vestige of a warm article of clothing."

Jenny might wear a jumper but it looks a little worn and I'm sure that it was provided by the school.

Mrs Tate is almost upon me as she points over her shoulder and speaks in a loud voice.

"She wants to see you."

Not sure who she refers to, I carry on.

90

"Good morning, Mrs Tate, rather a cold morning, isn't it? I'm pleased to see that you are burning the furniture to keep the children warm."

She stands and looks at me for a moment and then repeats, "She wants to see you."

I try to talk to Mrs Tate about Patricia and school, but I don't think that much has soaked in; her agitation about the mysterious person who wants to see me grows by the moment. Jenny has answered most of my questions, and has assured me that she will inform her father when he next comes home. I don't seek further information on Mr Tate's whereabouts; today I need to establish the fact that Patricia should be at school and that she should have an injection against diphtheria and tetanus before she starts

We have now completely lost Mrs Tate who has been to the door and back at least a dozen times and each time she repeats, "She wants to see you".

It turns out to be a piece of serendipity. I had discovered a card for a child named Robert Roberts who lives at Number 3, Court 19, Park Lane. His mother, it happens, is "her as wants to see me," and having been escorted to the house by Mrs Tate, I now enter the living room of Number 3 via the front door. The small piece of garden, from which the door had opened, had a few straggly blades of grass and the remains of some daisies adorning it; these were indeed rare prizes and I had stopped to admire them.

It had taken time to convince Mrs Tate that we could manage alone, in fact, that we *must* be alone as our conversation will be private. She had placed her finger to her lips, nodded in a conspiratorial manner, and remained standing between us. It had needed all Mrs Roberts' effort to see her out of the door.

The woman who stands before me is tall, thin and very pale. The room, while not palatial, knocks spots off that of her friend's. There is furniture, and an oil burner burns in the fireplace. I am becoming accustomed to this form of heating and while it does tend to produce a distinctive odour, it is quite cheap and very warm and many people are using it. I am seriously considering it for our flat. A child rises from behind a settee and scampers to the woman's side.

"I assume this is Robert," I say as I smile down at the child.

He, like his mother, is tall, thin and very pale; maybe a family trait, I think. We discuss Robert's pending entrance to school and his mother tells me that he is called Bobby. He nods agreement, does not speak to me, but mumbles to his mother.

Having completed all the details on Bobby's card, and having been assured that Mrs Roberts will make every effort to bring Bobby to the clinic for his injection before he starts school after Christmas, I get around to the issue that had so taxed Mrs Tate.

"You asked to see me Mrs Roberts. Was there something that you particularly wanted to ask, or discuss?"

Exactly on cue Mr Roberts enters. Like a Jack-in-the-box he appeared through a door at the far end of the room. He does, in fact, look rather like a Jack-in-the-box. He is even taller than his wife and is more than thin — he is skeletal. The thin, pale clothes, which seemed to hang on him as though he were a clothes horse, look as if someone else should be wearing them, someone who will fill them out. He seems to stand doubled over, and I am unsure if this is because he does not have the physical strength to stand upright, or because he wants to stop his clothes from falling off. His pale hair is wet and combed at the front, but it stands up in a fan at the back of his head, suggesting he lacks the energy to raise a comb that far. Like his skin, the hair looks almost transparent. Standing together they look like plants that have spent their lives in a darkened space and have grown long and thin as they seek the light.

Mrs Roberts is speaking.

"This is my dear Robert; it is him that I want to talk to you about."

We are now all standing by the door. A rather broken settee lies across the room, but no invitation to sit has been offered, so we stand. At the sound of his name, Robert's shoulders seem to droop even further, but he does not speak.

Mrs Roberts gives me the information or, should I say, tells the story. Her husband has been ill with a bad chest; he has been "under the doctor and up the hospital". The doctor has said that it would do him good to get a job. On this count I am in total agreement with the doctor, as my father would have said "a little work never did a man any harm." The doctor had sent him to the Department of Employment, or as Mrs Roberts said, "up the Employment." The Employment had made arrangements for him to attend one of their training courses. However, it seems that Mr Roberts is having some difficulty in finalising the arrangements.

"What sort of course is it?" I speak to Mr Robert in the hope that I can engage him in conversation, but Mrs Roberts again replies, "It's about flowers and grass and that sort of stuff; likes that sort of thing, he does."

She smiles up at her husband; he just replies with a bemused look.

"Oh, horticulture. I see that you have managed to grow a few flowers by the door, Mr Roberts." I smile up at him. "Must have been hard work in the poor soil. But how can I help you?"

His face has become a little more animated and I am sure that he is going to speak, but his wife gets in first.

"Well you see, miss, he has to go to this place and stop there for two weeks. They have sent a list of stuff that he must take, like pyjamas, and some clean clothes — you know shirts and stuff to wear under . . ."

She nods her head towards her husbands lower reaches, and he bends over even further. Until now, her voice had been loud and rather raucous, but now the voice becomes soft and whining.

"Well, he can't go without some clothes to go in, now can he, miss?"

For a moment I stand bemused; how can I provide clothes? Then "Aladdin's Cave" comes to mind, and with every confidence that I can solve the Roberts' problem, and get Mr Roberts on the road to gainful employment, I speak.

"If Mr Roberts comes up to the clinic on Lancaster Street on one Thursday or Friday afternoon I'm sure that I will be able to help him."

CHAPTER
SEVEN

Thursday, 20th November

3.30p.m.

It is my week for weighing the babies at the clinic but few have arrived; the cold wind is keeping them and their mothers at home. I am taking the opportunity to catch up on some of my clerical work, and I sit in the hall by Miss Haines' desk. The silence explodes as the door bursts open. For a moment I am unsure of what is happening, and then I hear an unmistakeable voice.

"Come on, Winnie, I'm sure this is the right place."

She stands just inside the door. A brown velour hat, which must once have been quite expensive, sits at a rakish angle over one eye and a pheasant's feather hangs down the other side of her face. Her long, brown, heavy coat almost touches her plimsolls, and I hope upon hope that she wears more than just a flimsy dress under it. Mrs Roberts comes through the door pulling the Tates' dilapidated pram behind her. Miss Haines is now on her feet, and I am sure that she is going to tell them not to bring the pram into the hall, but I put my hand on her arm to halt her. I have no idea what will be in the pram, and if it is children, how they will be dressed.

As they get nearer, I see that Simon sits in the pram, a bemused look on his face. He wears a woollen coat, which is many sizes too big, and a large pixie hood covers not only his head, but most of his face as well. The Roberts' boy wears a coat and the flat cap, which hangs over his ears, must have belonged to his father, or grandfather. The Tate children, although barelegged, wear an array of coats, hats and shorts, which are a mixture of both the winter and summer variety and their shoes are equally varied. The odour that I have become used to at their house comes with them; in the present environment it is rather obvious.

Chaos, too, has arrived with them. The few mothers who had ventured out to the clinic for a stretch of their legs and a chat to another adult, have left at speed. One woman had been attracted by Mrs Tate's cultured accent, but she had departed rapidly when the coat had been taken off and just the usual summer dress remained, complete with its distinctive odour that could vie with all the glories of Parisian sewers.

Miss Haines is trying to register the children who have never been to the clinic before. As she does so, she finds that she has a cold and must have her lavender perfumed handkerchief at hand.

"My goodness, what have you brought in on us?" she sighs as she drops back into her chair.

With Mrs Roberts' help, and my visiting cards, the children are identified and fuller notes established. Mrs Burns comes up trumps; this type of situation is not new to her and one of her neatly permed curls drops over her eyes and the Irish accent shows, just a little, as she tries to make sense of what Mrs Tate is saying. Dr West, I am pleased to say, is the doctor on duty at today's clinic. I dash in to see him while Mrs Burns tries to weigh the children. It's the first time that I have ever heard the Tate children make a sound and they do it with a vengeance, but Mrs Tate's voice pipes out constantly over the entire ruckus, "Where are the clothes?"

Baby Simon is examined and Dr West draws breath through pursed lips as he looks at the scarred back. Mrs Tate does not attend the examination; she remains in the weighing room and continues to become more agitated and belligerent about the clothes.

I remain with the child.

"He'll have these for life I think," Dr West says as he holds the now silent Simon over his hand, and touches his back.

"You should have seen him a couple of months ago," I say.

He sucks air through his lips again, but declares Simon fit; well, as fit as he can be under the circumstances.

"What's with his mother?" he asks.

I have to say that I have no idea, but that it is the father and an older sister who do most of the caring.

4.15p.m.
Finally, all the children have been seen to and we stand in Aladdin's Cave. Mrs Tate is not selective; she just

98

dives into the piles of baby clothes and starts scooping them into her arms. But Mrs Roberts is more careful.

"No, wait a minute Pat. We came to get some clothes for my old man, let's sort some of them out first."

To my amazement, Mrs Tate halts, drops the clothes she is holding into a heap on the floor, and steps behind Mrs Roberts who, rubbing her fingertips together, peers down to the few clothes that have been designated as belonging to the men's section.

"That's a nice suit," she says as she bends her long thin body over towards a navy-blue suit jacket which hangs on a rail by the back wall. She mumbles to herself as she pulls the jacket open and looks at the label. Dropping it closed she picks it up and holds it high. "This should just fit our Robby." She turns it around and examines its back. "Yes, this will do very nicely."

I had been looking for pyjamas but now look towards her, knowing that the gentleman who had last worn that coat had been quite a different shape to Mr Roberts. "Don't you think that it might be rather large around the chest for him?" I ask.

"No, he's bigger that he looks, it's being so tall that makes him look thin."

The trousers are now across her arm and I attempt to tell her that they might be a tad short for her old man, but I am no match, I am in the presence of an expert. A small leather case is found, dress shirts, black socks, a pair of good, but small, leather shoes, and a black bow tie are placed in its bottom, along with the navy-blue suit. I am about to ask whether she feels that

99

Mr Roberts will be dining out often, but without a word she has moved across the room. The pram, which I had claimed for Mrs Broses, but which had not been delivered, has been ensconced in this room and now rests behind its door. The door had swung shut a little and now she spies the prize. Without a moment's hesitation, she has rounded on me and the voice rings out, loud and raucous, "I'm pregnant you know." She smiles at me and rubs her emaciated abdomen as her voice becomes softer. "Only about three months yet."

I manage to get them out of the room with Miss Hampton's help. She had returned from a meeting to find her clinic in chaos.

"I will consider finding you a baby carriage and some appropriate clothing for the infant when the midwives assure me that you are in need of them," she had said and shooed the two women out of the room, removing an armful of baby clothing from Mrs Tate, who was stating in a loud and adamant voice, "I'm pregnant as well, you know," as she pushed her belly forward.

I had seen her shoving children's clothing up her dress, but I pretended not to notice, or try to retrieve them; who would want them after they had been there?

5.00p.m.
Miss Haines is spraying the rooms with a rather potent rose-perfumed spray, and Mrs Burns has returned to our office to escape the roses and to repair her hair. Dr West walks into the hall; he wears his outdoor coat.

"I don't think that we will have any more excitement today, do you, Miss Compton?" As he speaks, he places

100

a two shilling piece on the desk and pushes it towards Miss Haines. "Do you think that will buy a new rabbit, Miss Haines?"

I look from the coin to her face, which has now turned scarlet.

"I . . . I didn't intend that you should pay for the rabbit, Doctor, I was just a little overcome by those children."

He smiles down at her and pushes the money forward again.

"Put it in the toy fund."

I learn the story from Miss Haines, who, working hard to overcome her embarrassment, is talking faster than I have ever heard her talk before. "The baby, what was his name?"

"Simon," I remind her.

"Yes, yes. Well, he took hold of a green woollen rabbit that was in the toy box. When he was going he wouldn't put it down, he just hung on to it. Doctor said that he should have it, said he didn't have much to love and a green woolly rabbit wasn't much to ask for." She sighs. "Then the other children started taking things and I couldn't get them back. That nice fire engine has gone."

She raises her hands as if in despair. In my mind's eye I see young Master Arnold Wilberforce playing on the clinic floor with the toy.

"I don't think that he will miss its presence," I tell myself.

One of the cleaning women comes in; crinkling up her nose, she heads towards her store cupboard.

"Had a few customers in today, have you?" She stands by the desk and looks from Miss Haines to me and smiles. "You didn't give them some stuff, did you?"

No one replies.

"I'm certainly not letting anyone in there any more. Miss Hampton is right; in future I'll decide who gets what," I tell myself.

The voice continues as the cleaner walks away, mop in hand, "Only I think you might find most of it down in the pawnshop. On my way in just now, I think I recognised that good suit that came in, hanging in the pawnshop window, it is."

For a moment I stand, unable to take in what is being said. Miss Haines draws in breath and speaks through an expulsion of air, "Oh! Miss Compton," and then she laughs.

I have never heard her laugh before. For a moment I stand watching her, and then it is my turn to have a red face, only mine is red with anger. Grabbing my coat from the peg, and shouting over my shoulder to Mrs Burns, I head for the door.

"You'll find them in the pub — the kids are on the steps!"

The cleaner's voice follows me as the door slams.

The rain has stopped but there are many large puddles. Ignoring all, I dodge the traffic, head across the road, and at full sprint race down towards the pawnshop.

The cleaner is right. In the dull, late afternoon light I can see the suit hanging in all its glory. In the back of the window, baby and children's clothes are spread, and the leather suitcase, with a note pinned to it proclaiming that it has had only one careful owner, takes pride of place beside the fire engine.

"Where is the green rabbit?" I shout out loud. "I'll kill the pair of them if they have taken his green rabbit."

A man looks at me and steps off the pavement to pass. But I am not hanging about. Throwing open the shop door I bound in. A bent, grey-faced man, straight out of *The Old Curiosity Shop* steps through a thin curtain behind the counter. In the half-light I can just about discern him. I have not planned what I am going to say or do, I am running on pure adrenaline.

"You have stolen property for sale in your window, sir, and if you don't return it to me at once I will be forced to take the necessary steps."

In the almost-dark shop the man stands unmoved, then pressing his lips tightly together he speaks. For his stature and demeanour his voice is louder and more authoritative than I had anticipated.

"That is a very serious accusation, madam; on what grounds are you making it, may I ask?"

I swing around, my hand waving towards the shop window, for a moment he has caused me to lose my words.

"In the window — in the window you have articles for sale which should not be there."

He has walked around the counter and now stands beside me looking over the rail which divides his window from the shop. A strong smell of thin-twist tobacco comes with him and as he pulls himself up to look over and into the window, his jacket, which passes close to my face, smells as though it has spent much time amongst unwashed, second-hand, clothes.

"So which articles are you saying have been stolen?"

He speaks into the window, but there is still a strong smell of tobacco. I take the sleeve of the suit and shake it.

"This, for one thing."

I push to get near to the window to try and collect the objects which I know had left the clinic only minutes before.

The thin, bony elbow sticks in my chest and equally thin and tobacco-stained fingers lift my hand from the sleeve of the suit.

"Please do not touch objects that you do not intend to buy."

The grey, hooded eyes hold mine as he blocks my way.

My voice rises an octave. "Sir, less than quarter of an hour ago I gave . . ." My voice fades as I realise what I have said.

The thin lips move into what I assume is a smile and he steps back into the shop.

"Right, madam, unless we have any further business to conduct . . ." He waves his hand towards the mouldering rags that adorn his shop. "No? Then I will wish you good day."

With a sharp ring, the shop door is opened and I am standing once again looking at the purloined articles through dirty glass. I picture Miss Haines' face as she tells me that the fire engine has gone and I remember the green rabbit. I had not asked about it. Where is it? Where are the children and where has the money gone?

The hooded eyes watch me. Turning my back on the hopeless endeavour I try to make up my mind in which direction to run. The anger has subsided, but now I seek cold revenge. The cleaning lady had waved her hands towards town when she mentioned the public house where she had seen the pram. During my travels I have paid little note as to the whereabouts of public houses; they have not registered high on my list of important establishments. But now once again I run, this time up the hill and this time I seek a pub. The rain has started to fall again and now it has turned into a downpour; my face is wet and my hair is glued to my head. At last I see the pram outside an ugly, Victorian building, from where a gutter pours water. The three Tate children and the Roberts' boy, who were sitting on a concrete step beside the pram, jump to their feet and the water misses them. I grab the pram just as a gust of wind catches the water and changes its direction. Baby Simon and I are soaked.

In tears of anger I drag the pram up the concrete steps. Thick glass panes, set in a heavy wooden door, proclaim that the building is named "The Two Horseshoes" and as the door bursts open at my push, I know that it is a public house.

Several men in work clothes stand beside a long oak-topped bar; each has one foot resting on a metal rail, which runs beneath the bar, and each has a pint pot of beer standing before him. But the only sound I hear is Mrs Tate's voice. Its tones ring out, clashing violently with the dull, faded and smoky environment. Pushing my hair from my eyes, I stand still for a moment. Then, finding my direction, I lift the soaked child from the pram. He, I am pleased to say, hangs on to his green rabbit. I push them towards the mother and speak as I walk towards her.

"This, I think, is yours, madam."

She stands, glass in hand, the brown coat is unbuttoned, and with each swing of her arm it falls open. Now I realise why all the men stand at one end of the bar; Mrs Tate's dress leaves little about the female anatomy unanswered. Mrs Roberts has downed her drink and now apparently feels an urgent need to find the ladies. Her son follows her, screaming loudly.

Ignoring Simon, Mrs Tate pushes her glass at me, her voice now laughing.

"Ha! The Welfare; come and have a little drink."

Knocking the drink sideways I shout into her face, "Will you control yourself, madam? And will you take these children home?"

Her three other children stand behind me in a huddle; they have not run to their mother.

I had not heard anyone approaching and until she walks down the bar towards me I had been unaware of the landlady's presence. Now her voice is sharp, authoritative and has a definite London accent.

"Who has brought these children into my bar?"

She directs the words to the barman who stands polishing a wine glass as he watches events unfold. He jumps to attention and the men leaning on the bar suddenly find need for another swallow of beer. But no one is leaving; in fact, more custom is arriving.

Before I can claim responsibility for the children Mrs Tate's voice rings out.

"She did! The Welfare brought them in; I left them outside and —"

"Where you had no right to leave them," I say, finishing the sentence for her.

The barman has hastened along the bar to serve a new customer, and now watches events from a distance but the landlady holds her ground. The red-dyed hair stands up off her head and her heavily made-up eyes look like steel.

"She has every right to leave, on the pavement before my establishment, whatever she does not wish to bring into my bar." The eyes challenge.

My voice is cold as I hold out Master Simon and his green rabbit.

"This is not a 'whatever'. This is a human being for whom this woman has total responsibility."

"And this is a public house for which *I* have responsibility, and there are laws which say that children may not enter it, and I am the landlady who will uphold those laws." While speaking, she serves Mrs Tate with another drink and takes money from the counter.

My anger rises cold. This is *my* money which she takes; money made from pawning the clinic's donations.

"There are also laws, madam, which say that no child shall be allowed to be placed in moral or physical danger."

Her face lights up as she almost shouts, "Well get them out of here, then, they are in moral danger."

The men at the bar roar with laughter and she almost glows.

Now I am at war, a war in which I have been involved since I was a child, a war against drunken poverty; a war which I had seen, and heard, my father fight. His impassioned words come readily to my lips.

"I would indeed say that they are in moral danger, there is certainly little morality in this place. You encourage men to come and spend their wages before their wives and families have even seen the money. You allow them to drink until they are out of control and then return home to abuse their wives and children. You should be ashamed of your laws — they should be rescinded."

Now I feel quite exhausted and Baby Simon is watching my face with some alarm. But a small victory has been won. Mrs Tate and Mrs Roberts have left the bar, mumbling under their breath "We'll see who gets rescinded."

The sorry caravan heads down the road. Fresh air has not done Mrs Tate much good; she has already vomited twice. Mrs Roberts appears to be quite sober and I am sure that she had made the bullets and had left Mrs Tate to fire them.

5.30p.m.
Relieved to part ways with them, I re-enter the clinic a damp and pitiful soul. Miss Haines is bent over a filing cabinet and just glances at me as she speaks.

"She wants you to go to her office as soon as you get in."

She nods her head towards Miss Hampton's door. I tap and wait to enter.

"Ah, Miss Compton, I am pleased that you were able to see me so promptly." I know the sarcasm heralds a lecture. "This clinic is not a place of refuse for clientele who require custodial or medical care. It is not a place where you can bring those who have moved beyond the remit of your care. It seems that today Health Visitors are seeing it as an establishment of other than preventive medicine."

The lecture on professional behaviour, bringing my professionalism into disrepute and my responsibility to the public, is short, sharp and to the point.

"Were those children safe in the hands of those two drunken women?" she says as I stare at the floor.

"Safer than abandoned on the pavement. And Mrs Roberts wasn't drunk, she is a strong woman she will get them home."

The voice that replies is softer than I have heard before.

"You know you don't have to take the whole world on yourself, Miss Compton. There are others around, and while we do not have your energy, we do have a great deal of experience. It would be valuable if you would allow us to share it with you."

The lecture had done little, but this struck home.

"Thank you, Miss Compton."

I am dismissed.

With bowed shoulders I pass the desk and offer Miss Haines my apologies on my way past.

"Maybe you had better warn us when they're going to come again," She smiled as she struggled into her coat. "By the way, did the poor little baby keep his toy?"

"Oh yes, he hung on to his green rabbit."

"Good." I hear a drawer open and money ring into a tin.

Mrs Burns puts a cup of tea in front of me and turns to pick up her coat.

"Been taken for a ride, have you?" I look at her over the rim of the cup and raise my shoulders. "Take you for a lot of rides, do some people, seems to be their only pleasure. I've been led up the garden path so often I've almost worn the stones out, but as Father Michael says, that's the joy of working close to people, you never know what to expect next. Thing is, you must not let them find your soft centre." She picks up her black bag and holds it in front of her. "Don't forget it's a job, always keep something between you and them, and don't forget, they have the right to make their own decisions. See you tomorrow," she calls as she heads out the door.

The room is empty, the tea is cold. I put my head on my arms and cry. My mother's voice speaks in my mind, "Dorothy, stop trying to make everyone's decisions for them."

I say the words that I have said a thousand times, "Sorry, Mum."

Now I smile as I remember the green rabbit and think to myself, maybe it was worth it all to get Simon a friend.

"Goodnight," I shout as I pass the cleaning lady.

"Night, miss. My old man's just bin in, says you gave that landlady a run for her money — thinks she can show us with her cocky London ways, does she."

She bursts out laughing and holds the door open for me. My step is lighter, and as I pass the door to The Two Horseshoes, I think that I could do with a drink, but maybe not in there, I tell myself. Maybe I'll be more welcome in the university bar.

CHAPTER
EIGHT

Monday, 24th November

10.30 a.m.

It hasn't stopped raining for over forty-eight hours. I have visited a couple of families, and I have had a couple of no replies; where do people go in such appalling weather? Most of the drains on the main road are blocked with goodness knows what; I have not tried to investigate. Suffice it to say that some of the dirty puddles have been too wide for me to jump, hence the state of my feet.

Mrs Burns had said that the women often congregate in one house, their mother's, a friend's, a neighbour's or anyone who has coal or wood to burn. Miss Winthrop, who managed to stay with us long enough to say "good morning" today, said that sometimes they go up to the big shops to keep warm. Most of her cases are resident in the southern section of our patch and I think that Miss Hampton's area is next to hers because they seem to work together a good deal. However, as I turn the corner into Sutton Street and fight the rain and mobile grit, I am quite sure that I have not passed any large shops on my morning travels — so who knows where *my* families are hiding.

Baby Nat is now six weeks old so today I will carry out his PK test, more commonly known as the wet nappy test. The door opens and Mrs Brown junior stands in the entrance. For a moment she looks at me and then calls, "Come in, miss, come in."

She closes the door behind me and rearranges the heavy curtain.

"Mother, mother, it's the Welfare."

Her voice is loud in my ear as she directs me to sit. A shiver runs through me as the heat from the fire hits.

I had visited the house a couple of weeks ago and Nathan had then been home for three weeks. Mrs Brown senior had decided not to breastfeed, and for once I agreed. The midwives at the hospital had given her a couple of samples of half-cream Cow and Gate milk. Instructions on how to mix the milk were written on the packets, but not being prone to much reading Mrs Brown had ignored these and, having been overwhelmed by hospital procedures, had understood little of what she called "this modern stuff".

"You had your babies proper when I had the others; you had 'em at home like you should, none of this crowding together and all the babies crying at once."

She had made this proclamation as she presented me with the screaming red mass named Nat. Because he had cried all night, the junior Mrs Brown had suggested a change to full-cream milk, proclaiming, "I bet he's hungry."

In her confusion, Mrs Brown Senior had mixed the full-cream powder to the same proportions as those prescribed for the half-cream. To make matters worse, Baby Nat's niece, the young teenager who loves her sweets and chocolate, had suggested to her grandma that the concoction might not be sweet enough for Nat.

"After all, this is my uncle," she had rationalised.

A full spoon of sugar had been added. No wonder the poor mite was wailing!

I had quickly returned the baby's intake to half-cream milk, and had prescribed an occasional drink of cool boiled water.

"If he awakes between feeds, give him a little drink of water; a less rigid feeding regimen might be better for him as well."

Some ointment from the chemist was prescribed for his very sore buttocks. Now, a fortnight later, I am anxious to see how little Nat is faring.

Through the curtain at the far end of the room Mrs Brown senior enters. She looks ten years younger than she had at my last visit. At that time I had wondered if she would last the year out, never mind Nathan's childhood.

"Hello miss, hello miss." She pats her hands together as she approaches me.

"You are looking well, Mrs Brown." I speak as I stand, and from an almost eye-to-eye position I see her smile a half-toothed smile.

"So have you seen him?" she says as she steps around the settee.

114

There, lying fast asleep, his two hands above his head and his lips in a tight grip, is Master Nathan, not a care in the world.

After a welcome, warm cup of tea has been drunk I suggest that the baby might now be safely returned to full-cream milk. But Mrs Brown senior almost spills her tea.

"Oh no, no, no, miss, him upstairs has just managed to get his first good sleep in. I think that he might leave home if the baby starts screaming again."

Both Mrs Browns had looked up at the ceiling during this speech, and I had assumed that Mr Brown senior was on nights.

"I'm afraid that I might have to waken him now. The baby that is, not your husband." Everyone laughs and Mrs Brown junior reprimands us by pointing to the ceiling.

Nathan has been lifted up. The arms, now not quite so thin, stretch out and the legs point upwards. He has certainly provided us with a wet napkin and Mrs Brown junior is busy ensconcing him in a dry one while Mrs Brown senior holds the wet one. I press the small stick of litmus paper into the wettest part.

"That's fine," I say as I read the resulting changes in colour on the stick. "Master Nathan, you have passed your first of many tests."

I speak to him as he is passed back to his mother and the sharp eyes, still almost covered by swollen lids, watch my face and move with me as I move my head, I take the hand, which grips mine, and putting my face closer to his I speak and smile. "Hello, Nathan, hello,

115

Mr Nathan." The eyes hold mine and the mouth stretches. Without altering my position I speak to his mother. "Look at him smiling, look at his first smile."

With eyes wide both women look down on the little face.

"Can he hear you?" Mrs Brown junior asks.

"Course he can. Just you keep talking to him. I think that you have a bright little chap here, Mrs Brown, an afterthought he might have been, but I think he is the jackpot."

I have been recording the results of the test as I speak and now as I look up, tears are running down Mrs Brown senior's face.

"Do you think that he might be clever, miss?"

I am rather lost for words, then I remember the old adage.

"Well, it's not unusual for older parents to have a bright child; quite often the last is the cleverest." I look down at the little face again; the eyes are definitely watching me. "But first we must fatten him up a bit and get him going. If the weather picks up do you think that you could get him up to the clinic? A bus runs from the bottom of Park Lane."

I pass a card with clinic times and dates written on it.

Mrs Brown junior sees me to the door.

"We'll bring him up to the clinic, miss. A genius, hey? Have to start putting some money in the Post Office for his education."

I smile up at her as I step from the bottom step. "You never know." Then say to myself, "I hope you live up to

116

it, Nat, but a bit of a helping hand at the start won't do you any harm, will it?"

11.00a.m.
Down the road, the puddle before the Roberts' house is large, the whole area more akin to a reservoir than a road and pavement. I give up on my attempt to circumnavigate it; what the heck, my feet are already soaked. What had once looked to me like an attempt at gardening, today looks like an ill-kept mud patch with weeds growing from it. Mr Roberts opens the door, just a crack. The pale face does not enjoy even this amount of daylight.

"Not at work then, Mr Roberts? Or your training course?"

The eyes look at me hesitantly, the lids blink and then he remembers. The mouth drops open and he shakes his head. The door remains two-thirds closed and I assume that this is to be the extent of our communication this morning. Then the face almost disappears behind the door.

"Her's not in now. Nothing for me to go to this week but her said there might be one of those training things next week, if I have some clothes, that is."

A leg, wearing the lower half of the pyjamas that I had so carefully selected, appears around the door. At least one item of clothing hadn't ended up pawned. The clay-coloured face splits into a semi-toothed smile and hope shines in the colourless eyes. To argue, or to fight, with this man is impossible.

"OK, Mr Roberts, leave it with me."

I turn, almost slip on the mud, and head back down the path, the path up which I have been so easily led. Mrs Roberts passes me as she tries to circumnavigate the opposite side of the puddle. She is only a couple of feet from me but, as if unaware of my presence, she passes me by. Bobby gets a smack at the back of his head when he says, "Hello."

She shouts over her shoulder, "Got a good price for them clothes — we'll have some more when you are ready."

She is starting to laugh when Bobby pipes out, "Going to school soon."

Now I turn around and look at them. Young Bobby is being dragged along by his arm, through puddle and mud, but as the thin legs stagger and he struggles to keep his balance, he looks over his shoulder and smiles.

"Great, great stuff, Robert," I shout. Now my step is lighter, and I say to myself, "I must keep my eye on that boy; he has the makings of a revolutionary, sticking up to a dragon of a mother."

11.30a.m.

Lighter steps I might have, but they are of little use to me as I stand before the door to the Tates' house.

"Come in, miss," a voice beyond the door calls, and I am glad to hear that it is the voice of Mr Tate.

The house is very dark; precious little light comes through the window today, but I am pleased to see some glimmers of light in the fireplace; that is, the part of it that I can glimpse through the crowd of small bodies. I am gratified to see that all the children are clothed, though they are still in the clothes they had worn to the clinic. Even Baby Simon, who sits in his pram at the other side of the room, is still wearing his oversized coat. Mr Tate puts a few more pieces of broken fruit box on the fire and then stands. His overalls are dirty, and he wears heavy work boots.

Hardly knowing which problem to deal with first I find myself verbalising neither, but say to myself, "I hope that he doesn't tread on those little feet, and you really should have a guard around that fire." He raises his shoulders and walks away from the fire, I speak to his back. "So they got home OK last Thursday?"

"Yes." He speaks as he nods his head in the direction of the adjoining room. "Her's in there, been in a sorry state since."

I nod my head.

"Sorry, I didn't know they would do that with the things I gave them."

He turns to me, and for the first time since our initial encounter, I see anger in his face and I step back in alarm. But the anger fades, he drops his head, lowers his shoulders and, raising his large, work-worn hands, speaks.

"It's not your fault, miss, but you see, she will sell anything that she can get her hands on to buy drink. I can't bring anything into the house, she only sells it, and then I have to come home to this." He lifts his large hands encompassing the whole house. "But there you are, miss, can't do much about it can we? I think I'll be home for the next couple of days, can't do much building in this weather." He smiles a half-toothed

119

smile, and I realise that he must have been a handsome man a few years ago. His voice crosses my previous thoughts, "If you can get one of those guard things I'll put it round the fire when we have one." He laughs again. "If it's made of iron she won't be able to carry it out of the place, will she?"

His laughter arouses Mrs Tate, she staggers through the opening between the rooms and leans upon his shoulder, without looking he turns her around and redirects her back from where she came.

12.15p.m.

I squelch my way across the hall; my coat is wet, my hat hangs around my ears and I am cold. It is dinner time; thank goodness I remembered to buy some soup and a bread roll on my way to work this morning.

"Good, you've got back early, hurry and have your dinner; we've got to get off as soon as we can." Mrs Burns stands, sandwich in one hand and cup of tea in the other.

I look down at my feet; they are very wet, cold and covered in what, I have no idea.

"What's happened? Where are we going?"

Dropping my black bag on to the seat of my chair, as my desk's too full with notes awaiting this afternoon's clerical session, when I hope to write up essential information and re-file them. I had also hoped for an afternoon with my freshly washed stockings hanging on the radiator and my shoes and coat drying beside it.

120

"Come on, give me the soup while you hang up your coat." Grabbing my soup, and eating her sandwich as she goes, she exits the office.

"What's happened now?" I ask myself as I hang my coat on the peg by the radiator.

It is unusual to see Mrs Burns hurried or flustered. I can't say her voice sounds particularly anxious now, more like excited, so undoing my suspenders as I go I head for the kitchen.

"So what's the rush?" I ask as I drop my shoes over each end of the small radiator and remove my stockings. She watches me as she stirs the soup in the large saucepan.

"You are not going to have time for that; we've got about ten minutes before we have to go out."

I switch on the warm tap and hang the feet of the stockings under it.

"Then I'll put them back on wet; tap water has got to be better than what is on them now."

She smiles and nods as she passes me a beaker of hot soup.

"Bad as that, hey?"

12.30p.m.

With feet still wet, but now at least warm, coat still damp and hat misshapen, I scurry after Mrs Burns. We skirt the boundary of the Health Centre and head down Vessey Street. This area is new to me, but its roads resemble those I had been lost in when I first arrived. Grey walls, topped by rusty corrugated iron, drip water on to us, and the smells which exude from broken windows do not make for a pleasant afternoon stroll. Now I know why the Virgin Mary guards the tightly fastened window in our office with such determination.

"So who is this Sister that we are going to see? I mean, why the rush?" I am almost running to keep up, and all but fall over my feet as I lean forward to hear what she is saying.

"We used to conduct mothercraft classes and advisory sessions at the maternity hospital, but we had to stop when we were one Health Visitor down. The new Chief Health Visitor has made arrangements with the Matron at the hospital so we can restart them."

"So why the rush?" I think.

We have come to a halt in an arched doorway. The patterned, glazed tiles, against which my coat now brushes, are very discoloured, I realise that they must be old, but they look to me as though they could do with a good wash, and the cracked, red-tiled floor needs replacing.

"The Sister who is in charge of the antenatal clinic is not very fond of Health Visitors, so we have to tread carefully, including turning up promptly. Follow my lead; I've worked with her before."

To my amazement, as she speaks, she straightens my coat collar and readjusts my hat; my mother could have done no better.

Hospitals and I have never got on well together, I've always preferred being out on call. But I'm determined not to let Mrs Burns down. Pulling my hat back into the position it had originally held, I follow her inside.

122

The sign "Antenatal Clinic" leads through well-used swing doors, and into a hall. Lines of upright wooden chairs, arranged facing the four corners of the compass, furnish the space; some of those facing east are occupied, all remaining points stand empty. A door in one wall opens and a midwife steps out. Confronting the expectant women, she calls a name, stands for a second and then calls again. A woman, who is trying to manoeuvre at least one extra human being in front of her, struggles to stand.

"Yes, nurse," I hear her mumble as she passes.

I notice Mrs Burns has gone; my loitering has done me no good, and there is no time to stand and stare in such places. Seeing the navy-blue coat vanishing around a corner, I skirt the chairs and head across the hall. Making every effort not to trip over feet, mine or other people's, and not to bump into important-looking staff, I reach her side. The Sister sits in her office; it is a small space and her ample form dominates the room. After few words, none of which I hear, she rises. She is shorter than expected, but I still feel that I am being looked down on, and, to my horror, find that I am straightening my own hat.

The door to another small room, which had long ago been allotted to the Health Visitors, is now unlocked. Mrs Burns and I stand and survey our territory. Everything looks as though it needs a good clean, but that will present no problem. With gusto we rearrange the furniture and soon the room looks more like a Health Visitors' premises.

"I'll do the advisory clinic on Friday morning, ten to eleven, and you can do the mothercraft class, also on Friday, say eleven fifteen to twelve fifteen. That OK with you?"

Without waiting for my reply or ceremony from the hospital staff, Mrs Burns heads for the outer door, and in haste I follow. The rain has not stopped, and with some determination we march back to the clinic.

CHAPTER
NINE

Monday, 22nd December

9.30a.m.
Christmas looms. Christmas day will be Thursday; this is good because it means that we have a four-day break: Christmas Day, Boxing Day and the weekend. Alan and I have decided to spend Christmas in our flat. Mrs Pointer is going to her sister's house. She had stood before me, her tight mouth firm and her arms folded before her.

"I'm going to be away for Christmas and Boxing Day and I hope that I can trust you two not to mess the place up while I'm away."

We had both reassured her that we would be doing nothing but resting before the fire for the whole time. However, we are to be in charge of the premises, so a small party has been arranged for Boxing Day, but we are determined that any interlopers will be thrown out. We have bought a small carpet in the sales, and have found a good settee in a second-hand shop. We do not want anyone spilling drink, or vomiting, on our new furniture because we are very proud of it. Alan has managed to get the introduction to his thesis written, and now it sits in the hands of his supervisor. It took a lot of persuasion to get him to part with it, but with help from his mates at the university we made it and hopefully we can forget the thing for a few days.

"I've got a job in the sorting office at the Post Office for the week before Christmas."

Alan had made this announcement last Tuesday when I returned home from work. I had made a few appropriately rude comments, and he had picked me up and thrown me into the air, laughing. I'm sure that he misjudges my height; he is one foot taller than I, and I don't think that the ceiling will take many more bashes, never mind what will happen to various parts of my anatomy. But I am delighted about the job and the little bit of extra income. We have decided to buy a record player for our combined Christmas present, and there followed much banter about who will pay for the turntable and who the cabinet. I have been allotted the cabinet, which means that I will have the job of polishing it, apparently. I have bought Alan a long-playing record with some excellent classical pieces and I can't wait to give him his gift.

It had been one of those cold nights where your feet never seem to get warm, and you wake up in the morning with cramped legs and the feeling that you haven't really been to sleep at all. The early morning had offered a slate-grey sky and an icy cold wind, and a man standing beside me at the bus stop had cheered me up considerably.

"Looks to me like we will get a white Christmas."

He had smiled as he had spoken and my returning smile was more of a grimace. I had spent my childhood in the hills of Derbyshire and it always snowed there; every Christmas was white. I had three brothers, and deep snow was their joy, it wasn't mine; as the only girl in the mob I usually became the snowman, or woman, and was usually the first to be pushed on to ice to see if it would hold. And now, as I stand at the bus stop which lies across the road from the clinic, this year's first flakes of snow fall.

I had asked Mrs Burns if we would be able to put up decorations in the clinic.

"We didn't do much last year; just had a few silver stars and a couple of angels hanging from the clock."

She had made this reply without much enthusiasm, so I felt that I was on my own. Miss Haines and I found the box containing the little glamour and glitter that we had at our disposal.

"It looks a bit shabby, doesn't it?" Miss Haines had commented whilst lifting a falling star, well, a falling-to-bits star.

Miss Hampton had said that Mrs Burns, Miss Haines and I could do what was possible, if we were not too busy, at the Thursday clinic. The silver stars were repaired with Sellotape, the angel was given a new lease of life with a bottle of clear nail varnish which Mrs Burns found in the bottom of her handbag, and some coloured crêpe paper was hung over the doors leading to the weighing room.

So the hall remains pretty much as it has always been, clinical as ever, just a few fallen stars draped here and there. But this morning different kinds of voices echo through the office: women's voices, soft, clear and kind of determined, several of them all talking at once. It is almost time to set off visiting and I am ready to don my heavy coat.

I stand for a moment, coat in hand. Should I walk into the hall? Mrs Burns has obviously been waiting for these ladies, and now I can hear her voice amongst theirs. Miss Winthrop has no such reservations. Squashing down the red mop of hair and grunting to me, she heads out. I hear Mrs Burns introducing her to someone; there is a mumble of voices and then silence. Mrs Burns' face appears in the doorway, cheeks red and eyes bright.

"Hello, I thought that you had gone, come and meet the Sisters."

In grey habits and white cowls, four or five nuns stand in the centre of the hall. The tables, I can now see, have been rearranged; they had stood scattered around the hall but now some lie in line under the clock. Mrs Burns stands beside me and raises her hand; one of the figures breaks from the group and approaches us.

"Sister Margaret, this is Miss Compton, the new Health Visitor I have spoken about."

The blue eyes look down at me. Why do nuns always have to be tall?

"I am pleased to meet you, Miss Compton, we have heard much about you."

"Some good I hope . . ." I manage to squeeze out the words.

"Oh, yes, many good things." The eyes lighten and the face creases into what I assume to be a smile.

There is much chatter and, rather unsure as to what is happening and what my part in it might be, I just smile and nod. Eventually they leave, and now the hall is still. I see the small tables are high with boxes, about the size of a large shoe box, and each is tied with white string.

"Right, do you have families who might welcome a parcel of food from the Sisters, Miss Compton?" For a moment I hesitate, I don't yet know my area well enough for all the names of needy families to come readily to mind.

10.30a.m.
I am allotted three of the boxes, and two of them now lie in a large leather bag which stands at my feet. The names that had come to mind had been firstly Mrs Watts and her extended family. It had taken some time to convince Miss Hampton of their need.

"No, if they have a wage coming into the house they can supply their own Christmas food."

It had taken some force of argument to convince her that the food will go to a dozen children, who, unless Mrs Watts provides it, will see no Christmas fare. The Tate family had, of course, been high on my list, but I know that I cannot hand the parcel over to Mrs Tate; I now know that its contents would be out of the door almost before I am. The third parcel I will offer to Mrs

Parkin's family. I had only been introduced to them a few days ago but I know that I must call again before the Christmas break, and taking the parcel will give me a good reason to do so.

On Park Lane, both the Watts and the Tate houses are in sight. To whom shall I give the first parcel? I have no idea what they contain but Mrs Burns has assured me that it will be good, wholesome food. I sigh; the parcels weigh heavy on several counts. What will Mrs Tate do with good wholesome food? Will she sell it if she gets a chance and get drunk for Christmas? Will Mrs Watts accept the parcel? She is a proud woman; I have faith in her eldest daughter's common sense, but will it prevail, or will it cause a family argument? I have gained the impression that mother and daughter do tend to fight for top cat position. I really do not know either of these families very well, and do not wish to encroach upon their privacy. The dilemma is solved when the voice speaks.

"Hello, miss, you look weighed down."

Margie Watts, Mrs Watts' eldest daughter, steps out of the corner shop and almost knocks the parcels from my hands. As the saying goes, speak of the devil.

I explained my mission as we walk the last few paces. Margie has already claimed the heavy bag and I continue to gabble.

"The nuns, from a convent somewhere near town, brought several of these parcels into the clinic and asked us if we knew anyone who could make good use of some extra food this Christmas."

130

Whilst I talk she opens the door and now I stand before four feet ten inches of power and determination.

"No, no, no, miss, we don't accept no charity in this house. Make our own way, always have and always will. Take your parcel to them as needs it and thank the nuns, but say no, thanks."

I had expected this and now stand with the heavy bag in my arms, and I have to admit, it weighs heavier than before. Ellie, the younger of the two grown-up daughters, has skirted around her mother and now guides me forward.

"Here, miss, put that on the table."

The girl smiles across at me as she makes space on the crowded table. The bag is deposited, but the parcel has not been accepted. Seizing the handles of the bag, Mrs Watts throws it back towards me and turns on her daughters.

"I don't know who brought yo two up, like a pair of vagabonds yo are, yo'd go begging on the street if yo thought that yo could get something for nothing. Good job your brother isn't here — he'd box your ears for yo he would."

Her hand reaches up and touches the flowered picture frame. The small thin face holds just a hint of pride and determination, and the khaki uniform almost envelops him. Wally was her first child, the one she had before she met Mr Watts. He had been just eighteen on D Day.

"Lied about his age, said he wanted to do his duty. Didn't get chance to do much, died on the beach he did, but the officer what wrote said he was a man to be proud of. Always promised him that we would go to the seaside one day, me and him. We didn't get there, but my Wally did, didn't he?"

Tears had run down her face when she had first told me the story, and now the tears glint there again. Closing my arms around the offending bag I back towards the door.

"I'm sorry, Mrs Watts, I didn't intend to insult your family, I just thought that you would know the kids around here who might be able to use some food at Christmas."

She does not look at me; her eyes still rest on Wally. Her eldest daughter puts an arm around her shoulder but she shrugs it off and turns back towards me. With her feet planted apart and her arms behind her back, she faces me.

"What makes you think I know all the kids, and if I do, what gives you right to think I can't feed um without your help?"

But with a little bit of encouragement from the girls, a parcel is opened with care, coloured tissue paper is smoothed out.

"It would make a nice tablecloth, this." Ellie's voice sounds quite animated.

A small tin of pink salmon is passed around: the girls have never seen one before, then some spam is placed in pride of position, and the custard powder and the Christmas pudding are set together.

"We'll make the custard and mix the pudding in it, then everyone will get a bit." Mrs Watts pushes them even closer together, as if she will need to be reminded of her receipt. Spam, bloater paste, and jam sandwiches are planned, and I am forgotten until a voice shouts out, "Look what's here." A bar of Cadbury's chocolate shines bright purple; even in the half-light it sparkles. "That's our Christmas present to us three." The three women link arms and the mother kisses the chocolate bar.

As I am on my way out, Margie's voice halts me.

"Miss, miss. We'll have a party at Christmas. Tell the nuns thanks, and we'll make sure all the kids get a bit of the parcel. You can come if you want, miss, there will be plenty, as long as dad comes up trumps." There is laughter in her voice as she speaks.

"I'll tell the nuns," I say.

From out of the melange of older daughters and young children, Mrs Watts raises a hand and waves the Cadbury's chocolate; her pride is retrieved. Raising my hand I turn, and, with careful step, leave; the bag is now a little lighter, as are my spirits.

11.00a.m.

The puddle by the Tates' house still stands dark and foreboding, its depth unknown, I try to skirt it, but it encompasses the whole alleyway. My feet are already wet, so what the heck. The door to the black abyss stands open, and to my surprise I can hear the joyful calls of children's voices. No words but certainly laughter. I check the house again; yes, it's definitely the right one, no other could be like this. Holding the large shopping bag before me, I tentatively step through the open space.

"Mrs Tate, Mr Tate," I call loudly as I step into the living room.

The boy of four years crawls from beneath the table, his face more animated than I have ever seen it. Ignoring me he steps forward, pulls a large flat disk from beneath his arm, takes it in his hand and sets it spinning away into the other room. The five-year-old girl barks out a laugh and it seems to get stuck in her throat; maybe it is an act so rarely undertaken that it is yet to be learned. Setting the disk spinning again, she falls backwards, her body, naked but for a dress, collides with that of her other brother. On the floor the scrimmage continues and Simon, looking down from his pram, claps his hands and smiles.

I stand, taken aback; there are no adults in the room, just three small children, the baby, and the flying disks. One of the disks lies at my feet, I touch it with my toe, and it looks familiar. Checking that the table is in a fit state to take it, I lower the bag with its parcel and, bending, retrieve the disk from the floor. It takes me some moments to realise what I am holding. I have just paid a considerable amount of my hard-earned cash to buy Alan a long-playing record, a disk of short excerpts of classical music, and now here I stand holding Mozart's *Requiem*. I turn it over, The London Philharmonic offer several hours of wonderful music. Coming to my senses I look across the room as another disk whirls towards me. Recovering it just before the older boy arrives in its wake, I wipe dirt from its label: Beethoven, *The Halleluja Chorus*. I almost jump into the adjourning room as another disk hits me in the

134

back, and the children retreat. Vivaldi's *Four Seasons*. I am almost crying as I hold the disk.

"Hello there." A nonchalant voice behind me speaks; I know who stands there and I turn, for the first time anger in my motion. I hold one of the disks out towards Mrs Tate. The summer dress, now ragged, hangs only to her knees, the hair, even more unkempt, hangs askew across her eyes. "Oh, I see you are a music lover, too." Taking the Vivaldi from me she turns it over, screws up her face and says, "Prefer Beethoven myself."

I fight to control myself. I see Simon holding one of the disks but it is heavy and it falls to the floor. I have gathered up six disks and now hold them out towards her.

"Where did you get these?"

"Oh those, they are free, I sent for them, they came the other day."

I have almost crawled around the floor and found the remains of the cardboard box in which they were delivered. She had followed me around and now speaks.

"They are free, told you. Saw it in *The Times*, my husband brought the paper home."

Bending, she recovers screws of paper from the unlit fire, and pushing my bag and the parcel to one side, she smoothes the bits of newspaper out on the table. I stand, holding the long-playing records under my arm. The children watch me from their crouching position under the bay window, their attempts at laughter now ended. "Oh, what the heck, let them play," I think to myself. Her voice breaks through my thoughts.

"Here you are, 'long-playing disks FREE'." This part the company had written in large letters, the small letters said "for the first month, thereafter . . ." More money per week than Mrs Tate could spend on drink. Her voice is droning on, reading the advertisement.

"But Mrs Tate, you don't have a record player." I manage to get out the words as I press my free hand to my forehead.

The Christmas parcel has almost been forgotten, but Jenny's voice brings me back. She stands by the table, dressed in her school clothes, and with her hair tied back. I am surprised by how pretty she looks.

"What's this?" she asks as she lifts the shopping bag.

I explain the parcel to her and she assures me that it will be hidden away until her father returns. I discuss the records with her; she remembers them arriving, but can't remember who sent for them.

"Talk to your father; I will store the disks at the clinic. Check with him if he intended to order them. If he didn't I will return them so they don't charge you."

With the six records weighing heavier than the Christmas parcels had, I struggle back to the clinic. I am determined to find some children's toys to replace the disks I'd prised away from them. Even if the toys stay in the house for but a short time, it will be worth it. Stopping that laughter had pained me.

Repacked, the disks are eventually posted, filth and all. "Music Lovers Christmas Extravaganza" will receive an interesting New Year surprise. It's a pity I couldn't keep the disks as our record player is much valued, but it's not just Mrs Tate who lacks the money for such luxuries.

11.30a.m.
I am venturing into unknown territory. I have brought the map with me as I have not approached Tower Road from this direction before. The day is overcast and the afternoon light, already fading, gives me little help. On the bus I had reminded myself of Mrs Parkin's address on my small map but the street before me is long and straight and the houses fronting on to it stand in relentless rows, colourless and without definition. There had been no name on the street when I had turned off Park Lane, and no person to ask. I stare at the map. The wind whips down the street, my hat takes off and the map, cardboard and all, sails into the air. I run after both, catch and hold the hat, and my foot rests on the map. The crumpled map, which now resides inside my coat and the bottom of the shopping bag holding the third parcel, are wet, as I continue my walk up the street, looking for Tower Road.

I had been introduced to Mrs Parkin via the midwives at the maternity hospital. A couple of weeks ago she had collapsed in the street. When the ambulance men attended her they found she was bleeding, and suspected that she was pregnant. Their suspicions had been confirmed, and after a week in hospital the pregnancy had been stabilised. It was a shocked and surprised Mrs Parkin who had returned home. I had visited the rather timid and frail woman who, in her middle years, already had three sons all at school.

On my first visit her house had been, as many in the area, dark, cold and sparsely furnished. I had seen no one but Mrs Parkin and there had been little sign of other inhabitants, and most certainly no sign of other children. We had talked for some time and I had discovered that her sons, aged twelve, eleven and six, all attended a school for children with special educational needs; they were all classified as being "educationally subnormal". The school was residential, and the boys only returned home during the holidays.

Mrs Parkin had been sterilized after the birth of her last child because it was felt that she and her husband would keep producing such children. So she had been very surprised at finding herself pregnant again.

Someone at the hospital had said, "Had we found your pregnancy earlier we would have terminated it, but now it is too late; you must go to term."

At my first visit she had cried a good deal and had said, "I don't want to be no burden to society, miss."

I, planning to go to the hospital and murder someone, had tried to console her, and had assured her that we two would go through this pregnancy together, and if anyone said that this little person was anything other than a great blessing, I would speak to them. I had visited Mrs Parkin twice already, visiting the corner shop en route. I had notified my colleagues that I would not be in for dinner on two days of the week and on those days I had bought ham rolls and a bottle of milk from the shop and had shared them with Mrs Parkin.

The boys are to be home for Christmas and I am delivering a few extra goods. The front door is firmly closed against the wind and the entrance to the back of the house, which runs down the side of a factory, is dark and the steady thump of machinery and the sharp smell of hot metal do little to improve the general ambiance. The factory's galvanised iron roof drips rusty water on to a yard, which is about four feet wide, and from which three unpainted wooden doors open. At my first tap the middle door opens and Mrs Parkin's face peers out. She stands, and for a moment I wonder what has happened, then she stretches her mouth, nods her head sideways and says, "Come in."

The room, in which stands a mangle with a wooden top which forms a table, two upright wooden chairs and a large tin bath which hangs on the opposite wall, is small, cold and dimly lit. I put the shopping bag on the mangle top and trying to smile ask, "So how are you?"

Mrs Parkin does not reply. The little light entering from the adjoining room is blocked, and a rough voice asks, "What you got there?"

His dress is similar to that of Mr Tate's and his body size is similar, but there it ends. This man appears to be soft and gentle, or on second view I might say smooth, slimy and not too bright. Appearing to almost glide he crosses the kitchen in two steps, his large boots making no sound and his worn, loose, clothes seeming to slide with him. Paying no attention to me, he looks down on the bag and repeats again, "What you got here?"

The parcel is lifted, and without ceremony, torn open. No saving decorations or wrapping here, the box is thrown wide and the contents pulled out. The tins are dropped onto the table, but the Christmas pudding, in its greaseproof paper, is examined with more care. The sweet smell of fruit and spices rises as he tears open the outer cover, and with dull eyes looking at me from a be-whiskered face, he backs out of the room, devouring the cold and uncooked pudding.

CHAPTER
TEN

Tuesday, 20th January, 1959

11.30a.m.

"That must be the house," I tell myself.

This morning I have walked for what seems miles, up New Town Row and back down again, but there is no sign of number 35a. Ahead of me lies the narrow dark road; on my left lies the broken derelict remains of a factory and on my right a continuous grey wall, into which patterns of windows and doors are set to fool me into thinking that I have found human habitation, I hurry down the road, but again there are no houses, just the grey walls with their wartime camouflage.

I stand defeated, my feet are soaked, my hat hangs limp and useless, and a flurry of snow hits me in the face. I am cold and wet, my throat aches and my nose won't stop running; the small handkerchief is of little use. The warm Christmas Day, just three weeks past, seems to have been in another world and now just cold dark days spread before me. Then I remember the mothercraft classes which are to start this Friday; a morning doing what I enjoy most, talking with expectant women about future events. For a moment I feel cheered, and at least for one morning I will be out of this awful cold. But for now the immediate problem still remains.

I had received a message from a school nurse. A child had been booked to start school after Christmas; he had not started, and the school wanted to know if he still needed the place. I had looked in my box and had found a card for a child named Maximus Went who lived at 35a New Town Row and whose fifth birthday had been in November. I should have visited him before he started school, so I feel rather guilty and am determined to make amends. However, the address that I had been given and the address I have on the card seem to be non-existent. There are no houses on this street. I turn and look back down the rainswept, empty street. A sheet of rusty corrugated iron lifts and sways. I assume that it is the wind which has moved it, but two men in heavy overalls and boots emerge and shuffle off down the road. Unheeded I stand and watch them, then I come to my senses — maybe they will know where number 35a is. Hanging on to my hat and my black bag I chase after them.

The two men look down at me with surprise, and they both nod their heads.

"Yo none goin' to find no houses here, miss, just factory and rubbish."

He points to the grey wall and the mounds of corrugated iron and broken concrete. The men turn to leave and I turn too, defeated.

Then the voice calls out, "I heard say as how a family live on that rooftop above the factory."

We all look up to where he points. The grey wall, which edges the road, has ended and another, of a slightly differing colour starts. Above its straight red-grey side there rises a pointed roof with small windows cut into its sides.

"Don't know as how it has a number, but it might be 35a." The man smiles down on me, the other nods his head knowingly and, rolling his cigarette across his mouth, turns. The two are gone.

The galvanised iron steps are attached to the red-grey wall, or at least some parts of them are attached, some parts aren't. It is a precarious journey, but I make it. A gantry travels off to my right and heads towards the pointed roof. It consists of iron strips joined together by intermittent bands of iron. Iron tubes, attached on one end to the stairs which I have just ascended, and on the other to the wall by the roof, act as handrails. Below this precarious bridge lies a chasm some thirty feet in depth; I cannot see the bottom. Taking a deep breath I set off. The bridge is firmer than I had expected and a small platform lies before the tall, narrow door cut into the side of the pointed roof. No number resides on the door, so more in hope than in expectation I tap on its unpainted surface. I am unsure who is more surprised, the woman who opens the door, or the woman who waits on its other side.

Introductions have been made, and now I stand on the other side of the door in total darkness. The voice speaks beside me, "Maximus is not here at the moment, but I expect him back shortly."

A diffuse light then fills the space, as a tall, very thin, youngish woman holds up a grey army blanket, and reveals the space behind it. For a moment I think that I am back in my Girl Guide days in a bring-and-buy sale in the church hall. Certainly the half-light and the large space in which we both stand equates in size to a church hall. Screens and hangers, covered in clothes in various states of disintegration take up much of the space.

"Do come in! How lovely it is to have visitors, please do take a seat and I will find some refreshment." The woman stands before me, raising and lowering her hands as she presses me backwards.

"Thank you," I murmur as I look behind for someplace to sit.

The backs of my legs hit something hard and I sit down on what I had thought was a mound of clothes, but which I now realise is a long settee. I am almost lying in mounds of cloth, my feet off the ground. To my surprise, I feel warm, and I settle back and start to relax. The smell in the room is unusual, but not unpleasant; it reminds me of something, but I can't decide what it is. "Oh well, it doesn't smell unkempt," I tell myself.

The lady of the house had disappeared, but now she reappears on a narrow mezzanine floor, which runs around the room just below the small windows, many of which are broken and covered with cardboard or wood. When I attempt to take stock of my surroundings

I find that I can't see the end of the room as another grey army blanket is suspended across the space.

As if by magic, Mrs Went reappears on my level, sits on what seems to me to be another mound of clothes, and lifts two flasks in the air. The flask in her right hand contains something dark red in colour and the one in her left hand contains a clear fluid. The smile splits her face as she produces two glasses from somewhere.

"You will take a little of my homemade wine, won't you?" Before I have time to say yes or no the glass is in my hand. "It is made of pure fresh blackcurrants — I noticed that you had a snuffle when you arrived, that's why I chose the blackcurrant." Again the smile as she raises a glass. "I have also chosen an elderberry, as this is also medicinal."

The clear fluid is held high. These are indeed medicinal substances, ones that my grandmother, an excellent herbalist, always had available in her arsenal on cold winter days. I have issues which I need to discuss with this lady, but maybe a little cordial, for cordiality's sake, would be good. The blackcurrant cordial slips down; it warms my throat and my nasal passages feel renewed and refreshed. Afterwards the elderberry takes the ache from my throat. Mrs Went's home is warm, soft and comfortable and her voice is soothing. But with no sign of young Maximus, soon it is time to try and rouse myself from the effects of the warmth and the wine.

Mrs Went moves the blanket by the door to one side ... The gantry lies before me. It had looked rather rickety when I crossed it for the first time; now it seems to be moving up and down, as well as from side to side, and the steps down to the pavement take long to descend. I lean on the factory wall to recover, hoping that the two men don't choose this moment to return. It takes me about an hour to get back to the clinic, although it is only about a ten minute walk.

"Did you find that child?" Mrs Burns asks as I return.

"I found the house, well, the place where he lives; I'll have to return to check where he is."

She smiles across at me.

"Is she the woman who makes good wine? Father Michael said someone brought some pretty strong stuff to the church bazaar."

I think it best not to reply to that, but ask instead, "What does she do with all the clothes?"

Mrs Burns laughs. "She and her mother sell clothes at markets, seems they do quite well for themselves — her mother has a house on Victoria Road."

"Does the child live in the rooms above the factory?" I ask.

"I don't know. Father Michael thinks they only keep that address so that the boy can attend the church school, and so that they can have someplace to store the clothes . . . and the wine." She adds this as she looks sideways at me and grins.

CHAPTER
ELEVEN

Friday, 23rd January

9.30a.m.

I call in at number 35a again on my way to the hospital on Friday morning. This time I am prepared. I politely refuse the wine and in just a few minutes I elicit the information I need. Master Maximus is with his grandma and will be returning here on Saturday. I hand over a card on which is recorded the dates when clinics will be held and remind Mrs Went that Maximus should have his injections before he starts school. Once again I note the sweet and not unpleasant smell, which I now assume is a chemical used to cleanse and preserve clothes. I glance up to the mezzanine; bottles line a long wooden shelf and I am amazed at how many there are. However, I have also noted that all signs of my cold from the other day have disappeared.

"Here's to you, Grandma," I think as I descend the steps.

CHAPTER
TWELVE

Friday, 13th February

9.30 a.m.
Today is the day for our hospital work. The Health
Visitors' sessions at the maternity hospital have been
well received. Our little room has been converted and
posters informing women of their rights, both financial
and physical, line the walls, and comfortable chairs
have been squeezed into the room. Equipment from the
health education department at the council arrives
every week, as ordered, and the attendance has been
good, in fact it is verging on excellent — we can hardly
squeeze everyone in, and I usually sit on the desk to
teach.

I often manage a couple of visits before I head for the
hospital, but I usually check times with Mrs Burns
before I head out. Today she has not arrived at her
desk.

"Have you seen Mrs Burns this morning?"

Miss Haines mumbles "no" into a filing cabinet, and
I return to the office, unsure as to what I should do.
"Maybe she is ill," I tell myself. But Miss Hampton
would have told me if she had reported in sick, I look

down at her desk as I pull on my coat. "I'll leave her a note," I tell myself. "But then that won't help; she won't be able to find you if you are out visiting." I stand, coat half on, half off, then my problem is solved.

Mrs Burns stands in the doorway, her body slumped forward and her hand pressed to her forehead.

"It's Mrs Blunt. I told her not to have him back, but there you are, he is a very forceful man, she can never stand up to him." She lowers her hand and accepts the cup which I offer her. Without drinking she turns and places the cup on her desk. Turning back towards me she almost shouts, "But he's gone too far this time. Goodness knows what would have happened if I hadn't called around." Lifting the cup from behind her she takes one sip. "She didn't answer the door; I thought she was in, so I looked through the window. She was sitting on the stairs and I could just see her bare legs and the poor children." She stops speaking and turns back to her desk. Picking up a set of notes she looks at them and nods her head. "Four, two and a baby of six months; you should just have seen the state of them. I think that the boy had tried to defend his mother — he has a real black eye and they will have to X-ray his arm, it might be broken. She was naked, they were *all* naked, no clothes left in the house, he had taken them all, and there is hardly an inch of her body that is not bruised."

Picking up the now cold tea she takes a swallow and then turns over her hand to look at her watch and spills tea down her coat. I take the cup from her as the crashing of doors and the sound of voices resound from the hall. She is gone, wet coat and all.

149

Two nuns stand in the hall. A swollen-faced woman with a blanket draped around her body and a sleeping baby clutched close leans heavily on one of them and a small, bloodstained child, covered in a similar blanket, lies in the arms of the other. Miss Hampton has greeted them and now turns to Mrs Burns for an explanation. Some talk and then the entourage disappear into the weighing room, as Miss Hampton's voice calls out.

"Tea, I think, Miss Haines."

This morning the hospital sessions will all be down to me.

12.30p.m.

A car is leaving as I return to the clinic after the classes. Miss Haines is carrying cups and an empty biscuit tin from the waiting room.

"What happened?" I whisper to her.

She looks across at the closed door and mouths, "Tell you at dinner time."

I find out later that the woman and the two children had been taken to the convent, which stands by the Catholic cathedral, and the four-year-old boy had been admitted to the children's hospital. Mrs Burns held his hand while they administered the anaesthetic — she had been right, the arm was broken.

CHAPTER
THIRTEEN

Thursday, 19th February

9.00a.m.

As I enter the Health Centre loud laughter startles me. So much humour at this time in the morning is, to say the least, unusual. A tall, well-built man rises to his feet as I approach. This morning Mrs Burns is animated, and bright roses colour her cheeks and smiles wreath them as she, too, stands and makes the introductions.

"Father Michael, this is my colleague, Miss Compton."

The green eyes smile down on me as the strong hand takes mine.

"A pleasure to meet you at last, I have heard so much about you, most of it good." The voice laughs again, young and strong.

Mrs Burn's voice holds laughter as she speaks.

"Father Michael has solved our problem for us — that is, the problem of Mr Blunt; we don't think that he will be bothering the nuns again, or anyone else." Her eyes smile as she looks up at the man who wears the cloth.

"Just took a little imagination and a firm hand." He pats her arm, and looking at his watch, steps backwards. "Must be getting along."

"Thank you, Father, it has taken a load from my mind."

"No problem, never thought my ill-spent student days would be of such use." So saying he heads towards the door.

This time last week Mrs Burns had not looked her usual self.

"Are you all right?" I had asked.

With a despondent shrug and her head lowered she had replied, "He went round to the nunnery last night — Mr Blunt, I mean. He was drunk and made an awful noise and threatened the nuns, said he would get them if they didn't send his wife and children out. The police moved him on, but he said that he would be back. Maybe I shouldn't have got them involved, he is a violent man and he's been in prison twice for causing harm to someone."

I tried to reassure her that she had done what was necessary, but she was not convinced.

"My Arthur says that he will come round and give him a good hiding if he touches me, but dear Arthur is not strong so I do hope that he doesn't get involved. What do you do with a man like Blunt?"

Tears had welled up in her eyes, and my arm had been of little comfort.

Now I stand by my desk, not wanting to start with today's work; I want to know what has happened. Mrs

Burns enters the office, her face still bright as she continues to chuckle to herself.

"Come on then, tell me what happened," I say as I drop down into my chair and face her.

"Oh, I don't know if I should tell you — he could get into trouble if they found out."

"Found out what?"

She turns around, hands pressed to her face. Eyes sparkling with laughter above latticed fingers she manages to speak.

"Oh! I hardly know how to tell you, but you won't tell anyone else, will you?"

I reassure her and she settles into her chair.

"Well, you know that Mrs Blunt is staying at the nunnery because her husband had beaten her children."

"Yes," I murmur. This is an old story and I want to know the new episode.

"You know Mr Blunt went to the nunnery and threatened the nuns, said he would see to them if they didn't send his wife out?"

"Yes, I remember. You were worried that your husband would get involved if he threatened you."

Now we sit leaning close, her voice almost a whisper.

"Apparently, Mr Blunt went round to the nunnery again. Mother Superior said he was pretty drunk; he bashed at the front door, but it's tightly locked and didn't move, so he threw a half a brick through one of the side windows. Then he shouted through the broken window, said that he was coming back the next night to force the window and fetch his wife out." She bursts out laughing.

I, as yet, cannot see the joke and tell her so.

"I don't see anything funny in that! I think the nuns should have sent for the police again."

"Oh, you wait a minute, then you'll see the joke. Father Michael said the Mother Superior told him what had happened and asked for his advice. He said that he had told her that he would try to have a word with Mr Blunt." With her hands to her face she starts to laugh again and mumbles, "I really don't think that I should be telling you this."

I am becoming a little exasperated. I don't see anything funny in the events to date.

"Oh! Come on," I almost shout, "you can't stop now."

"Well, Father Michael said he didn't know how to get hold of Mr Blunt, but he knew that he drank at the Three Tons public house, so he went round at closing time, thought he might speak to him when he came out. The pub is not far from the cathedral, so Father Michael waited by one of its walls, on the road which leads to the nunnery."

I work to bring her back to the story. "So did he see him?"

With a smile stretching across her face she replies, "Oh yes, he saw him. Had to stand for a while and he'd just pulled his big black coat around him, when he heard this voice singing and shouting. It was very dark on the corner and he stepped out into the road holding his arms out to attract the man's attention. As he said, he was only intent on stopping the man so that he could speak to him. Father said he couldn't be sure what happened next, but the man must have been very close, because as Father lifted his arms and his coat fell open, the man walked straight into his arms. He said Mr Blunt just went into some kind of drunken panic, whirling around and shouting 'Get away from me you demon'."

Mrs Burns pushes her chair back and laughs out loud again.

"Mr Blunt was so drunk he thought he was seeing a demon. Father tried to control him, to save him from hurting himself, but he was so overcome that it took a left hook, as Father Michael put it, to stop him."

Now I start to see the humour in this, and ask, "So what did he do with him, take him to the nunnery?"

Now she has to dry her eyes as she continues.

"No, Mr Blunt was on his knees begging Satan to give him another chance and Father said that he couldn't let Satan take credit for this redemption, so he put on his deepest booming voice and said, 'The Archangel Gabriel is not pleased with your behaviour, and he has sent me to return to you that unbecoming form of action, which you deem it necessary to direct towards women. He demands that you do not go near the nunnery again and that you leave your wife in the care of the nuns.'"

We are both laughing so loudly that Miss Haines pokes her head into the room to see if all is well. Mrs Burns wipes her eyes.

"Just discussing a case, no problem," she manages to say.

When we are alone again I ask, "*Did* he keep away?"

"He didn't go that night, but Mother Superior said that he was outside the main door on the next night, shouting something about it taking more than the Archangel Gabriel and all his bullies to stop him. So Father Michael waited for him again. He said that Mr Blunt was on his knees begging for forgiveness before he'd hardly set eyes on him but Father said he thought it could go on forever because it seemed this man only understands violence. So he said, 'The Archangel Gabriel has heard your words and has seen your deeds. He is very displeased, and he asks me reward you with like deeds.'"

"Did he give him another left hook?" I am starting to enjoy this story.

"No, he said that his old boxing training came to the fore and he gave him, as he put it, a tickle around the ribs, and a tap at the side of the head. He left Mr Blunt being sick in the gutter. Father said he called out as he left, 'That was a reward from the Archangel, do not raise his wrath again.'"

Tea is made and as we stand in the kitchen drinking, I ask, "Did he go back to the nunnery?"

She replies over the rim of her cup, "Well, he went back yesterday to say sorry, and to ask if he could say hello to his wife and apologise."

We both laugh out loud again. "Wow, I bet that startled them."

"You haven't heard the end yet," she says as she washes the cups. "Father Michael said that Mr Blunt has also been to confession, and asked if angels were able to forgive. Father had said that he was sure they were, but he was also sure that they remembered. Father said he was pleased that Mr Blunt had been to confession, as he was worried that he was starting to enjoy the boxing bouts."

CHAPTER
FOURTEEN

Tuesday, 3rd March

10.00a.m.

The morning is cold; most mornings are cold at the moment. I had left Alan in bed, and he hadn't moved when I left the house. His thesis must be presented to his supervisor before the end of June, as he has to defend it at the end of August. His time, and more importantly his grant, will then run out. He now spends all his time shuffling through sheets of computer printouts and accusing me of having rearranged them while he was out. As if! The rest of the time he spends at the university doing punch cards and arguing with the women who put them on the mainframe computer. I don't know which of us will have gone mad before this thing is finished.

I alight from the bus in town. For the last couple of weeks there has been rubble and broken window frames in front of the old red building which stands across the road from the bus stop. A man who was climbing off the bus had said that it was an old warehouse and that they were pulling it down. I had asked if he knew what they were building in its place.

"Nothing for the likes of me and you, you can bet on that," he had said.

Today half the building has been pulled down and the pavement is covered in broken bricks and red dust.

Work at the Health Centre offers little respite; it seems that our recorded number of visits and clinic attendance are not up as they should be with one new Health Visitor; maybe I should walk a little faster between clients, and give less time to each of them when I do get there.

On this cold damp morning the long dark streets look very inhospitable and possibly jogging long Park Lane would keep me warm. This street seems to go on for ever; maybe it would be a good thing to run because its edgings of tall grey houses make it feel like a tunnel, a wind tunnel that is.

At last Clifton Road appears. The large, unpainted door, which rises above two concrete steps, stands firm and no one responds to my knock. I had received a set of notes from the Health Department, which tell me that a family of three young children, the youngest only a few months old, have moved into this address. I step back into the road and look up at windows; three stories rise above me. There is no sign of life, not even the flick of a curtain. Two houses along, an alleyway runs between the houses and offers a way to the back of the house I need to visit. A high, broken fence, with gates whose laths have been torn away — no doubt for burning — edge the gardens behind the houses that front on to the road. A broken number tells me that this

159

garden — well, this space, leads to the rear of number 77, the one I seek.

Steps lead up to a closed door and a heavily curtained window looks out on to the broken, unkempt yard, where the overflowing drain has left a supply of food for more than the local birdlife. My rap on the door causes no disturbance within, but my visit has raised some interest. A rattle of the fence between the houses alerts me to the fact that someone is in next door. A face appears in a gap in the fence; the turban, holding any stray hair firmly from the face, is the only colour in sight.

"Yo'll non find anybody in there at this time, gone at ten they are."

The face is gone and I realise that the rattling has been caused by her broom, which she now shakes high above the fence.

Hastily I return down the steps and approach the fence. "Good morning, I'm the Health Visitor, and I wonder if you could help me. I'm looking for a woman who I was informed had moved into this house with several young children — a Mrs Betts?"

The broom continues its work and she repeats her words, "Yo'll non find anybody there at this hour, gone by ten they are."

"Why are they gone by ten?" My words sound silly as I speak them, but they gain her attention.

"Bed and breakfast, that place, have to leave at ten in the morning, and they can't come back in until four thirty in the afternoon."

I look down at the cards which stand in front of my bag; yes, the youngest child is four months old.

"I think that you must be mistaken, this woman has a very young baby, and it shouldn't be taken out for long periods in this weather."

I raise my hand towards the dark threatening clouds to emphasis my statement. She raises her shoulders and carries on sweeping. Leaning the broom on the wall she turns to me.

"Look, miss, I don't know nothing about them, I just know if yo want to see um come back at four thirty."

Now the road looks even darker and the rain has started. Where can a woman with a child so young go? Maybe she has relatives nearby, I tell myself. I look down at the notes, thinking I'll return after I've finished my other calls.

At my next visit on this road the large door is opened, but just a face appears around it. I watch the face, expecting the door to open further, but it doesn't; in fact, it closes. Now just the eyes peer at me.

"What you want?"

The voice is sharp, it does not invite conversation.

"Um!" I look down at the card to check the name, my foot falls off the step and I walk backwards on to the road. The door closes. In haste, I jump the two steps back up and hammer on the door. I manage one bang; the door opens and I stand, with fist raised. A large lady, dressed in a floral nightdress and large felt slippers, looks down on me, her face red and her mouth tight.

161

"What yo making all this noise for? I was in bed trying to get some sleep." I step back and try to smile at the woman. "If yo selling something I don't want any, and if yo preaching God, I got my own inside."

The door starts to close, I have to move fast.

"No, I'm looking for a Mrs West."

The face reappears.

"Her's gone out to work, what yo want her for?" Now she stands before me, her interest aroused and her long nose twitching.

"I'm from the welfare clinic and I wanted to know if she has registered Thomas for school."

Her mouth curls up and she nods her head.

"Don't know, he don't live here no more, lives over Nechelles with his gran."

"Do you have an address?"

My voice echoes back, I am shouting at a worn and broken door once again.

12.00p.m.

It has not been a successful morning. I am very cold and I am hungry. I look down at my watch, just after midday.

"Time to give up, not many numbers added to the books today," I tell myself.

As I turn, a boy of about twelve years of age whirls out of a door opposite, and we just miss colliding as he turns back to the house he had left, pushes just his head inside and yells, "Yo blind as well as daft, yo silly old bat, yo got all the change."

162

Throwing back his head he roars with laughter, narrowly misses me again and, jingling money in his pocket, he skips across the road, his large, studded boots sending up sparks. I look after him as his flying jacket disappears down one of the alleyways. The high-pitched cry of an older woman's voice reverberates from behind the still-open door. Children, in their early teens, walk up the road towards me.

"Come back here, come back you vagabond!" the voice behind the door screams.

A boy of the same age as the one who has just departed pushes the door open wider still, puts his head in and shouts, "Drink your bottle and shut up!"

Other children, boys and girls, pass by, ignoring me as they go.

The door, which opens directly from the pavement, remains wide open, and the voice has quietened. Thinking I had better investigate, I venture inside.

For a moment I can see nothing; the only light entering seems to come from the open door behind me. However, I do know that there is human inhabitancy, the odour alone tells me. I had thought to shut the door and close out the cold wind but when my senses kick in I turn and seek the fresher air of the icy gusts which follow me into the room.

Having recovered my equilibrium I turn again and review the space before me. As my eyes become accustomed to the pale, grey light, I see that most of the space before me is taken up by a king-sized bed. At least, I think that it is a bed; all I can see is a confusion of colourless shape. I step forward and the undoubted odour of human decay is now overpowering. I am just about to place my handkerchief across my face when I see a movement within the grey mounds before me. Eyes watch me, their sharp brightness reflecting the only light in the room.

"What you want?"

The voice, just audible, sounds croaky, only half the volume I had heard out in the road. Now I can make out the shape of a figure as it lies buried beneath the chaos, just the head exposed.

"Oh! I do beg your pardon; I was passing your house when those boys came out of your door." I turn and direct my hand towards the still-open door.

"What you want?" the voice repeats.

I realised that I had not answered her question and step forward as if to introduce myself as I speak.

"I am the Health Visitor for this area, I was in the street when I saw those youths leaving your house in haste, and they were speaking in a very impolite manner." The eyes watch me. "Are you all right? Have they stolen from you?"

I lean towards her and my breath is taken away. To my embarrassment I find myself gagging. Putting my handkerchief over my face I turn and pretend to cough.

"Do excuse me, this awful weather."

Keeping the handkerchief across my mouth I turn back towards her.

She has not moved and once again asks, "What you want?"

With the handkerchief just under my nose I can breath.

"I have called to see if you need any help." She does not reply. "To see if you are well or if I can arrange some care for you."

The eyes watch me, and I know that far from being the silly old bat the boy had accused her of being, a sharp brain is at work behind those eyes.

The voice is firm and it startles me. "You police?"

"Oh no, I'm from the Health Department."

I move further into the room as I reply; maybe someone else lives in this house and I should speak to them.

"Well, if you're not the police you can get out, don't want any health here, and I've got all the care I need."

As she speaks she rises up and I see that she holds quite a large object in her hand, which she raises above her head. There is a loud clanging of glass on glass and in the half-light I think that she holds a missile to hurl at me. Lifting the black bag to my head I retreat backwards across the room, sitting down heavily on something hard. From this vantage point I see her more clearly; far from throwing the object she now nurses it in her arms as if it were a small child. She seems to have forgotten me and, caressing what I now see to be a bottle, murmurs, "My little babies look after me don't you?"

So saying, she pulls a cork from the bottle she holds, and with both hands raises it to her lips. She takes a swig and the rattle of glass on glass continues somewhere in the bed.

Now she is calm. It seems that far from being her adversaries, the youths are her friends — in fact, her

165

contact with the outside world. Between imbibing what turns out to be sweet sherry, and nodding off to sleep (the lady in the bed that is — not I), we have an informative and quite lucid conversation. A large secondary school lies just around the corner, and, for how long she has no idea, the children have visited her on their way to and from school. They collect her pension for her, do a little shopping and most importantly fetch her the bottle of sherry which she says keeps her alive, one bottle a day. She knows how much money they take from her; it is a kind of game which she plays with them.

"Who pays the household bills? Does someone else live here?" I ask as I try to peer further into the house, but beyond this room total darkness regns.

"Oh, just me and my babies live here," she says, tapping the bottle.

Again the glass rattles as she moves her feet. Now I can see well and I note with some concern that the skin on her arm is encrusted, split and bleeding.

"May I come to see you again?"

I ask this as she closes her eyes, and the face, grey, lined and sunken, sleeps. I move the bottle from under her cheek but leave it by her side — her baby.

2.00p.m.

I have searched through the cards filed in my box and have found one for a Mrs Wainwright who lives at the house I had visited. The card had been set up five years ago when Mrs Wainwright was seventy-five years of age. At that time she had fallen down the stairs and had

166

broken her arm. From what I read, there had been no complications, and after she came out of hospital only a couple of home visits had been made. It seems she owns the house and, at the time of the broken arm, took in lodgers. I turn the card over. There is little written on it — too little to give me any idea why she has become such a recluse. Although I think those tenderly cradled bottles of sherry give me enough of a clue. But that is not my most pressing problem. With this lady, I think her physical condition is the main issue. How do I get her out of that appalling bed, bathed, and the bed covers changed?

Not yet familiar with all the local health services that my patch can offer, I seek advice. I can see that Mrs Burns is busy but I risk a quick question.

"Can I pick your brains for a minute?"

As quickly as I can I explain the situation.

"So do you know of any organisation where home visits are made to help people bathe?" I say to her back as she rises from her desk.

"No, I don't know of anyone who will go to her home, but if she lives near Victoria Road you might try the public baths." She taps the telephone directory as she passes on her way out of the door.

The Victoria Public Baths is listed under Local Authority Services. The phone rings several times before anyone answers, and I am just about to give up hope when a man's voice speaks.

"Victoria Road Public Baths, can I help you?"

"Oh, I do hope so," I reply.

Having explained who I am, and Mrs Wainwright's position and condition, I wait for him, and whomever he has to consult, to make a decision.

"We don't make no home visits," he explains, "but we can go and pick her up in a car. A lady bathing attendant can come with us, and she will help Mrs Wainwright when she gets to the baths. She'll have to bring her own towel and soap; we don't provide them any more."

"Oh, that will be fine, I'm sure that we can arrange that. When will you fetch her?"

There is a moment's silence, and then voices mumble before he returns to the phone.

"Will Thursday afternoon about half two be OK?"

"Yes, that will be fine. I'll let Mrs Wainwright know that you'll be coming, and thank you very much."

"That's all right, miss." The phone goes dead, and I am almost jumping with delight, the problem being solved so easily.

2.30p.m.

I head back to Mrs Wainwright's house. The door was open again and she still lies in the bed. Her eyes are closed, but I know she is awake because she can't resist licking her lips for a taste of the sherry drying on them.

"Mrs Wainwright I've got some news for you."

I lean over and press her shoulder as I speak; I had thought that I had become accustomed to the odour, but when she turns to look at me I have to step backwards. Heaven help the bath attendant, I think.

I have riffled through the box which stands at the far side of the room — the one I sat down on so abruptly earlier in the day. It holds goodies reminiscent of better times. A white nightdress, clean cotton sheets and a bath towel are unearthed and I have provided the soap and some baby lotion for her skin. I explain over and over what is going to happen and reassure her that I will be here when she returns, and will put the clean sheets on her bed. She nods her approval of the arrangements, and repeats the time when the car will arrive. The towel, soap and nightdress are on the top of the box, and I look back with a satisfied eye as I leave her to wait for Thursday. As I leave, my only concern is that her final action is to raise the sherry bottle and offer the cheers sign to me, her long, broken fingernails clinking on the glass.

Walking back down Clifton Road, the wind is now behind me, and it is cold. I glance down at my watch, and in the near darkness note that it is 4.15p.m.; again I have the cards for the three Betts children in my bag, and recall that the neighbour had said that Mrs Betts would be able to return home at 4.30p.m. The house is in sight and the door at the top of the steps stands open. I quicken my pace and in a couple of minutes arrive before it. Climbing the steps I look to see if there is a doorbell that I might ring, but before I have time to see anything a man appears before me and fills the doorway. He is a short, thin man, his grey, pinched face is narrow, the narrowness being accentuated by a long pointed nose. His lips, straight and pressed firmly together, speak no welcome, and the eyes, which look directly at me, hold no spark of warmth. It is, I feel, beholden upon me to make the introductions.

"Um, um, I am looking for a Mrs Betts; I have been informed that she lives at this address."

He stands straight, his thumbs rest inside the front of the waistcoat, which lies over a white long-sleeved shirt.

"Who told you that she lives here?"

Lifting the black bag forward I reply.

"I received cards from the health department to say that her address is now this one." Turning the cards towards him so that he might see the address, I smile.

Still standing high above me he ignores the cards, but steps out of the doorway and nears me as he speaks.

"Who are you? And what do you want?

A challenge is something that I have never been able to resist; I've had a lot of practice with my father. Stepping up the step towards him I push the black bag at him as I ask the question, a false smile on just my lips.

"Are you Mr Betts? If you are not, then I think that my business is not with you, but with Mrs Betts." So saying I step up the last step, turn sideways and squeeze past him. My heart is beating loudly, and I am pleased to note that only his cheap aftershave follows me.

A gaslight burns on the first-floor landing, and the smell of cooking is strong. The back of a woman fills the alcove over the stairwell, and I realise that it is she who is cooking.

170

"Good afternoon, I wonder if you could tell me if Mrs Betts lives in this house?"

I have spoken to her back, and she does not turn. Two gas rings stand on a bare wooden table and both are working at full force, a frying pan on one and a saucepan on the other are being worked at full speed by the hands of the young woman. Her concentration is total — at least, she manages to ignore me.

"I'm looking for a Mrs Betts," I repeat. "Does she live here?" I now touch her arm, but she does not turn, just raises and drops her shoulders.

Turning from her, I look around. Three doors open from this landing; each has a number painted on it in red, a narrow passageway continues on towards the back of the house, and I hear water running somewhere in that direction, but there is little light to direct me to where any activity might be. Stairs continue upwards, and suddenly flat shoes, topped by thick lisle stockings, appear almost at the level of my head. The legs descend the stairs to reveal a woman of indeterminate age who carries a large enamel bowl pulled in close against her flowered apron. I am sandwiched between the two women. The one who had been cooking now turns, her red face bearing down into mine. Pushing her hair from her sweating brow, she manipulates her own large enamel bowl around me, and without speaking, leaves. Squeezing past me the second woman descends upon the two gas rings and with speed and practiced dexterity, proceeds to work. Through all of this I have turned this way and that, but have not spoken; now I speak to the woman who has just arrived.

171

"I am looking for a woman who has just moved here with three small children."

She does not speak but, raising the spoon which she is holding, she points it towards the door with a number three painted on it.

A woman of no more than twenty-two opens the door. We stand for a moment looking at each other, two women of similar age.

"Mrs Betts?" I enquire.

She does not speak, but opening the door a little wider she peers out on to the landing; the woman who is cooking ignores her. With cheeks blazing red, she opens the door a little wider, and I take this to be an invitation to enter. The room is hot, very hot, and it is of medium size with a small bay window, which I assume looks over the road. A double bed takes up most of the space before the window, and a double-sized wardrobe, whose doors can't close because of the number of articles hanging over them, takes up all the space behind the door. The room is silent, and then I hear the rustle of paper. Two children sit cross-legged on the bed, their backs pressed hard against its head. I step further into the room in order to see them. Neither speaks nor makes a sound, they both just look at me. The door clicks closed, and with her face still burning red, the young woman faces me. She is about my height, but under the large apron, which covers most of her body, I can see that she is incredibly thin.

"You Welfare?" she asks.

The smallest child, a girl, who I know to be two years of age, starts to cry, and with great speed her mother scoops her up. The older child, a boy of four, stays with his legs crossed and his back pressed against the back of the bed. He holds something in his hands and I realise that it is a children's book. I smile at him; he does not return the compliment, but in silence his eyes watch me. The girl stops crying and her mother lays her on the bed by her brother.

Introductions have been made; the baby, who sleeps in a carrycot in the bay window, has been seen; all three children are well-nourished and well-dressed, but I have discovered why the room is so hot. The familiar smell of paraffin should have warned me, the oil burner stands bright red and unguarded in the corner of the room.

"You really need a guard for that fire, it is very close to the bed." I follow her around the room as I speak.

"Must hurry, it's my turn for the cooker in ten minutes, have to get it done in quarter of an hour or I miss my chance."

The large enamel bowl is pulled out from beneath the bed, and a shopping bag is poured into it.

"Where do you go during the day?" I ask.

"Oh, you know, here and there, to the café, and often to the library." The boy offers me his book as evidence.

"Does your husband live here?" I ask.

"No, miss, he lives at the hostel, just see him at the weekend, he's got a job you know."

I move around her as she gathers things from the room.

"Can't you get somewhere bigger to live?" I ask the question as we almost fall over each other. The look on her face I can best describe as panic.

"Oh no, miss, we must stay here. We are on the housing list; if we move they'll take us off and we'll never get back on again. Must go now, miss, or I'll miss my time."

The baby murmurs, the girl has fallen asleep, the boy rustles the pages of his library book, and I am hustled out of the room in silence. The man, who I now take to be the landlord, watches me leave.

CHAPTER
FIFTEEN

Thursday, 5th March

3.00p.m.

Today the sun shines, not very warm, but at least bright and cheery. The Child Health Clinic is busier than I had expected. Over the winter months things tend to be rather quiet because it's hard for women to leave the house on a cold afternoon, and assuming that would be the case today I had asked Mrs Burns if she could manage alone so I could get back to Mrs Wainwright. But Mrs Brown has just come in with Nathan. Baby Nat, as he is called, is as bright as he had first promised to be; Dr West had seen him last month and declared him to be well up on all his tests. I am delighted to see him today, but every time I see him I am reminded of Baby Dean. I have been back to the house on Upper Thomas Street several times; I think another family lives there now but I haven't seen any children. I constantly look for Mrs Broses and her baby, but have seen no sign of them and can find no relatives. The baby's cards have been returned to the Health Department with "address unknown" written on their front.

But I can spend little time in the clinic with Nathan today. If all has gone well Mrs Wainwright should now have arrived at the public baths, and I will be able to change her bed linen. I have retrieved a woollen shawl from the Aladdin's Cave, and I intend to use it as a blanket. All of this depends, of course, on whether I can find a bed under the tumultuous pile.

I phone, and on the fourth, or fifth, ring a man's voice speaks.

"Victoria Street Baths, can I help you?"

I explain who I am and ask if Mrs Wainwright has arrived. I am intent on explaining why I need to know at what time she will be leaving, but the man stops me.

"Excuse me, miss, are you the lady who made the arrangements?"

"Yes, I am," I reply, sorry for not having introduced myself.

"Then, miss, I'm sorry but she wouldn't come."

"Wouldn't come?" I repeat.

"No, miss, she threw a bottle at the woman who went to collect her, and said a few abusive words. We can't force them to come, miss, can only collect those who want to come, but aren't able to make it alone." There is a moment's silence and then the voice says, "Sorry, miss."

My mind is struggling with the facts. Thrown one of her babies at them! She must not have understood what I had said.

"Hello, hello, are you still there?"

"Yes, miss," the quiet voice replies.

"Um, if I see her today and explain things, could you try again tomorrow?"

"Well, I suppose we could try again, miss, but we can't take her unless she wants to come."

"I'll go and see her." I say.

"All right, miss, same time as today then, thank you."

I hold the phone in my hand and look at it.

"She couldn't have understood," I tell myself.

I call to Mrs Burns, reminding her that I must shoot out for an hour. I have been informed by the cleaning lady that if I stay on the bus for one more stop I will be able to get off at the bottom of Clifton Road. This has made my journey much shorter, and now I am half walking and half running along Clifton Road. All is quiet and the door to number 61 still stands partly open. Stepping through it, I accustom myself to the half-light and the odour. She lies in amongst the mounds, eyes closed, but I am not in the mood for polite introductions and go straight in.

"Mrs Wainwright you promised me that you would go to the baths today. I made all the arrangements and what did you do? You threw a bottle at the lady who came to collect you."

She watches me, just her eyes showing over the mound which supports the bottle on her chest. Now she heaves herself up the bed, and gives me a glare.

"Somebody come just now, said they was taking me away; me and my baby soon saw them off, bleedin' idiots."

Pulling up a chair I sit by her bed and explain everything again.

CHAPTER
SIXTEEN

Friday, 6th March

10.45a.m.

This morning I am taking the mothercraft class at the hospital. I am delighted to see Mrs Parkin is one of the first women to arrive at the class. She is now seven months pregnant, and attends all the classes, although I am sure that she already knows much of what I teach. She has been a regular attendee at all the antenatal clinics, determined to do the best for this surprise baby. I have visited her home on as many occasions as I could manage and together we have eaten ham rolls, bought at the corner shop, and I have obtained her milk tokens for her and free vitamin coupons. Now I must rely on her to do the rest. Most of our transactions are carried out in the small dark kitchen, as Mr Parkin is usually to be found in the only other downstairs room, where he sits over an empty fireplace. On one occasion he had entered the kitchen, had taken the half-eaten bread from his wife's hand and, pushing it into his mouth, had disappeared without a sound.

Ten expectant mothers have arrived today and, with much laughter, we all squeezed into the small room to

178

discuss the layette, which the new baby will require. I have already invaded Aladdin's Cave for Mrs Parkin. Having reluctantly accepted that Baby Dean will not be using the pram which Mrs Wilberforce donated, I have asked if Mrs Parkin may have it. At last one thing seems to be going well, I can tell myself.

The session ends and Mrs Parkin retires with other mothers; a cup of tea in the hospital café is always acceptable, and the environment is more welcoming than her kitchen.

3.00p.m.
This afternoon I should be catching up with clerical work, but other things fill my mind. Picking up the phone, a man's voice answers my call, and now he knows my voice, and he answers my question before I ask.

"No, miss, I'm sorry but she was very abusive this time, we couldn't get anywhere near her. The attendant said that she looked as though she needed some care, but I'm afraid that we can't try again." He is silent for a moment and then repeats, "I'm very sorry."

The phone goes dead.

The clerical work is on the back burner and once again I push open Mrs Wainwright's door. The afternoon is cold; one of those dark, cold afternoons when daylight seems to fade at noon. The inside of the room is like a morgue — I have only been in one hospital morgue, but this is how I remember it. The figure on the bed does not move, and for a moment I think that my attempts to improve her condition may have caused her demise. My hand on her cold head does not give me hope. But the eyes shoot open, and their belligerent stare convinces me that she was awake when I arrived.

"Get out, bugger off. No one is going to take me away."

With these blunt words she disappears beneath the mounds and I am left with no part of her to communicate with.

With the feeling that I have completely failed this woman, and at a loss to know where to move next, I almost whisper, "I'll call to see you again."

I back out of the door, pulling it closed behind me.

The street is now almost in darkness, the gas lamps on time switches take no account of the weather and have not yet lit themselves. Shuddering inside my heavy overcoat I pull up the collar and tighten my scarf. The face of my watch comes into view; just gone three o'clock. I stare along the deserted, bleak road, and question whether the movement I see further along is Mrs Betts and her three small children.

"Surely she can't be expected to stay outside in these conditions." Mumbling to myself I hurry down the road.

The figure has disappeared, and now the door of number 77 stands firmly closed above its concrete steps. Convincing myself that I had seen Mrs Betts entering these premises, I rap on the door. Before the sound has died the door is thrown open, and the man, still in white sleeves, but now with cuffs well soiled and waistcoat buttoned, stands above me.

"Good afternoon." I start to speak as he moves forward to fill the doorway. The face is as grey as I remember, the mouth as tight, and the eyes, if possible, are even narrower. I try to smile. "If you will excuse me, I would like to come in to see Mrs Betts." He does not budge; only the hands, which he holds before him, tighten to form fists. I look down at the black bag, which I hold before me, as I speak. "I need to see her as I gave her a clinic appointment which she didn't —"

"She's not in. She's gone, don't live here no more."

For a moment I am taken aback.

"But I saw her here only a couple of days ago, she has three small children, how can she have gone?"

"Husband got a new job, she's gone with him."

He steps out on to the top of the steps and towers above me. His threatening nearness pushes me down one step and throws me off balance.

Regaining my balance I shout up at him, "But I would like to see her room! I'm sure I saw her come in."

In one move he steps down on to the step on which I stand and, with his fist still clenched, hits me in the chest. I step backwards. The blow has knocked me off balance and, with a thud, I land seated on the cobbled pavement. Still he stands on the bottom step his fist clenched.

"Bugger off, you nosey cow, and if you come back, poking your snout into my business, you'll get more."

It has been a long time since I have cried, and certainly a longer time since I have cried for my father, but now I wish he was here. I know well his opinion of men who hit women.

5.00p.m.
The office is warm as I throw my bag on to the cluttered desk.

"You must have smelt the teapot," Mrs Burns says as she holds her cup out towards me.

Without replying or removing my coat, I sink on to my chair. The fall had hurt my back, which now aches, and the punch had completely knocked the wind out of me; my chest aches and breathing is not easy. Miss Haines had watched me walk through the hall and now I hear Miss Hampton's steps. The injuries have been examined and fortunately the heavy coat and the scarf had deadened the blow; just a red mark over the sternum records the damage. The back, I am assured, will be fine after a hot bath.

"Do you think the woman is still in the house?" Miss Hampton asks as we finish our tea.

Feeling a little calmer, I take the children's notes out of my bag.

"These are the people I am worried about."

She takes the envelope with its cards, and looks at them as she asks, "Are there other families in this house?"

"Oh, yes, I saw several women, but I didn't hear any other children. It was completely silent, even the women didn't speak, and now I know why, with a landlord like that around."

182

Turning she says, "Leave these with me, I'll ring the Housing Department and see if they know this house. You get off home now, and get that hot bath before your back goes stiff."

6.30p.m.
My living room is as hot as the clinic office had been. Think of the electric bill, my mind screams. Alan and a woman stand over the work table, their heads almost touching, their arms crossing, their voices murmuring. For a moment I feel insanely jealous, not of their physical intimacy, but of their mental closeness. In our youth I had been Alan's source of inspiration, his confidante. Now he has moved so far away from me in his studies, but obviously not far from this woman. I realise that it is Judith, the Jude I had been introduced to at the Students' Union hop, when I was doing midwifery and Alan had just started writing.

"Hello, you two busy?" I ask as I remove my coat.

"Is it that time?" asks Alan, without looking up.

I'm about to say, "I'm early" when Judith intercedes.

"Goodness, look at the time! Must fly; give me a shout if you need to talk anything else over."

"Don't you want a cup of tea?" I ask.

"No thanks, Dot, must fly. Bye, Alan."

Feet clatter on the stairs as she descends. I stand, face flushed. I am tired and I hurt. Physically I hurt, and emotionally I am angered by the indiscriminate use of our resources; funds, which I earn by my hard work are being wasted, I feel. Judith's perfume lingers and I feel her furtive presence around my chap. I am irritated

183

and aggrieved; I came home for consolation not confrontation.

"You could have lit the coke burner, it's Friday, the weekend." I speak as I lean over and switch off one bar of the electric fire. Pain shoots up my spine and I shout out.

"Be with you in a minute," Alan murmurs.

Giving him a cup of tea I take two Aspirin and, feeling as low as I can ever remember feeling, I fall into bed.

8.30p.m.

I can hear the sound of the television through the wall. For a moment I can't think where I am; it is dark and I am still dressed and in bed. Realisation dawns, and with my back so stiff that I can hardly move, I creep into the next room. The settee is drawn up in front of the coal burner and flames now dance behind its glass. The room is not yet very warm, but I know that it soon will be.

"Better now?" Alan's eyes watch me over the back of the settee. Before I have time to answer he continues. "If you've got flu you can keep away from me, I haven't got time to be ill."

"Thanks," I say as I lower myself slowly on to the seat. "I don't have flu, just had one hell of an awful day."

"Join the queue," he says as he turns back to the television.

My back hurts badly and I feel angry.

184

"Maybe, but you didn't get beaten up by an aggressive man, did you?" Just mauled by a possessive woman, I want to add, but my back jabs and I want care, not conflict.

"What?" Now he is up from the settee and looking into my face. I can no longer hold the tears and the story is told.

"You know what there is in the cupboard, left over from Christmas?"

With Alan's arm around me and a double tot of Johnnie Walker's whisky in my hand the world seems better. A hot bath is followed by egg and chips, and we spend the night lying in each others' arms, the first for a long time. The back is not better in the morning, but it has improved.

CHAPTER
SEVENTEEN

Monday, 9th March

9.30a.m.

"So what do you think I can do about Mrs Wainwright? I can't just leave her, now can I?"

Mrs Burns is not really listening to me, she has problems of her own and Monday is always a busy day.

"Has she got any relatives? You might ring them, or drop them a note." She pulls on her coat, standing behind me as she wraps her scarf tight. I look down on to Mrs Wainwright's notes; Mrs Burns' manicured finger taps them. "What's that number, is it a phone number?"

I am unused to seeing phone numbers on clients' notes and this lightly pencilled number had not registered.

"It could be," I murmur as I look closer.

"Well, try it and see if it rings." She is gone.

"Erdington 472."

For a moment the cultured voice silences me, maybe I have rung a shop or even a bank.

"Um! I am looking for a Mrs Wainwright. Am I through to the right number?"

Before I have finished speaking the voice replies, "Sorry, you must have the wrong number, goodbye."

I almost sigh as I speak, my only avenue of enquiry now closed.

"Sorry to have disturbed you."

The phone hangs in my hand and then I hear a crackling sound as the voice shouts down the phone, "Hello! Hello! Are you still there?"

"Yes, I am here," I shout.

"My maiden name was Wainwright — has something happened to my mother?"

Mrs Parkinson, as she reveals herself to be, sounds sharp and clipped.

"We have seen little of each other since father died. A forceful woman, my mother; I tend to leave her to her own devices."

I have explained the present situation, including my attempts at arranging a bath for her mother. It seems Mrs Parkinson and her mother had parted company many years ago; a quarrel over money had split them. Her mother's present address has been confirmed and my credentials and telephone number have been passed to the daughter who, with a deep sigh, says that she will pay her mother a visit. I almost hum to myself as I set about catching up with clerical work, relieved to have someone else looking in on Mrs Wainwright.

4.30p.m.
"A Mrs Parkinson rang just after you went out this afternoon, said could you please ring her back this

evening," Miss Haines calls over her shoulder as she closes the door to her small food office.

I wait until 5.30p.m. and then ring. Again the crisp polite voice replies, "Erdington 472." She has visited her mother and the full extent of the problem has been revealed; now Mrs Parkinson's voice is less assured.

"I see what you mean about a bath, but she hardly knew *me*. I don't think that she will let strangers help her."

For a moment there is silence and then we both speak together — maybe the idea is conveyed telepathically across the phone line; whatever, arrangements are made for us to meet at her mother's house and together attempt to offer Mrs Wainwright a bath.

CHAPTER
EIGHTEEN

Tuesday, 10th March

10.00a.m.
The door to the pavement is closed and when I tap a voice calls, "Come in." The odour has lessened; a gas mantel throws a yellow light across the room and I am surprised to see pieces of pretty good furniture. Mrs Wainwright now rests against pillows and the mounds appear as blankets, pretty soiled, but recognisable as blankets. Her long-nailed hands clutch the edge of a blanket and not a bottle, and for the first time I see the extent of her condition. Her colourless, sunken face appears like a round blue-white pebble, which lies, beached, within a drift of rotting seaweed. From the gloom of the adjoining room a figure emerges. As the gaslight encompasses it I see a dark apron stretching from black high-heeled shoes to white silk sleeves, and a tall, straight woman stands before me. Pushing hair from her face she stops.

"Oh my goodness, what a mess, what a mess. You must be Miss Compton; I am Mrs Parkinson. What a mess, what a mess, where do we start?"

She had held out her hand but had withdrawn it before we met.

I am about to say, "With the bath, I suppose," when a voice from the bed pipes up.

"Always was a fussy child, fussy, fussy Freda. Never could take joke." The voice ends with a cackle. Mrs Parkinson is not amused.

A long tin bath has been carried from the yard at the back of the house, and has been placed in the room next to the one Mrs Wainwright uses as a bedroom. Water is already heating in a boiler in the kitchen and, removing my coat and rolling up the sleeves of my blouse, I set to work. Getting the bath prepared presents little problem; the nightdress is produced, and the towel placed ready, but now the real work begins. Despite Mrs Wainwright seeming to have lived on sherry for the last however long, she is not frail. We have her standing by the bed — she must have got out of bed from time to time when no one was there, because her feet and legs take her weight. Mrs Parkinson assures me that, according to the state of things in the remaining rooms, she has taken frequent trips out of bed. I ask no questions.

The steaming bath lies before us; we stand either side of our patient. The yells and cries almost waken the dead, but the nightdress must be removed; its torn shreds cling to her back, and seem almost to be removing her skin as we lift it.

"Let me go, let me go, you thieves!" she shouts as she flails her arms around.

"Come along, Mother, and stop shouting before someone sends for the police."

"That's it, I'm being murdered, send for the police!" Her voice is loud and croaky, and as she hits out at her daughter she falls backwards.

Letting a patient fall is a crime; no nurse can allow it. Instinctively I make a grab for her. She fights to hang on to me and, as she does, my face goes under the bathwater and I know that she has succeeded in her plan. Struggling to get my head above the waterline I push against the soft mass, but it now presses my body down. One of my feet remains on the floor; I push with all my might and press my free hand on the side of the bath with all the force I can muster. The body above me rolls with me and, to my great relief, the bath tips sideways, water sloshes out and I can breath.

Mrs Parkinson is screaming, the cultured accent forgotten. "Oh my god, are yo all right, are yo all right?"

Her arms pull me and I am free. The remaining water steadies itself and, half-clothed, Mrs Wainwright sits in the tub, the water lapping around her waist. Her eyes meet mine as I struggle to stand, only one arm and one leg of my body not soaked.

Now she smiles. "There, managed that. Not too bad, was it?"

3.00p.m.
The phone rings. I am in the clinic advising mothers and Miss Haines pokes her head around the door.

"Phone call for you, Miss Compton."

I smile to acknowledge that I have heard, and finishing the interview I walk to the office.

"Miss Compton speaking, may I help you?"

"Miss Compton, Mrs Parkinson here." The refined accent is back and I have to smile. "Just thought I would ring to let you know that I am taking mother back home with me — I think that we will be able to arrange things better when we have her under our roof." For a moment there is silence then the voice, a little less formal, says "Thank you for your help, um, and thank you for alerting me to the situation. Goodbye."

Before I have time to reply the line goes dead. For a moment I think of Mrs Wainwright lying in her bed, all her young visitors calling to see her, a non-stop supply of company because the secondary school at the bottom of the road will never run dry and she would have died before she ran out of friends.

"Maybe she'll go into a home, eventually," I tell myself. "Plenty of clean sheets and people to talk to, but I wonder if she will ever get her 'babies' again?"

"Not your problem." Mrs Burns reads my mind.

CHAPTER
NINETEEN

Monday, 23rd March

11.00a.m.
The door onto Tower Road is opened to my knock.
This is a bit of a shock, and when I see that it is Mr
Parkin who has opened the door my heart flips a beat.
Has something happened to Mrs Parkin? She had not
attended the last mothercraft class and had missed a
clinic appointment. She is now seven-and-a-half-
months pregnant, and although I have had no
notification that she has had the baby, I am concerned
that she might have gone into early labour and might at
this moment be lying in the hospital. Mr Parkin's
presence alone in the house does little to allay my fears.
Without speaking he has turned and slithered back into
the room. I follow, pulling the door closed behind me.

"Is your wife in, Mr Parkin?"

I speak to his back; he sits on a vegetable box, as
usual in front of the empty fireplace, yet he holds his
hands out towards it as though the memory of a fire
might warm him.

After what seems to me to be a considerable length
of time he turns glassy eyes towards me and, looking as

though he has just discovered me standing in his house, he asks, "What you say?"

I repeat, "Is your wife at home?"

Still looking at me from his seated position he shakes his head from side to side. Now I feel a chill in my spine, but then he adds, "Her's gone down to collect her money."

With relief I realise that she is just out collecting her maternity allowance.

"Oh, tell her that I called and that I will be back sometime this morning." He does not move and I am unsure if he has heard, so I decide to try to get his attention from another angle. "You not at work this morning then, Mr Parkin?" I have seen little of him until now, and am unsure what work he does, if any.

He shakes his head, and the glassy eyes turn on me again.

"Only wish I could get some work, miss, her being in the family way, like, but not much around." Shaking his head again he turns back to the empty fireplace.

I am back on the pavement, and with head down against the stiff cold wind and a brisk step to keep me warm, I set off down Sutton Street, but my route is barred. A petrol can filled with concrete stands on the pavement. A piece of wood sticks out of the concrete and string, tied to it, barricades off half the pavement down which I must walk. Several men, in rough jackets or overalls, stand or dig in the bottom of a trench, which runs on the other side of the string and which extends out into the road. With care I step around the damp earth which has spilled on to the pavement.

194

"Mind your legs there, missus, don't you go hurting those legs."

I look sideways, the man's face is almost level with my waist, and in front of him another man is swinging a pickaxe over his head; it lands with a resounding thud into the ground in front of him.

"Charlie, never mind women, you get this lot moved before the foreman gets back. You know what he's like this morning."

The man raises his eyebrows to me and sets to work with his shovel.

I have walked a few yards when the thought hits me; turning back, I approach the trench.

"Um, excuse me; are you looking for anymore workmen?"

Heads rising from their work, the men look at me.

"Can't say, miss, the foreman'll be back in about ten minutes. We are a bit short — are you offering?"

There are catcalls from his colleagues and I smile and shake my head as I speak.

"No, but I might know a chap who could use a job."

The man in the overalls asks, "Has he got a strong back?"

"Oh, yes," I reply as I turn back towards the Parkins' house.

Mrs Parkin opens the door to me.

"Hello, I called to see why you missed a clinic."

She does not reply but just nods her head to direct my attention towards the fireplace. Mr Parkin is now busy breaking up the box on which he had been sitting. A couple of the pieces of wood already blaze in the fireplace. I feel quite pleased with myself as I step towards him.

"I've got some good news for you. There are some workmen on Sutton Street, digging up the road. I asked if there were any jobs going and they said that the foreman will be back in ten minutes. If you go round then there might be a job."

The smile I give him stays on my face; as the sudden pain of a blow across my head freezes it there. For a moment stars dance and loud voices shout; I stagger sideways as an arm pulls me. After shaking my head and blinking my eyes a couple of times, I bring the world back into focus. A diminutive figure carrying a seven-month pregnancy has come to my rescue and now is beating the life out of a large six-foot man.

Protecting his face with a piece of wood, Mr Parkin is walking backwards as he shouts, "Well she had no right to go insulting me. Getting me job — who asked her to do that?"

An arm directs me to the door, as Mrs Parkin's quiet voice murmurs, "You better go, miss, I'll have to calm him down; a bit sensitive about work he is."

I stand outside the closed door; my head still rings and I feel rather light.

I think I should have taken a course in boxing not in Health Visiting to do this job. I must check if Father Michael is giving lessons. But at least I know that Mrs Parkin is fit and well, for the time being at least.

CHAPTER
TWENTY

Tuesday, 24th March

9.30a.m.
The card lands on my desk; the address is familiar, Tower Road, but the name is unfamiliar — Singh.

"This is an unusual name. Have you got any family with this name?" I show Mrs Burns the card; she glances sideways at it.

"No, I can't say I have."

A voice speaks behind me; Miss Winthrop is paying us one of her rare visits.

"Let me see." Taking the card in her hand she stares hard at its front. "Yes, my fiancé works in the Housing Department; he said that some Sikh families are being housed around here, it must be one of those." With a brief smile and no further information she returns the card.

10.30a.m.
I have walked up Upper Sutton Street, and now set off to my right and head down Tower Road. The numbers get higher the further I go, so it must be the other way. As I turn around, ice-cold wind hits me in the

face and I'm not sure if it is rain or snow that comes with it.

"This winter must end soon," I tell myself.

The aching throat and running nose seem to have been with me for ever and last weekend had been no better. Alan had paper all over the flat and when I moved some to get near to the fire he had the most enormous temper tantrum. If I had had some place to go I would have walked out on him.

Eventually I find the right front door but my knock brings no reply and so I head down an alleyway which has the usual sign hanging at its entrance, pointing to some court or other. But I stop, realising that there's something unusual here; the smell is quite overpowering, and it is one that I have never encountered before. I step into the small yard where water runs into a grate by my feet. Steam rises into the cold air and I realise that it is the water from which the smells are coming. Stepping carefully around the grate I head for the back door which stands, like so many around here, off a small yard. I knock and wait, black bag held before me.

The door opens just a crack. I can see a pair of eyes looking at me, but I can pay them little attention as I am almost bowled backwards by the aroma. Now more of the figure appears, and I face a woman whose like I have only ever seen in films before now. She is tall and strongly built. Her upper body, leaning towards me out the door, is clad in a brown tunic which closely fits her body and which stretches from her shoulders to her thighs. Above the tunic a strong face, oval-shaped and

198

brown-skinned, looks directly at me and the dark eyes ask the question, "Who are you?"

I realise that I have not spoken as yet, but as I look again at the child's card I'm clutching, she addresses me in an authoritative voice. I do not understand the words, but before I have time to speak she leans back into the house and calls loudly in the same language. Now the door is opened wide and, as a braid of black hair falls over her shoulder, she leans towards me, takes hold of my coat sleeve, and with a forceful tug pulls me across the threshold.

The door has closed and I stand just inches from pans that boil furiously on the old gas stove. She steps around me and, moving me backwards, she mumbles and attends the pans. I can not see what she does, but I can certainly smell the effects. The redolence fills my lungs and I feel that I am eating the spicy steam that rises over her. There is little light in the small room because both window and door are covered and there seems hardly air to breathe. A voice calls from the adjoining room; she replies with musical words which almost ring in my ear. Wiping her hands down in one move she turns, opens the door to the middle room and with a flick of her arm propels me through it.

I know the size of this room; all houses on these roads are the same, and I have been in many, but as is common in houses around here, near-darkness reigns. A red glow lights up the fireplace and I realise that I am standing beside an oil burner whose filaments are glowing at full force. Now it hits me how very hot the room is. My face already burns and, pulling off my gloves and unwinding the scarf, I look at the figures who sit but a few feet from me. My eyes are becoming accustomed to the light, or lack of it, but I can not distinguish who they are or on what they sit. Shouting loudly, the woman from the kitchen whirls into the room and busies herself with something on the wall. The sound of gas hisses, and a mantle, attached to the wall by the fireplace, comes to life and its yellow glow fills the room.

Now I can see my surroundings — well, at least I think that I can see them; it takes some time to absorb them. Sitting on low chairs, their feet drawn beneath them, four women look at me from across the room. Apart from being excessively hot, the room is incredibly crowded. Pieces of soft furnishing and piles of clothes fill all the space around the women and I realise that a second oil heater has clothes hanging over it at rather precarious angles. My patroness springs to life and with words that I do not understand, but whose meaning I know, she pulls what I see to be a girl of about sixteen years of age to her feet. I now see that each of the women is sitting cross-legged on a chair whose wooden legs have been cut down to about six inches from the ground. The girl, dressed similarly to the older woman, but with bright-blue tunic and multi-coloured shawl, is pushed, complaining loudly, into the kitchen, having been relieved of her shawl on the way. The woman I assume to be her mother sinks on to the vacated chair and, pulling her coloured slippers up beneath her, throws the shawl around her head and shoulders and looks at me.

I, in the meantime, have started to melt and, having undone my coat, make an effort to move a little further from the very red oil heater, but without success as vacant floor space is limited.

Pulling my black bag up in front of me I look at the card. "Yes, this must be the Singh family, or part of it," I tell myself.

Not moving, the line of women sit, heads covered, and watch me in silence. The door to the kitchen bursts open again and I am almost bowled over as the young woman who had been thrown out returns, walking backwards into the room. A bowl of something warm is placed in my hands and, talking all at once, the women each take a bowl, and all eyes are again on me.

"A cup of tea, hooray!" I think.

I smile my thanks, and as my mother always does when she is lost for words, I bow my head. All the women smile, and heads are bowed. We have something in common — a cup of tea — the words we can sort out later. The tea is a little different to what I'd expected and though I do like sweet things, as I sip it I realise it contains a substantial amount of condensed milk, even for my tastes. But what the heck, it's warm and drinkable.

Now I must ask about the baby, so taking a breath I speak to the lady who seems to be in charge.

"Mrs Singh?"

All eyes look at me, but silence reigns. I lift the black bag and take out Baby Singh's card, check the details and smiling towards them I rock the card in my arms as if I were cradling an infant. Now the oldest lady of the group springs to life and the voices rise. A young woman, who sits at the other end of the row, gets up slowly. She is quite tall, but very thin, and from what I can see of her, she looks pale. The first woman I met rises with her and, bowing to me, they both leave, returning moments later with Baby Singh carried by the lady in charge. She peels back several layers of blankets and passes the baby to the young, thinner woman. I am beginning to sort out who is who; the woman who now holds him must be the mother, and the boss lady, his grandmother, and no doubt the grey-haired lady is great-grandma. With care, the baby is unveiled and as I examine him all the women stand. He is a long thin baby with feet which are almost as long as his legs.

"Going to be tall," I tell myself.

Now I must remove his nappy, and everyone talks at once as I try to solve the riddle of the napkin. The elderly lady stands before me. She is about my height with, as I can now see, steel-grey hair, much wrinkled skin and piercing sharp eyes. With careful, work-worn hands, she opens the nappy and remains holding it open while I examine her great-grandson. Smiling, I confirm that the infant appears to be fine. All are wreathed in smiles and the young woman, now surrounded by much chatter, rewraps her son and disappears.

I am unable to find out the child's name, or how he is being fed, but this I can find out later, I tell myself. He is obviously being cared for by several able women and, as my mother says, "You can die of too little love but rarely from too much." After a hand-washing ceremony I head back out into the winter cold, just as I was becoming accustomed to the heat.

Back at work, my reception at lunchtime surprises me. As I pass the desk in the hall Miss Haines looks at me askance, and Mrs Burns, and asks what the smell is. I had become used to the rather tempting cooking smells in the house but even Alan noticed that evening — it must have been strong to penetrate through to him.

CHAPTER
TWENTY-ONE

Tuesday, 14th April

I have been back to the Singh family several times. On one of my visits a boy of about thirteen years of age, Kuldip, was home from school and he could speak a good deal of English. Through him, I found that the baby was called Ranjit and was named after his father, and grandfather. With what sounded like much arguing between the boy and the boss woman, who it turned out was his mother, and also the mother of the baby's father, he told me that the baby was being breastfed. A card with clinic dates was given to the boy, and after receiving a smart clip around his head, the young man translated the information into Punjabi, and, at the behest of his grandma, wrote a full translation down on the card.

I take most of my walks alone in the park as Alan must present his thesis to his supervisor at the end of this month. I have tried telling him that a walk in the park will do him good, but I get no reply, just another whirl of paper.

Overall I am beginning to feel quite depressed. Miss Hampton had put a message on my desk at work. It seems that a visitor from the Housing Department has been to 77 Clifton Road — the supposed bed and breakfast. He had found the house to be multi-occupied, but reported that although the accommodation was rather crowded he did feel that the facilities provided were adequate. He had found no Mrs Betts living there, and there were no small children in evidence at his visit. I looked at the note in disbelief.

"What time did you go?" I ask the absent inspector, thinking "If you went between ten thirty and four thirty all young children would be out walking the streets."

I had taken the report to Miss Hampton.

"Just send the children's notes to the Health Department; we can do no more Miss Compton."

The notes have gone; where the children have gone is anybody's guess. Whatever has happened, I desperately hope my intervention has not lost them this meagre accommodation. The last time I had walked along Clifton Road, the house had stood as blank and closed as before.

I had also passed Mrs Wainwright's house; it too was closed and the door was locked. A boy in short trousers and heavy boots gave it a kick.

"She's not in, gone away with her daughter," I had told him.

"That the tart in the big car?" he had asked.

I didn't want to speculate about her occupation, so I had just nodded.

My other charges all seem equally tricky at the moment. Mrs Parkin had missed a clinic appointment, and it had taken another visit to get her attending, though again I was not well received by her husband.

I have also visited Mrs Watts on several occasions; two of the children should be starting school, one after Easter and her daughter's child after the summer holidays. I have left cards on three occasions, and have asked her to attend an immunisation clinic. She just replies, "Yes, miss, I'll see to it," but nothing happens.

"Maybe I am in the wrong job," I tell myself. "Maybe I should just go back into hospital and stop poking my nose into other people's lives."

CHAPTER
TWENTY-TWO

Wednesday, 22nd April

Now the air has turned a little warmer; the trees in the park are starting to look quite green and the dark streets of my area are a little lighter.

This morning the immunisation clinic had been quite busy, and now the last child is in the doctor's room and the final notes are being filed. Miss Haines and I both work at the desk in the hall. The glass door creaks and a draught blows across the hall. I look up from my work and towards the door. A face looks at me — just the face. It peers around the door and a smaller face appears below it. The face at the top disappears and a voice calls, "It's here, I think we've found it."

A hand appears and the small face, which has been smiling at us, vanishes. For a moment I watch the spot, nothing happens, and then a voice calls out, "Come on our Margie, I think we are here."

I had thought that spring was about to arrive, but as the door bursts open it is as if an autumn wind is bringing in a whirl of leaves. Mrs Watts, her short frame filling the doorway, enters first, her billowing skirt alive with leaves of green, brown and gold. Her youngest, now quite a strong chap of fifteen months, sits high in her arms, resplendent in another suit of leaves. They are followed by a matching sea of green, brown and gold as Mrs Watts' other children follow. Two women I do not recognise, each with one or more children in tow, bring up the rear. Each child is dressed in identical clothing: the boys wear trousers and bolero jackets, the girls are clothed in skirts and similar jackets; even the adults appear to be attired in similar dress of autumn leaf pattern. The hall is filled with noise and chaos, and then above it all the voice booms out.

"There she is, have we come to the right place, miss?"

I regain my equilibrium and step forward to meet her.

Doctor has been warned not to put away the clinical equipment, and the children have found their way into the weighing room and the box of toys. Mrs Wilberforce, who had just come out from the doctor after Arnold had received his school jab, now sits back and watches the parade. Arnold is soon doing battle to hang on to the train, which he has, until this moment, always claimed as his own since the Tates took off with the fire engine. Mrs Watts sits beside the desk, her feet planted firmly apart, the leafy skirt at full stretch. Miss Haines, who is starting to get used to such invasions, has taken some of the women to a table at the other side of the hall. I have recovered all the visiting cards from my box, and now we start to enter each child into the clinical records.

"Sorry we're a bit late, miss, took some time to get um all into their new kit." She looks down at her leaf-bedecked skirt and, brushing her hands across it, smiles to herself as she says, "Not bad hey?" Her youngest child returns to her side, his leafy trousers now rather damp, and without taking her eyes off me she strips him of his trousers and nappy and sends him running. "So what do you think of um? You see, miss, you kept on saying that we should come up here for the kids, and we felt that maybe it would not be safe for um to start at that school if they hadn't been up here first. But we coudn' a come 'cause we hadn't got proper clothes for um to come in. The old 'uns can come in worn stuff, but not the kids."

Now she smiles at me and suddenly I feel quite ashamed of myself. I hadn't understood what I had been asking for.

The scraping of chairs against the wooden floor resonates from the other side of the hall and footsteps sound. She is speaking again, her voice now soft and kind. "But you see, miss, Nelly over there ..." she raises her hand to the approaching women, "she had the answer, didn't you, Nelly?"

A thin woman, with a frizz of self-permed hair, approaches us. "You mean the curtains, hey, Winnie?"

Others have arrived and all laugh, I sit, at a loss to understand.

"Well, you see, miss, Nelly had been shaking dust out of these old curtains, which hang, or should I say hung ..." Once more they all laugh. Mrs Watts begins again. "You see, these curtains had hung by that big window ever since you moved in, hadn't they, Nelly?" Nelly nods her confirmation. "Well we took um down, there were four of um, a bit torn in parts but a lot of good material." There was much affirmation of this statement. "So we washed um and Nelly there, and Jan over there, well they both work in the factory, make seat covers they do, cars or something." Both women nod their confirmation.

"And so we did a bit of overtime and ran up these," Nelly finishes off the story at speed, and everyone bursts into laughter. And now I see the old curtains brought back to life and dancing before me, and I have to laugh with them. Miss Haines isn't so sure.

"That was stealing," she whispers.

"No," I whisper back, "Just reclamation and ingenuity."

All children are immunised, and appointments for follow-up immunisations are given. I have talked Miss Haines into making the women a cup of tea, and a bottle of concentrated orange juice has provided refreshment for those too young for that. Mrs Wilberforce has made a donation towards the cost, and she and Mrs Watts now sit in animated conversation, while the smallest boy's trousers dry on a radiator. Miss Hampton has arrived back. The children are still rather active, and with an authoritarian look at me, she heads off into the weighing room. I hear her words, stern at first, as they change tone, "What is . . .? Oh, er, good day, Mrs Wilberforce."

With Miss Hampton silenced and the children all inoculated, I smile — a good day's work done.

210

CHAPTER
TWENTY-THREE

Monday, 4th May

10.00a.m.

Spring has come in with a bit of a rush and now it feels almost like summer; the temperature has risen considerably. It had rained pretty hard in April, but far from washing these streets, the deluge of water has caused drains to overflow, and garbage, which has been washed into corners, now sets like papier mâché modern art. The streets down which I walk have that strange "getting dry" smell, like a well-worn, damp woollen garment placed before the fire to dry.

Easter has passed, Alan's thesis is with his supervisor and, like a mole blinking in the light, over the long weekend he has returned to walking with me around the park. The blackthorn blossom did much to raise spirits and a bottle of wine and a visit to the cinema lifted them even higher.

With my heavy winter coat back in the wardrobe, and my less-than-waterproof raincoat hanging open, I set off down Park Lane. I have not been to the Tates' home for a couple of weeks and now something looks different. It also smells different; a powerful chemical smell fills the air. Goodness, has Mrs Tate been doing some cleaning? In the kitchen there is daylight; is it this which causes the apparent change, or is there more space?

I poke my head around the door. Mr Tate stands in the middle room, reading a sheet of paper. To announce my presence I say, "Good morning."

He looks across at me and smiles.

"Well, they came, then." He makes this announcement as he holds the sheet of paper towards me.

Before I have time to ask, "Who came?" I am being directed back into the kitchen.

"They shifted it all, and then they washed everything down, done it yesterday."

He stands with hands on hips, and surveys his new, rubbish-free, bright, clean room. That is why there is daylight in the room, the window has been washed. He smiles down on me; his hair is slicked back and new overalls, smart and unblemished, cover his ample form.

"They come like you said they would."

Again he smiles at me, and waves the paper. Now I remember. In January I had rung the Public Health Department and been put through to the Vermin Control Officer. I had explained the condition in which the Tate children were living and had asked if he could do anything about getting the landlord moving. His only reply had been, "Leave it with me." I had told Mr Tate that someone might come to see him, and I had heard nothing more, but now it looks as though they have done more than just contact Mr Tate. He is busy explaining to me what happened, but I am already looking for the children.

Mrs Tate walks down the alley, the sun shining through her usual see-through dress. The family follow; Simon, now walking, hangs on to Jenny with one hand and his green rabbit with the other; the other three children now wear clothes, I am shocked to see.

Mr Tate, still trying to read the instructions which the Vermin Control Officer had left, waits in the yard to greet them.

"Been stopping with Winnie, they have, slept there last night."

Mrs Robert's pale face looks at me around her door, and I raise my hand to her, memory of my last skirmish with her still sharp in my mind. Mrs Tate passes me without word, and I follow the children back into the house. Jenny brings up the rear, and I am surprised how mature she looks, quite the young woman, and when she turns to smile at me, I think "quite a looker". If only she'd clean those teeth. Without making any comment on the state of the kitchen and the yard, Mrs Tate has passed through into the far room, and turning on me, calls out, "How long you been here then?" I am about to reply, when stepping towards me, she raises her fist. "I know why he wanted me out of the way; you were coming to keep him company."

Putting his arm around her Mr Tate redirects her back into the far room. He calls over his shoulder, "I should go now, miss, I'll get her calmed down a bit."

I am well used to Mrs Tate's moods, so giving the assembled children a smile I depart, not even bothering to refute Mrs Tate's jealous imaginings.

As I swing back into Park Lane a sports car pulls to a sudden halt beside the kerb. Cars on this road are few, red sports cars are unheard of. Walking backwards I watch a young woman climb out of the vehicle. Removing a scarf from her head she leans back into the car, and after a few minutes, stands up again holding sheets of paper. I can smell her perfume from this distance, and her pale green-and-primrose coloured dress moves around her legs as she walks down the alley beside the Tates' house.

11.30a.m.

I have visited several houses, and now pass three women who stand gossiping on the corner of Upper Thomas Street. When I meet local women I usually say hello, and am just about to do so when one of the ladies swings to face me. In voice loud enough to compete for town crier she announces to the whole street,

"They sent for the Black Maria, reckon they will be taking her away now."

For a moment I look at her and then I speak.

"Sorry, I don't know what you are talking about."

Now the tight group breaks open, and all three women speak at once. From this gaggle of voices I gather that there has been a fight in one of the houses in Park Lane. I ask the question — "Which house?" — but I already know the answer. The reply, "Hers, that

214

daft bugger, her as walks around half dressed, as mad as a hatter" follows me into Park Lane.

Half walking, half running I turn the bend in the road. An ambulance is just drawing away from the kerb and a police car remains there. Now I cut out the walking steps and just run. A red-faced and limp Mrs Tate is being led down the alley; I have fought my way through the crowd that has already gathered around the sports car and lines the pavement at the front of the house. Now I come face-to-face with a young policeman.

"Can't come in here, miss, not unless you live up the back."

He nods over his shoulder as he speaks, and I see the long white face of Mrs Roberts; with hands waving and mouth wagging she tells her tale. I approach the young policeman again, and with as much authority as I can muster, I speak.

"I visit this family, I know them well. May I go to see the children?"

"No, miss, the police are dealing with it."

2.30p.m.
I had returned to the clinic to see if any messages had come through, but all was silent. Mrs Burns returned as I tried to ring the local police station.

"What happened?" she asked as she pulled off her coat.

Speaking as fast as I could, I told her all that I knew — which turned out to be very little.

"Calm down, eat your dinner and then go back and see what has happened to the children," she told me.

The advice was good, and as I now approach the house an hour or two later, all is calm and quiet. Treading carefully I step through the kitchen. No sound of children, or of anyone for that matter. Mr Tate sits in front of the empty fireplace, his head held in his hands. At my approach he looks up and, recognising me, he lowers his head again. For a moment I stand behind him, and then I hear a sound in the next room. Jenny, eyes red and face bloated from crying, walks in. I hold my hands out towards her and, falling over her feet, she almost lands on top of me. Stepping back to get my balance I hang on to her as the sobs start again. Mr Tate looks up at us, but does not speak. After some moments I manage to calm Jenny a little, and after much searching in the cleaned-up kitchen, we make everyone a cup of tea.

"I knew she'd do something one day." Mr Tate speaks through gulps of tea. I don't speak, and Jenny, now a little calmer, leans on the wall beside the fireplace.

"I didn't know who she was, said she was from the Children's Department, or something. The Public Health, who came to shift the muck, had told her that they had been to our place." He stops and sighs.

I put my hand to my head, in trying to help, had I caused something bad to happen again? I mumble, "Sorry."

"Not your fault, miss, I should have done something for her long ago, but you know how it is, you just hope if you leave it, maybe it will go away." He rubs his hand across his face, and the room remains silent. "You see, miss, in the war, when I was a lad of seventeen and hadn't been called up, I worked on clearing bomb sites. One night there had been a raid in the middle of town and some big houses got bombed. In the morning we was clearing up, as best we could that is, and digging for survivors. She was there, with a baby."

He stops, struggles into his pockets, produces a cigarette end and lights it.

"Wouldn't leave, kept fighting everybody, said she had to find her husband. She come to me, asked me to find him. She had blood running down the side of her face and it was running in her eyes, I wiped her face with this rag, and held the baby while she went for a pee in the rubble. When she come back she went off, mumbling to herself, so I followed with the baby, pretty little thing she was, even then." He smiles up at Jenny, who, wrapping her arms around his neck, kisses the top of his head and remains standing behind him. Now he stands and rubs his hand across his face as the cigarette stub sparks its way to the empty fireplace. "Well, things sort of went on from there; bit of a mess it was after the war ended. I don't really know who she is — I don't think she knows either, always has been sort of posh, but we've rubbed along since then."

He walks across the room and back, then pressing his lips together he looks at me.

"Should have done something about her years ago, got some help. She's never really been all there since the night we met, but now she's gone and done it, hit the woman she did. I had to drag her off; she said her from the Children's Department had come all tarted up to take me from her."

In the silence that follows, he puts his hand to his face and I ask, "Where are the children?"

"Don't know," his voice mumbles, and as he snuffles and rubs his hand across his face I see tears on his chin.

CHAPTER
TWENTY-FOUR

Monday, 8th June

Over the last couple of weeks the weather has not been warm; in fact, for June it is quite cool. But for me, the weather is not of much consequence: weekdays are work and the weekends are taken up with Alan panicking. He has found an external examiner and in August he must go to Leicester University to defend his thesis. He has to make one or two alterations before the work can go for binding, and a chap I don't know, and Jude, seem to be his main supports. All I really know is that when they are in the flat I am expected to provide a non-stop supply of tea.

10.00a.m.
A large black car stands outside the Tates' house.

"What is that doing there?" I think as I quicken my step and head towards the house. "Don't say they are going to take Mr Tate away," I mumble to myself as I head toward the rear door. There is a distinct smell of perfume, not the smell I associate with this house, but it is there. I tap the door and step into the house.

An educated and distinctly posh voice speaks.

"Well, Patricia, I had expected many things, but this beats them all. How could you want to live *here*?"

A tall man in a smart grey suit stands in the middle of the room, his nose is raised and a white handkerchief floats in his right hand. Mrs Tate walks in from the far room — well, I think it is Mrs Tate — her dress is of a flowered material, but not the usual see-through one. Her hair is cut in a short bob, clean and combed, and she wears sandals on her feet. Her eyes search the room with a concerned gaze as, in a quiet voice she asks, "Where are the children?"

Jenny stands behind the man, wearing her school dress, but none of the younger children are there.

"Where are the children?" Mrs Tate repeats, and this time the question is directed to Jenny. Jenny is about to speak when Mrs Tate sees me, and with a smile and hands outreached she heads towards me.

"Oh, *you've* got the children, where are they?"

The man turns and now I see him properly. Sleek and smooth, with gleaming white cuffs showing, he looks down on me; his lip curls up and the eyes stay still. His smooth hair glistens and his cufflinks sparkle; for some reason I do not like this man. Mrs Tate has now walked past me and into the kitchen.

"Where are the children?" the voice calls again.

I smile at Jenny and I feel the man's eyes follow me.

"Mrs Tate," I call.

Turning, she looks at me, and the eyes repeat her question. I feel lost as I face this woman, I hardly know her — so transformed is she from her usual self — and I feel that I am approaching her for the first time. "How

220

nice to see you again, Mrs Tate, and how well you look."

Jenny has walked to her mother's side and together we direct Mrs Tate back to the middle room.

"Is your father here?" I ask Jenny as we stand on either side of her mother.

"No, he has gone to do some shopping. My uncle brought Mother home, and he is going to wait until Father returns."

The man stands, long cigarette holder in hand and perfumed smoke pouring from his mouth and nose.

"And you are?" His voice is cultured, and I feel that he is patronising me.

I step forward, hand extended; he steps back and ignores the hand.

"I am a Health Visitor and I look after this family."

His mouth stretches and his eyebrows rise, and waving his hand around he speaks in sneering tones. "Well, I can honestly say that you are not doing a very good job."

Mrs Tate has returned to the kitchen once again in search of her children and I am more than pleased when the familiar voice of Mr Tate rings out. A large shopping bag is dropped on the floor and Mr Tate, accepting a cigarette from the man, puts his arm around his wife as she leans quietly against him.

"Well, Charles, are you staying for something to eat?"

The man looks around the humble room and says, "No, my man, I think I'll away and find a watering hole someplace. Bye then, Patricia, I will contact you if there is news." Picking up Mrs Tate's hand he kisses it, and

221

looking from under his lids at Jenny he says, "And I will most certainly be coming back to see you."

This is not lost on Jenny, or her father. Jenny blushes and Mr Tate looks from one to the other.

The car roars off, and those standing watching step back from the cloud of smoke. Mr Tate stands and savours his expensive cigarette; Mrs Tate still leans against him.

"Will Mrs Tate be staying at home now?" I ask as I make a note on the front of the card.

"She's not Mrs Tate," he says as he blows smoke into the air. "Her real name's Mrs Calverton." He looks down at the woman beside him, and smiles. "The chap you saw is her cousin. When she was in hospital they found him in London, and he came up to identify her. They had her down as dead, didn't they, my love?" He tightens his grip, and she smiles up at him.

I repeat my question, "Is she staying here now? Is she stable?"

"Her said that she wanted to come home to me. They got her on some sort of tablets now, said that she had some brain damage after the bombing, say she may never remember who she is, or who she was." Again they exchange smiles. Mrs Tate, or whoever she is, is now a different woman, calm and quiet and, in a sort of way, dignified.

"Will the children be returning?" I ask the question I've been trying to answer by all sorts of means. I have attempted to contact the Children's Department on several occasions; Miss Hampton has attended a case conference, and reported that a decision will most likely

222

be made when Mrs Tate has settled. The social worker has recovered, a small scar on one cheek, a scratch made by Mrs Tate's once-long fingernails is, apparently, all that remains to remind her of the attack. I don't think that she is going to take Mrs Tate to court; after all, she won't know who to summons, Mrs Tate or Mrs Calverton.

CHAPTER
TWENTY-FIVE

Monday, 15th June

Summer is in full swing and I look down at the cards which have just been placed on my desk; they are new to me, a batch just brought down from the Health Department.

I turn the buff-coloured card over in my hands. The name on the front is familiar and the address I know, but for a moment I can't remember the family.

"Who was expecting a baby in June?" I ask myself, and then I remember. "Of course," I almost shout out loud.

Mrs Burns looks up from her desk. "What?" she asks.

"You remember the woman who has three boys, who are all away at a special school, the one who was sterilized so that she would have no more so-called 'mentally subnormal' children? Well, she's just had a baby girl."

Mrs Burns' mind is full of her own problems but I am delighted with the news. I turn the card over. Weight: six pounds four ounces; a good weight I tell myself.

10.30 a.m.

Mrs Parkin stands by her bed in the hospital, her back towards me.

"Congratulations," I say as I reach her side.

She swings around and almost falls backwards on to the bed. We both laugh and she has more colour in her face than I have ever seen before.

"Isn't she wonderful?" she says as we both look down on the tiny infant who lies in a linen-sling crib at the foot of the bed and who acknowledges us with a small flick of her hand.

"She recognises your voice, all right." I speak partly to the mother and partly to the baby as I feel her head. All is fine, and as I touch her, two perfectly formed, minute hands rise and open like anemones beneath the sea; they close again with a slow, composed movement. "And she is certainly aware of the world." I again speak to both her and her mother.

Pride oozes out of Mrs Parkin as she looks down with tears in her eyes.

"Fancy getting a girl, miss, never ever thought about that. I had always thought that it would be another boy."

"What does Mr Parkin think about her?" I ask as I sit by her bed.

"Oh, I don't think he knows. The woman next door sent for the ambulance, he just stayed in bed; only just got here in time I did." She smiles and looks over to the cot.

"So when will you be going home?"

"Day after tomorrow, I think, miss, that's if Jean is up to weight. I was going to call her Clara after her grandma, but that's an old name, and she has got to be a modern girl."

Now we both smile and I have to agree with her. Saying goodbye, and assuring her that I will have the promised pram down at 141 Tower Road as soon as Jean and she return home, I turn to leave. Beneath their hooded lids the small bright eyes watch me, and I know for certain that I am being regarded.

Lowering my face towards her I say, "Welcome to the world Miss Jean."

The tiny hand tightens around my finger and the pink lips purse; they open and then close again. Her lids blink and her eyes follow me as I move. For a moment I stand and look at her diminutive form, "Far from being subnormal, Miss Jean, I think it looks as though you might cause your mother problems by being too bright."

"She all right, miss?" Her mother's face looks across at me, on her face the anxiety that all mothers feel when their child is being scrutinised.

"Oh, she looks pretty good to me — more than good, in fact." I smile at her mother and place one finger on Jean's head. "Bye, see you in a day or two."

CHAPTER
TWENTY-SIX

Monday, 22nd June

11.00a.m.

The door to the Parkins' house stands ajar. I am surprised to see this, but I am also very pleased. The walk from the clinic had been long and the journey up Thomas Street had seemed to go on for ever, but the pram has to be delivered, and I have to visit the Parkin family. Jean is now ten days old and I am keen to see her progress. I push on the door, calling out, "Mrs Parkin!" as I do so. The door opens a little way, but no one replies.

Pulling the pram up to the door, and holding its handle with one hand, I step into the room. I can just see part of the empty fireplace; a large male figure sits beside it, his bottom resting on a vegetable box that looks as though it will disintegrate at any moment.

"Excuse me, Mr Parkin, is your wife at home?" I call loudly as I attempt to manipulate the pram through the doorway.

To my surprise, large hands grasp the handle and the pram is almost lifted into the room as a young-sounding voice says, "She's upstairs with the baby, miss."

The face which looks down on me and the form which almost blocks my passage are familiar to me, but the voice and behaviour are not. This man is a physical replica of Mr Parkin, but there the resemblance stops; the smile, the clean dress and the communication, belong to a young man. I hear a door close and turn to see Mrs Parkin crossing the room.

Her very pale face holds a smile as she speaks.

"I see you have met my George then, miss." Her diminutive figure is almost enveloped as the young man, almost a foot taller than her, puts his arm around her. "He's sixteen now, leaves school this year. His dad's meant to be helping him to find a job." She nods her head towards the vegetable box and with a disdainful look says, "Though sitting on that's the only job his dad knows," then with a little pink showing on her cheeks she looks across at me and mumbles, "or wants, hey miss?"

I need no reminding; the echo of the blow her husband gave me still resounds.

The pram is received with great delight and I am amazed when the young man dashes off, only to return moments later carrying a small parcel with great care. Having experienced her father's explosive tempera- ment, I had had concerns about Baby Jean's safety, but now I see she has a guardian.

"He asked if he could come home to help me, and the school said he could if he looked for a job at the same time. Been up to the hospital and got a job as a porter he has."

Pride in her eldest son pours out of her. Baby Jean has been declared to be fine, and now her brother, with large, careful hands, deposits her in the newly acquired pram.

"I don't get a look in, he has just taken over and I don't know about a porter — *I* think that he would make a good nurse." Mrs Parkin sinks on to the vegetable box her husband has now vacated as her son rocks his sister to sleep.

"It takes a lot of studying," I murmur as I make notes on Jean's card.

"Oh — despite everything they said and sending him away to that special school, he did very well there. They were very surprised — took prizes, didn't you?"

The boy screws up his face, embarrassed.

"You can do a lot if you put your mind too it," I tell him. "But congratulations on getting a job at the hospital. It's a great start."

CHAPTER
TWENTY-SEVEN

Friday, 3rd July

Alan and I were meant to be going to France on a camping holiday this summer, but Alan's presentation date has been moved forward. He had hoped to present in September, but now the date is at the end of August. The thesis has been printed and bound; I went with him to collect it from the binders last Saturday morning. We had taken a large empty suitcase with us, and a leather holdall. It felt like going on holiday, except we had no clothes in the cases. The dark-blue bound books had stood in a large pile on a counter. Alan had nervously opened the top one and peered into its first pages. The man behind the counter had looked on, a fixed smile on his lips. After what to me seemed a long time, we had left, four of the substantial books in the case and two in the holdall. I had suggested that we might stay in town and have a coffee at the new coffee shop, but with the precious load we had returned home post haste. Jude came round that afternoon instead to look at the bound edition. I made tea.

So instead of camping in France, I am pounding the pavements as normal. The Tates' house looks cleaner; it even has curtains at the front window and when I walk in I am surprised to see a new rug on the floor and new chairs by the old wooden table. Mrs Tate comes to meet me, the dress decent and the feet still encased in sandals. She looks like a new woman and again treats me as if we are meeting for the first time. I shake the extended hand and thank her for the offer of tea. I wonder if it will be the same as the first cup that I almost drank here.

"Are the children here?"

I speak as I taste the almost-tea. It lies warm in my cup, and at least it has tea leaves in it, but the water has not boiled and most of the leaves now float on its top. Improvising, I place my teeth firmly together and use them as a tea strainer.

In the end, it is not Mrs Tate who answers my question but a young woman who appears through the door that leads to the upstairs rooms. For a moment I look at the beautiful woman who stands before me. The brown, shiny hair is piled high on her head; her lips are red, the colour maybe a little too red and not very straight, the brown eyes, dark with mascara and eyeshadow are maybe a little too heavily painted, but they are beautiful. She bends before me to straighten a stocking, which ends in an elegant shoe with straps and a heel, and I realise that I am looking at Jenny.

"Good heavens, Jenny, I didn't recognise you for a moment."

She looks up at me. The eyes, no longer uncertain and gentle, now hold a cold stillness, and the voice that replies to me is not that of Jenny. With a plum firmly in place the words come.

"Good, I'm pleased that I have changed so much. Mother, has Uncle Charles arrived yet?"

With heels clicking, she passes me, holding her flowing dress so that it will not touch any part of the house and looks out of the newly cleaned front window. A car horn sounds. She raises her hands and, almost skipping across the room, she grabs her handbag from the table, kisses her mother on the cheek and, with a waft of perfume, is gone.

"Gone to stay with her Uncle Charles for a week or two."

Mrs Tate or Calverton, or whatever her name is, glibly sends her just-fourteen-year-old daughter off with the man I had disliked at first sight, and who I wouldn't trust with a female sheep, never mind a young, impressionable girl.

CHAPTER
TWENTY-EIGHT

Tuesday, 4th August

9.30a.m.
My step is slow. The day has only just started and already I feel exhausted. It had been one of those nights, a night when it was too hot to sleep. A little breeze had crept up the road from the park, but it hardly had the strength to pass into the bedroom. Alan has been reading his thesis over and over for the last few days, and he is sending me mad — today he must defend it to the examiners.

I turn into Upper Sutton Street and the smell from the Midland Vinegar Brewery makes me retch; I pull my handkerchief from my coat pocket and hold it to my face. The road before me is narrow and dusty, no person, or animal stirs, and already a sultry heat hangs low, no breeze in this spot. Not a place to linger, I tell myself. I have not visited on this road before; indeed, I have done few visits to any of the back-to-back houses.

I had thought the term "back to back" to be quite poetic until I had visited one of these establishments, and realised why it was so labelled. Houses divided in two is the only way I can think of to describe them. The front house usually faces on to a road; in this front there is a door with a small window beside it, and behind this door is one small room. This contained all the living, cooking, toilet and ablution facilities for the whole family. From the corner of this room rises a flight of stairs, which open directly into a room of similar size to that below, with one small opening window. The stairs continue upwards to enter another, but smaller, room. This room is situated directly under the tiles of the roof, and in this room there is no ventilation, the cracks between the tiles being thought enough to provide that, and light, for its occupants. Behind this, and sharing a common back wall, is a house of similar style and size; this one usually opens into a court in which stands the latrines and wash house. These communal facilities are usually shared by over a dozen families, those living in the houses facing on to the street having to make a considerable journey in order to relieve themselves, or to wash their belongings. It is into such an environment that I make my way on this still and sultry morning.

The door opens very slowly. The noise from the factory along the road had made it difficult to hear any sound inside the house, and I had thought that no one was at home. The face that answers my knock is ashen but the eyes are bright; her form, almost indiscernible beneath the loose clothing, is hard to gauge. We stand for a moment without speech, my usual opening line — "I've called to see how you are" — appearing to be rather meaningless here.

Then I see the child. It lies limp, and as far as I can tell at the moment, lifeless in her arms. One small arm, and one soiled leg, hang down before her, and the small head, mouth open and eyes closed, rests on the woman's shoulder. Finding voice and motion together, I speak as I step towards her.

"What has happened? What has happened to the baby?"

Without replying she steps backwards, and leans against the edge of the door. For a moment I think that she is going to fall and, putting my arm behind her, I support her, and in the same move I feel the head of the child. It is hot, very hot, and dry. I slide my hand down beneath the chin and feel for a pulse; it is there, fast and weak, almost a flutter.

Now she speaks: "Can't get her to feed, she's sick all the time."

Taking the baby from her and holding it in one arm, I direct her back into the room. For a moment I can see nothing; the room appears to be in complete darkness, and then, from the light of the open door, I see a stool standing in the middle of the small open space. I lower her on to it and lean her backwards. Heat radiates from her, and I don't need to take a pulse — I can see it beating wildly in her neck.

"Have you been sick?"

She nods yes; I look around, for what I am not sure. The lack of ventilation, and limitations of space, have given rise to an accumulation of purulent odour, enough to tell me that there is serious sickness in this house. Returning to the baby I once again take the pulse. It remains as before. I know that if this child does not receive care it will die very shortly. I decide an ambulance must be called. Placing the child back in her arms I speak.

"I'll be back in a few minutes, try to stay awake."

I look up and down the road. Where is there likely to be a telephone, where have I seen one? My mind has gone dead. Then I see someone standing a few houses away, just up the road. From this distance, and with the light behind her, she looks like a square, with arms protruding from its top corners and legs from the bottom. I am heading towards her, calling as I run, "Is there a phone around here?"

Without speaking she points her hand up the road, and I continue running, the black bag, I realise, gripped tightly beneath my arm. The voice follows me.

"It's number thirteen Upper Sutton Street."

I raise my hand in thanks.

10.00a.m.

The call has been made and the urgency expressed and I am on my way back. The square woman still stands where I had passed her, and as I get near she speaks.

"She got the runs?"

I stop beside her, my breathing heavy. I nod the affirmative to her question, and then ask, "Have others got it?"

She nods yes, her eyes directing my attention to the alleyway.

236

Anxious to be back with the baby I walk backwards down the road as I call, "How many people have had it?"

Her voice carries. "One or two."

The baby is still, and the mother, eyes closed, hangs on to her. Now I hear another child; the cry comes from above. Frantically I search my mind for the family name.

"Mrs Borough, wake up! Is there another child in the house?"

Without opening her eyes she replies, "Jimmy's upstairs."

Having placed my black bag behind a narrow curtain, which runs partway across the far wall, I take the short flight of wooden stairs two at a time. As my head and shoulders pass through the opening I can see that no one lies in this room, where an empty mattress takes up most of the space. Turning, I follow the short flight of stairs upwards. The stench hits me as I raise my head into the room.

With white, gaunt face, round staring eyes and covered in copious vomit, a child stares back at me. Whacking my head on a roof rafter, I am by his side. The sun has just risen, but already the room is hot and airless. Throwing off my jacket, I gather Jimmy in my arms. I expect him to be as heavy as any four year old, but he is light, as light as a two year old.

"Come on, Jimmy; let's get you to where there is some ventilation."

He does not protest, and I hope that he does not vomit. He lies on the mattress downstairs, and with much pulling I force open the small window; a little air, with its vinegar flavour, creeps in — the sun's hot rays come with it. I hear the sound of the ambulance bell and, promising Jimmy that I will be back, I head down the stairs.

10.30 a.m.
The baby has gone in the ambulance, and I have warned the ambulance men that I might be calling them back, depending on what I find in the rest of the back-to-backs. Mrs Borough had stirred, but made little protest at the departure of her child; now she leans over the narrow stone sink and heaves, only water coming from her mouth. Sitting her back on the stool I search for drinking water. A small brass tap sticks out over the sink. I turn it and, expecting to receive the flow of fresh water, I hold a cup beneath it.

The voice speaks behind me. "Yo won't get no water out of that, unless yo wait about half an hour."

I turn. Her square-shaped form fills the door space and the room seems in near darkness. Turning back to the tap I note a fine pinline of water dribbling from it; pushing the cup under it I turn back to the woman.

"Is this all the water supply available to these houses?"

Pursing her lips she looks at me, the sort of look that asks, "Are you a marble short of a bag?" Then, turning sideways and directing her hand towards the outside world, in forceful tones she proclaims, "They got the wash house."

238

There is now about an inch of water in the cup, so waking Mrs Borough I give her the cup and tell her that she must drink it slowly. Grabbing a broken saucepan from the sink, I head after the good lady in the hope of collecting water for Jimmy.

Sunlight hits me and stench almost throws me backwards as, in my haste to follow the woman, I emerge at speed from the alleyway down which she had disappeared. Stopping in my tracks, I turn back towards the dark alley, maybe to gulp for air, I am not sure. Now large, black-stained cobblestones lie at my feet, with darkened gullies running between them. They extend backwards towards a pale-coloured brick building, before which the stones look worn. A row of three small brick-built sheds, whose stable doors are embellished with cut-outs of hearts, clubs and diamonds, lies before me. Two women lean either side of the sheds; bright anguished eyes watch me from tight-lipped, grey faces. One of the stable doors opens and a woman emerges, newspaper in hand. She speaks to one of the women, passes over the paper, pulls her skirt straight and, with waddling gait and slithering slippers, heads off to my right. My eyes return to the stable door and I realise that I am looking into one of the latrines.

The voice calls, "Welfare, water's over here."

To my right, a row of three back-to-back houses, each with an open door, faces the court. As I turn towards the voice I see what must be the wash house. Beyond the houses, a ridged, red-tiled roof juts out; three unpainted wooden posts, whose bases are almost rotted away, support this structure. The presence of broken tiles underfoot suggests that they are not doing their job, and the angle at which some of the tiles hang suggests that they won't be doing anything for much longer. My guide stands, arms folded, a tile leaning precariously over her head; I take my eyes from it.

"This is it, miss, this is what you can use."

A woman moves sideways, the lather from her green soap remaining behind her. My guide pumps a large metal handle and water gushes out and splashes on to the already-wet floor, a spout whose gaping mouth hangs over a smooth, shining stone sink. There are four such pumps, two on either side of the large washing stone, and my guide ably demonstrates the strength of each spout.

Stepping beyond the reach of the overhanging tile, I survey the surroundings. There is no lighting in this establishment, only the front of the stone slab is in light; the rear of the building which extends back, I should say, about the length of two of the conjoined houses, becomes increasingly gloomy the further you venture. The only green that I have seen in this region now lies underfoot, and its slimy surface makes walking precarious. My guide does another round of pumping and, as she extols the virtues of the wash house, her vigorous efforts cause more water to spill. For a moment I feel relieved that there is plenty of water and I invite the women — two more have arrived — to continue with their work. But as I walk around I wonder why the mouths of the water spouts are dark in

240

colour. In fact, when I look closely they are almost black.

"Where does the water come from?" I ask no one in particular.

"What you mean, where's it come from? Comes from the pump — just showed you." Again my large friend, who has obviously taken charge of me, pumps one of the handles. Another voice speaks behind me.

"She means where does the water that comes out of the pump come from, it don't come from the tap, do it?"

A tall, thin lady stands behind me, though to say that she is thin is to underexaggerate her skeletal proportions.

The two women argue and I am ignored for the time being. I am later to learn, incredibly, that the short square lady is named Mrs Long, and the tall thin lady is Mrs Short; they are inseparable friends and arch enemies. I'm sure this must be because they have got their names the wrong way round, or maybe it is because they have lived side by side in this tiny court for many years.

"Does no one have water in their tap?" I speak to another woman, who stands beneath the leaning tile. A small girl hangs on to her dress and, at the sight of me, she disappears behind her mother. The mother is as forthcoming as her child; she just shakes her head, no. It is my square friend who answers.

"Same as you saw, same in every house."

"Then we must get clean water from some other houses, if they have water," I tell myself and the assembled women.

The women who were washing stand back, water dripping off their elbows and wet clothes lying before them.

"You can wash your clothes in this water, but as we don't know its source, I think it would be sensible not to drink it until we find out what is causing the sickness."

"But we got to drink something," Mrs Long shouts.

Her thin friend interrupts her.

"Yes, she said as how we should see if any of the houses across has any clean water."

Another voice interjects, "Or on Park Lane. Park Lane might have some, them being down the hill."

"Bet that factory's not going short," two of the women mumble.

Mrs Long's voice sounds over the gathering murmur of discontent. "So what you think we are going to carry this water in?"

Before more is said, Mrs Short flourishes a large, flower-patterned water jug. It had obviously started its life in better times, possibly as half a jug-and-basin set on a washstand. Now others, who are still well enough to do so, head off in search of similar vessels. I watch, hoping that I am not in the process of organising a riot as these forceful women invade their neighbours across the road in search of water.

Mrs Borough is not downstairs when I return; she is with Jimmy. The little drink of water has improved her condition marginally, but the child retches, producing only water at each heave. The room is now sweltering; the sun is on the small window, and the child's skin is

242

on fire. With my hand on his head I speak to his mother, who has slumped backwards and sits in the corner of the small room.

"I think that we should take him downstairs, Mrs Borough, I think that you would both feel better by the open door."

With the child in my arms I struggle down the stairs and his mother manages to follow, dragging a blanket behind her. Before she reaches the door she doubles over and yells out. The bucket in the corner is reached just in time. Laying Jimmy down, I help his mother while I frantically look around for soap and hand-washing water. The tap is now dry and there is no soap in the sink. From my conversations with the women, I know that at least two other families are in similar condition in the back-to-backs and another child has started to vomit. There is no hospital near, and I know of only one doctor in the vicinity, and he only has surgeries twice a week. I must do something.

My grandmother had been a great herbalist, how had she controlled vomiting?

"Arrowroot," her voice shouts in my head.

I almost crash into Mrs Long as I whirl out on to the pavement, black bag before me. She doesn't stop — I feel that it would take a tank to stop her. With an enamel bucket half full of water she squeezes past me and heads for Mrs Borough's door. I hear her mumbling,

"Some mean old cows around here, half a bucket. I ask you."

An old man sits and watches me approach, his unlit pipe between his lips.

"Excuse me, do you know if there is a chemist shop anywhere around here?"

Without taking his eyes from me he nods his head sideways.

Smiling the thanks that I don't really feel, I turn and look up and down Park Lane. The gruff voice sounds and, with pipe wobbling and hand raised, he sends me in the best direction.

"There's corner shop as'll sell you aught you want."

Now nodding my real thanks I am off.

When I get there a thin, narrow-nosed woman looks at me with interest as I enquire if she sells arrowroot.

"You mean for cooking with?" she asks.

For a moment I have to think. Yes I have seen it used for thickening sauces.

"That will do," I reply.

I expect her to say, "Well we haven't got any," but to my great relief she returns carrying the familiar small tub.

"Can I have two please?" I ask.

She looks at me under her lids and disappears off into the back of the overcrowded dark shop. I stand and for a moment let the familiar childhood smells of turpentine, floor polish and bleach wash over me. I jump to attention at the thought — that's what we need, bleach for the undersink buckets and carbolic soap for the hands.

244

The woman returns, cardboard carton in hand. In my anxiety to get started with the bleach and carbolic, I lean over the counter towards her and almost shout, "I'll take two bottles of bleach, four tablets of carbolic soap, along with those two cartons of arrowroot."

Looking at me with some doubt in her eyes, she collects the goods and places them before me on the counter.

"That'll be thruppence for the arrowroot, a penny for the soap and three ha'pence for the bleach." I lay a sixpence on the counter. She looks at my offering and then, ripping a piece from a white paper bag, she lifts a pencil, licks the end of it, and writes. Then turning the paper back to me she announces, "That's each."

The total amount lies before me, one shilling and one penny. Putting down a shilling to join the sixpence I watch almost all my worldly money disappear.

11.15 a.m.

When I get back to the courtyard, drinking water is being delivered to all the houses; Mrs Long and Mrs Short are in command. I have mixed arrowroot in water and every one who has been sick is drinking.

"Should be mixed in hot water," Mrs Short announces as she pours water from her jug on to some of the powder.

"Oh, shut up, you old tart! Mrs Long shouts as she swings her now-empty bucket at her friend. "Knows better than the Welfare now, she does."

I smile to myself; maybe she does. Pushing my hair back, and wiping sweat from my forehead, I look at my watch. It is a quarter to twelve and I will have to return to the clinic, but first I must get the next strategy moving. The only shaded place is the wash house, and I stand, a handleless cup in my hand, the tea very welcome. The sun shines directly on to the cobblestones and a heat haze shimmers, making the straggly weeds, which hang over the brewery wall at the far end of the court, look like a bewitched, moving forest.

"There are now six families who have the sickness," I announce.

"Seven, miss. One more on the front," a voice announces.

"So almost half the houses have it," I say, almost to myself.

"So what we got to do to stop it, miss?" Mrs Long's face is serious as she holds on to her jam jar of tea.

Bringing a bottle of bleach from the sink behind me I announce, "All buckets that are used under sinks must be emptied, particularly those that people have been sick in. They must be washed out with bleach, and some bleach water put in each one before they are returned to the house."

One of the women waves her cup in the air. "I got some clothes bleach, will that do, miss?"

"Yes, that's fine. If any of you have bleach for clothes, use it."

Some move away, anxious to get going.

"Wait a minute, there's more to be done," I shout. Eyes turn on me. "Every house must have a bowl of water and a piece of soap standing on the sink. You can

246

use this water." I turn and point to the sink with its black spouts. "The water in the bowl is for washing hands; you don't have to use your drinking water, save that to drink." Retrieving a tablet of carbolic soap I hold it over my head. "Every family, where there is illness, must use this soap and others must wash as well, and if there is not enough carbolic to go around, you can use green washing soap, but *everyone* must wash their hands every time they go to the latrines, or use the bucket. If you've got some bleach, bring it here so that we can make sure that every one is OK."

Now they start to disperse and I take another look at my watch.

"You go if you want to, miss, I'll sort this lot out," says Mrs Long. Her voice is now quiet but it holds authority.

"Don't forget they must wash their hands after every visit to the bucket, or the toilet," I say as I pull on my jacket.

Mrs Short's voice interrupts my thoughts. "Don't worry, miss, I'll see to the nursing; I'll do the water and the arrowroot, she can do the ablutions." Arguing for all to hear, together they head out into the court.

12.30p.m.
The clinic feels cool and fresh — and possibly for the first time I value its antiseptic environs. Dropping my black bag and rather crumpled jacket in the office I head for the kitchen, where voices sound. In the cool half-light, Mrs Burns and Miss Haines sit eating. Both look up as I enter.

"You look as though you have been in a war."

Mrs Burns pats a chair which stands empty beside her, Miss Haines heads for the teapot.

After I have told them everything, and after washing as much of my person as I can, I return to eat. Miss Haines stands as I return.

"Mrs Burns says that you should notify the Public Health Department, so while you eat I'll try to get hold of someone there."

I am about to follow her but Mrs Burns takes my arm.

"No, you eat, or you will be the next one to be ill, and then you will be no good to anyone."

A few minutes later, Miss Haines returns.

"I got through to the Public Health Inspectors; the switchboard said they would be the ones you needed." Miss Haines hands me the phone and a quiet voice speaks.

"Public Health Inspectors, can I help?"

The situation has been explained and now the phone is silent.

"Hello, are you there?" I call, panic in my voice.

"Yes," the voice replies, "but there's no one here. I'm a student, the inspectors are out."

I let out a long sigh, remembering my own student days covering the phones, and then the voice continues, "But I've found you on the map and I'll let Mr George know as soon as he comes in."

"How long do you think that will be?" I ask, my voice now quiet.

"Should be back quite soon, he's just gone to get something to eat."

That sounds better and I feel more hopeful.

"I'm returning to Upper Sutton Street now and I will wait for him there."

I speak into what I fear is a dead phone.

2.15p.m.

Miss Haines has supplied me with orange juice, rusk and baby-rice samples, and above all, from Aladdin's Cave, half a dozen recycled nappies. She has also pushed a white coat into the top of the old shopping bag that, having been pulled from a kitchen cupboard, has been recommissioned and filled to the brim. Some of the white cotton sheets from the doctor's-room couch and a lot of sheets of paper, usually used in the weighing clinic, now fill it. On Mrs Burns' suggestion, and after a money collection from all persons present, I have called into the chemist and bought some Kaolin et Morph, a mixture known for its value in helping cure diarrhoea and stomach cramps.

I stand at the entrance to the court; the white coat covers me from head to toe. Heat meets me like a wall. Made impenetrable by the nauseating smell of the toilets, it almost blocks my way. Mrs Long sits by the door to her house, the shade of the wash house just reaching her. Several women, with small children, sit in the wash house gossiping and the court stands empty of life.

"You back then?" Mrs Long asks.

Pushing my hands into the pockets of the white coat I reply, "Yes, it would seem so. How are things going?"

She shrugs her shoulders, looks the white coat up and down, but does not move. Then with a snuffle she says. "Seems that the missus at the front is pretty bad; taken her some more water, but she's bad with the cramps."

I have left the full shopping bag on the top floor of Mrs Borough's house; I seem to have made that my office, or should I say storeroom. I had passed Mrs Borough and Jimmy, both asleep at the entrance to the house, and now I turn back in haste. Had they been unconscious and not asleep? Jimmy wakens as I step over his mother. He does look a little brighter, but Mrs Borough looks ghastly and I take her pulse as I speak.

"Jimmy, have you had a drink?

He replies, as he shuffles to a sitting position, "Yes, miss, but I ain't arf hungry."

"That sounds good," I say to myself and to Jimmy I say, "Drink some more, there's a good lad, and we'll sort the food out in a minute."

Mrs Borough opens her eyes as I attempt to pull her out of the sunlight; the shade is not much cooler but at least she won't burn.

"Have you still got the cramps?" I ask.

She nods her head and screws up her face. The bucket smells foul; she must have used it several times.

A sheet of the white paper covers the bucket, and I sprint into the court, Kaolin et Morph in hand.

"Has anyone got some warm water?"

250

Mrs Long still sits, and with languid movement points to the open door of her neighbour, Mrs Short.

"Her'll have some; just walk in, her'll be asleep, I bet."

I have no need to enter; Mrs Short stands at the door, large black kettle in hand. "It's gone off the boil, miss, but it's still hot."

That is just how I want it. "Do you know how many of them have got 'the runs'?" As I speak, I shake the medicine bottle.

"All on 'em as bin sick, except a couple of the kids." Mrs Long's voice echoes into the wash house as she rises from her chair.

I look at my two trusted foot soldiers, and hope upon hope that we can cure this.

"We have got to get this done pretty quickly," I say as I look into the faces of the two older women, "and with a great deal of care." I shake the bottle again and hold it out towards them. "This is medicine, and each person who has the runs is to be given a teaspoon of this in half a cup of warm water; children half a teaspoon."

Mrs Long puts out her hand to take the bottle, but Mrs Short steps in.

"I'll take the bottle, you'll be better with the kettle."

Already they are arguing. I call after them. "Tell them to sip it slowly, but make sure that they drink it all, and can I please have the first cup, with one good teaspoon of medicine?" I call after them.

Mrs Borough has taken the Kaolin et Morph and now rests against the door. I have been to the corner shop again; the old man still sits at the corner and nods to me, I nod back.

"Quite an entertainment for him," I say to myself.

The narrow-nosed lady behind the counter recognises me and asks, "Got a problem, hey, miss?"

I know the news must have travelled, so looking her straight in the eye I say, "Tell everyone to buy soap from you, and make sure that they wash their hands regularly."

With lips pressed together she nods her head; gossip this good comes rarely and now she feels she has a role to play in it. Turning her back on me she searches for the arrowroot biscuits I've asked for. But as she turns back, the face has softened. "Is it children wot's poorly?"

I nod. Putting her hand back in the biscuit box, she adds more to my paper bag and, shaking her head, she pushes me off when I offer money.

Jimmy receives his ration of biscuits with glee, and his mother has come back from the brink.

"Tastes nice does that, miss."

For the first time, I see her smile.

3.30p.m.
The bottle of medicine is half empty, and my helpers are collapsed in chairs.

"Did you shake the bottle before you poured it out?" I ask as I fall on to an empty chair beside them.

"Miss, you always shake medicine before you take it, you should know that."

I smile and relax; my lieutenants are trustworthy.

252

"Is anyone still being sick?"

Both shake their head.

"That medicine must be good," says Mrs Long.

"Yes, and treat it with care," I say as I look her in the eye.

Holding her head high she nods yes, and I half expect her to salute.

A car comes to a standstill at the end of the alley; we all lean forward to see what is happening. A shiny shoe and a grey trouser leg appear out of the car door and a man of obvious importance, as he still wears a grey suit jacket in this heat, follows them. He stands with nose raised and surveys the road; he is joined by a younger man who wears slacks and a linen jacket. Public Inspectors, my mind calls out, and leaping to my feet I head towards them.

The situation is explained, along with the present state of play, and my name, rank and number have been given. The white coat must have made an impression, for in swift order Mr George, the inspector, and Mr Bending, his student, have presented their credentials likewise.

Now we head down the alley into the court. My lieutenants have not been as duly impressed by the new arrivals as I, and have remained seated. Watching us as we enter the wash house, they remain unmoved. I wave my hands behind me, calling them to order. I had not anticipated the effect my call would have. Raising her large frame from the chair Mrs Long descends upon us, and stepping before me she takes over the proceedings.

"It's that water wot done it. Nothing to drink but bad water, and in this heat. If it hadn't been for the Welfare here we would have all been dead now."

My other lieutenant nods her head vigorously, and those who are still able gather around.

"Well, madam," says the inspector as he backs into the wash house and away from the belligerent stares and folded arms which are moving slowly towards him.

My other lieutenant comes to life and, touching his arm, she says, "You see, it's the lack of water in the pipes that causes the problem." She adds "sir" just in case.

It has the desired effect. Ignoring me completely, he turns towards her.

"So what exactly is the problem then, madam?"

With heads bent together they head towards her house.

"She is a tart, flirts with anything in trousers she does." Mrs Long stands, lip curled up and hands on hips.

The situation seems to have been clarified without my help, and the two inspectors collect water from the pumps, which Mrs Long flatly refuses to work. With his jacket in the car and his sleeves rolled up, Mr George faces his audience.

"I suggest that you do not drink this water until we can have it tested. Obtain your drinking water from taps attached to the mains only. I will leave Mr Bending here to offer you any further advice and help." So speaking, he turns and heads for his car, mumbling to

Mr Bending as he goes, "I should get those lavatory pans dealt with if I were you."

Children have appeared as if by magic, and with much shooing and a few words, Mr George is off, test tubes and all.

Mrs Long stands, arms folded, "Well, he was bugger all use! What *you* got to say for yourself, young man?"

The situation is reviewed in more detail and Mr Bending finds a bottle of Lysol, which had been hiding in the back of the wash house for years. He instructs that all buckets should be emptied, and that a little Lysol and water should be poured into the bottom of each. A large tin bath is found and, taking close instructions from the trainee inspector, who she now calls sir, Mrs Long, supported by several others, fills the bath and Lysol is added.

"Make sure that any soiled sheets are placed in this water; do not leave them lying around on the floor."

"What's a sheet?" one of the women asks.

"It's blankets what you've had under you," replies Mrs Short.

All nod their acceptance and understanding.

Having instructed my lieutenants on all details, and having handed over the clean sheets, nappies, rusks and cereal, I go and check on the sick. When I reach Mrs Borough, she looks a little brighter and, much to Jimmy's chagrin, she steals some of his biscuits.

"Can Mrs Borough have a cup of tea?" The call comes from Mrs Short, who stands teapot in hand.

"Give her more medicine first; she can try a cup of tea after."

I turn as the gruff voice calls in response, "Thank you for your help, miss. If you want a cup of tea any time call in." The teapot is held high. "That's if we've got any water." The gruff voice follows me and, turning, I see her smiling face. Giving my two worthy lieutenants a salute, I run to catch up with Mr Bending; he is giving Jimmy a penny to buy some chips.

Not the best thing he could eat, I think. But what the heck — he deserves a treat after a day like today!

6.00p.m.
I bound up the stairs; all looks dark. I call Alan's name as I rush from room to room. During my journey back to the clinic I had remembered that today is the day Alan is defending his thesis. Today is his great day and I had forgotten it completely among the chaos at the back-to-backs.

There had been a scribbled note on my desk, but I couldn't make sense of it and I didn't know if it was a message from Alan. Mrs Burns had left before I got back and Miss Haines had been at another clinic for part of the afternoon and so knew nothing of the phone call. Miss Winthrop was in, but she had been off before I could ask her, so I made my way home not knowing what had happened.

Now the house is empty; even Mrs Pointer is out, and Alan had been in such a panic this morning that he had forgotten to open the curtains. At least it has kept the flat cool. I look in the kitchen; milk stands on the draining board and looks like cheese; the bread has been left open and the butter has melted. There is no note from Alan, so he can't have been back home. I flop down on to a stool; two large flies fight to get through the closed window and a car passes down the road at the front of the house. Sweat stands on my neck, and I feel it on my forehead. I need a bath before I do anything else, I tell myself. Then I look at the blue-and-white clock that hangs on the wall over the table. It takes a couple of minutes for me to register that it is a quarter past six. The shop up the road closes at 6.30p.m. and there is not a thing in the flat to eat. The ten shilling note, which usually stands behind the pot on the shelf in readiness for midweek shopping, has gone. Alan must have taken it and I have no money left. It takes me five minutes to riffle through all the kitchen drawers and find the half-crown which has been hidden for such emergencies.

Racing down the road at full pelt I make it through the shop door just as the shopkeeper raises his hand to turn the lock. Snorting through his nose he says, "I hope you only want a couple of things, 'cause I'm closed now."

Grabbing the last bottle of silver-topped milk from the crate as I pass, I head for the counter.

"Could you slice me a bit of bacon, please?"

I talk to the back of his brown cotton coat as he lifts the counter and turns to face me. Blowing air out through his large lips he walks along behind the counter towards the meat slicer.

"Just four slices, please, and can you cut me a bit of butter?" I squeeze the half-crown in my hand.

"What's a bit, about two ounces?"

"Yes, that will be fine, and have you got a couple of eggs?"

I look over the counter at the bread tray; a large white loaf, squashed and broken, is its only contents. Taking a tin of beans from the shelf behind me, I turn as the perspiring shopkeeper places two greaseproof-wrapped food parcels and a small paper bag, which I assume contains two eggs, on the counter before me. I smile as I ask, "May I have that loaf please."

"That'll be two and eightpence." The eyes watch me as, opening my hand I look at the half-crown. "Oh, give me that — you can give me the other tuppence next time you come in."

Gathering my goods in my arms, I head for the door, smiling my thanks as I go. The door closes behind me and I hear the lock click.

I make it home and up the stairs without dropping anything and pour my load on to the kitchen table, the flies still buzzing around. Opening the window I shoo them out. I was feeling tired and sorry for myself, but as just a little evening breeze crosses my face I think of my friends in the court, and of Mrs Borough in her oven of a room, and I feel lucky.

7.15p.m.
I do think that I dozed off for a couple of minutes in my bath, because it is well gone seven when I return to the kitchen. Alan has not returned and I wonder if I should go down to the university and see if they have any news. My stomach answers for me with a very loud rumble.

258

"I'll eat first. If Alan comes I can soon cook him some egg and bacon," I tell myself.

The food is eaten, and waves of fatigue pass over me again; I had not realised how hungry and tired I was. The day had been both physically and mentally exhausting. In my dressing gown, I decide to rest on the bed for half an hour before going out.

CHAPTER
TWENTY-NINE

Wednesday, 5th August

7.30 a.m.

The alarm clock rings; I open my eyes slowly and then sit up with a start; it is morning! Alan lies at the other side of the bed in just his pyjama bottoms, spread out in a position of complete exhaustion. I had not heard him come in, but now I remember his thesis. Shaking him, I shout, "How did it go?"

Hardly stirring he raises one thumb in the air.

"You made it, you made it!" I shout as I leap on top of him.

With a smile from ear to ear he rolls his head towards me.

"Yes, I did, but now if you don't mind I would like to die for a few hours; I'll see you after work."

"Yes, Dr Bunting, most certainly, Dr Bunting," I sing out and tread on him as, climbing out of bed, I kiss his face and shoulder.

I have headed straight to Upper Sutton Street. It is only 8.30 a.m. but already the street feels warm; maybe the bricks of the houses, and the stones of the road, have not cooled off from yesterday. Mrs Borough already has the door open and I am delighted to see that she is up and about.

"Good morning, how are you?" I say as I poke my head through the doorway.

"Hello, miss, I must say that I feel a lot better now." Her smile is real, and there is even a little colour in her face, the smell of the carbolic soap is quite an improvement on yesterday's smells.

"How is Jimmy?" I ask as I step into the room.

She looks at me, grimaces, and nods her head towards the room above.

"Sick last night, he was, miss."

I look surprised. Now she smiled.

"Ate those chips too fast he did, told him to slow down, but they were almost gone before he got back from the shop."

Now I laugh with relief. "Boys will be boys," I say.

The courtyard is quiet, just a couple of women with their sweeping brushes, but the delicate perfume of factory and latrine still assaults the senses and makes it necessary to turn back for the last gasp of breath from the road.

Mrs Long sits by her door, cup in hand, and before I have time to speak she calls, "Cup of tea, miss?"

She is on her feet before I answer, and so I just pray that the water has been well-boiled and, if possible, collected fresh this morning.

"Mrs Short not around?" I ask as I look at the world over the rim of the best china cup.

"Oh! Her's gone to fetch another jug of water; take her an hour it will, can't stop talking, her can't."

"Are there any more cases this morning?"

She stands and takes my cup from me and, although I hadn't quite finished drinking, it disappears into her house.

"Not as I know of, miss," she answers my question as she returns, a large piece of sacking now tied around her comely waist. "Had a bit of activity in the night though."

She leans over the large tin bath, which stands before the wash-house door and its cloudy water now soaked up into discoloured matter.

"How many were there?" I ask the question as she pokes the contents of the bath with a long wooden stick.

"Three had the runs pretty bad, but her gave um some of the medicine." She nods her head sideways towards Mrs Short's house. "The little lad, the one as started yesterday, he was sick, but her had some of that stuff, the sort you used, had it in her cupboard. Seemed to work the same as your'n did."

The clothes rise from the water, and with a resounding slap she lands them on the stone slab. Water is pumped on to them and the strong hands turn them over and over. I meant to tell her that the Lysol will burn her skin, but I know that I will be wasting my time. I stand well back as a blanket and three sheets, which once covered the couch in the clinic room, and four of the recycled nappies are swung dripping over an improvised washing line, which stretches from the wash-house roof to the houses opposite.

I had not seen Mr Bending arrive, but now he stands beside me, his small frame clad neatly in a linen jacket.

"Good morning," I say and smile across at him. He barely smiles back; a very serious young man, I feel.

"Any new cases last night?"

Having asked the same question as I, he gets the same answer from the busy woman. She squeezes past him and we step backwards — she is not choosey as to where water from the dripping clothes lands. Looking down at the bath Mr Bending kicks it with his foot and says,

"That needs emptying."

Giving him a hard look, Mrs Long and a couple of the other women raise the end of the bath, and the foul water sloshes into the sump, down which all water from the washing slab flows. The water hits the sump at quite a speed and Mr Bending finds himself with one wet foot; this he waves vigorously in the air as he dances around.

"Oh! Sorry, sir, didn't see you there." Mrs Long drops the end of bath with a thud, narrowly missing his other foot.

The drinking water has arrived. Mrs Short has made tea and Mr Bending, having given Mrs Long a wide birth, now sips it as he hands Mrs Short a new bottle of medicine.

"I tell you, if it's got trousers on she's there." Mrs Long regards her friend, with narrow eyes.

All is calm, the day is starting to warm up and the odours from the lavatories are becoming overpowering. I view the scene and decide that I can now leave the company to their own devices and call back later in the day.

The loud clatter of metal on metal sounds and out in the road the engine of a lorry revs then stops. For a moment no one moves, then pushing his cup into Mrs Short's hand, Mr Bending springs to life.

"My goodness, my goodness, they are here." So calling he heads towards the alley.

Men's voices can be heard, and the sound of heavy boots hitting stone reverberates along the alley. Stopping beside me Mr Bending raises his hands to his face, and speaks through them.

"I almost forgot, I phoned the Sewage Department last night, asked them to come and change the lavatory pans, told them that it was quite an emergency because of the contagious infection. I didn't expect them to move this fast."

A tall man, dressed in leather apron, leather cap and high-topped leather boots, stands before us. He wears leather gloves, which almost meet the leather waistcoat which shows above the apron. Strong hairy arms show, and the overall look is that of a Nordic warrior.

"Called with the pans," the warrior says.

Two similarly dressed warriors pull trolleys on which lie smart and polished lavatory pans.

"Oh, very good, absolutely great," calls Mr Bending as he directs the warriors towards what are obviously the lavatories. A woman who had been occupying one of the stalls and sitting reading her scrap of newspaper, sees the approach through her small heart-shaped window and departs with all speed.

Now all watch with great anticipation; the smell is going to be taken away. The tall warrior enters a lavatory, but now he backs out, waving his compatriots backwards as he shouts, "What have you put in these lavatory pans?"

The obvious answer comes to mind, but I don't verbalise it, Mrs Long does.

"Shit, what do you think we put in them?"

"Never smelled shit like that, missus." The warrior heads towards us across the cobbled court. Reaching us he repeats, "What you put in those pans?"

It is Mr Bending who has to come to our aid. "Um . . . Um . . . Did the buckets get poured into the lavatories last night?"

"Yes, where else should we pour them?" asks Mrs Long.

"What had they got in them?" asks the warrior, ignoring Mrs Long, and addressing Mr Bending.

"Um, er, just a little Lysol." Mr Bending's voice is now rather quiet; all his lectures on sewage and fermentation having flooded back, he knows that he should have given instructions not to pour Lysol into the latrines.

"Well, we can't take those, can't pour that stuff in to the tanks."

The taller warrior heads towards the alley as he waves his troops towards him, the trolleys rattling as they prepare to leave. Mr Bending stands, head bent and lips pressed tight, as the trolleys pass him. But they don't get into the alley. With arms folded across her buxom form, and an apron matching that of her combatant, Mrs Long stands, her frame filling the entrance to the alley.

"You from sewage?" Her voice is loud and authoritative, the voice I remember from my first approach.

"Move over, missus, we got a job to do."

She stands firm.

"If you don't move, *I'll* move you." He turns to demand the support of his colleagues but instead he faces a group of women.

"Listen, missus, I don't want no trouble, but I can't take those pans with that stuff in them — it would destroy the fermentation tank." The man stands firmly and looks down on Mrs Long.

With chin raised and face pushed forward, she challenges him.

"No, *you* listen, my lad. We all been really sick in this place; a young baby has gone to hospital, might die yet. If these two hadn't come and helped us we could all have died because we didn't know how to stop it. So we made a mistake. Three pans is nothing compared to all the muck that comes from Brum; you telling me that you lot can't handle that?"

The warrior stands unmoved; she tries to push past him.

"All right, if you can't deal with them we'll just have to sit it out, and we'll hope no more kids die."

Silence follows, and then the voice shouts, "All right Bert, change them. Don't know what the boss is going to say, but I'll just blame the Public Health and the Welfare." Retreating with the soiled pans the lead warrior shouts back along the alley, "Don't put any more disinfectant in the pans."

Silence reigns, and then all descend to pat Mrs Long's back, even Mrs Short joins in.

"So what are we going to do with the buckets that were used last night?"

Mr Bending looks across at me as we stand under the shade of the wash-house roof. The temperature has started to rise, but today just the smell of boiling vinegar fills the air. Compared to yesterday, it smells like French perfume.

"Don't know."

I speak as I rub my hand under the rim of my small navy-blue hat; I'm sweating already. We had not heard Mrs Short approach, but now she stands inside the wash house and, having pumped water into the sink, she watches it whirl around the gully. The gully runs below the sink top, and continues until it has passed all the plug holes, which leave the sink at several points.

"We could pour them down there and swill a lot of water after them." She speaks quietly, her intelligent mind working as we all examine the drain.

"Don't know where that goes to," Mr Bending says as he stoops over the already Lysol-smelling hole. "But we'll soon know if the Sewage Department come back to see us."

Everyone laughs, and with coats off and sleeves rolled up we carefully supervise the disposal of last night's waste.

"Please use just a little water in your buckets if you're not ill, and they can be disposed of in the latrines," Mr Bending advises. "And please empty your handbasins down the sump as well."

The Lysol bath is finished, and washing with green soap is established. Having taken quite a liking to arrowroot biscuits, young Jimmy sprints down the road ahead of Mr Bending, whose penny gift will be spent more wisely today. Recovering my black bag from its hiding place under the sink, I reassure Mrs Borough that Baby Jean is holding her own and will be home within the week.

CHAPTER
THIRTY

Thursday, 10th September

"I think that we are going to have an Indian summer." Miss Haines speaks as she fans herself with a set of clinic notes. Turning, she files the notes in the cabinet; the Thursday clinic is coming to a close.

August had ended as August often does: with a period of rainy weather. Alan and I had been on holiday to Wales. We had taken a room in a farmhouse and it had rained for most of the two weeks we were there.

Alan will collect his PhD in October and at present he is waiting to go for an interview at the Rover Car Factory. He has applied to work in the research-and-design office though the arrival of the confirmation of interview date had not thrilled him.

"Didn't think that I would end up working in a car factory," had been his only remark.

I think that he is on a low; after all the stress of passing exams and dissertations reality is hard to come to terms with.

Miss Haines' voice continues, "Always seems to turn warm at the end of September, but I don't know why they call it an Indian summer."

On cue, and as if part of a scene in a film, a man enters. The door creaks a little, and a slim figure, wearing a blue turban and cream-coloured long coat emerges through the narrowest of slits. For a moment the dark eyes regard us, and then, with hands held before him, and the tips of his fingers just touching, he speaks.

"Good day, is this the place for caring for babies?"

Miss Haines had heard me talk about the Singh family, but this is the first time she has met any of them. For a moment I don't recognise the fellow who stands before me, then as he smiles and I realise it is Kuldip Singh. I had met him at his home on one or two occasions; in fact, I had tried to time my visits to coincide with his school breaks and he had always been my interpreter, his grasp of English being good. But Kuldip normally had his hair tied up on the top of his head, and I wasn't used to seeing him in a turban. Coming to life I step forward and smile broadly to my young friend.

"Yes, yes, sir, please do come in."

He pushes the door wide open and, turning, calls out to those outside. A babble of chatter ensues, and a kaleidoscope of colour fills the doorway of our establishment.

Baby Ranjit's grandmother leads the way, resplendent in a large turquoise-coloured cotton shawl and talking as fast as always. His mother, in lemon dress, holds her son; he, now seven months old, sits straight and firm in her arms. Carrying small children, two more women enter.

270

With a flurry of forms Miss Haines sets to work and my visiting records are produced. We need all the help that we can get, and Kuldip stretches his knowledge of English to its limits. He is not helped when his grandma demands an immediate translation of every word of English that is spoken, including those which Miss Haines directs to me. Her demands are taken as law, as she had entered leaning on the arm of a man whose appearance had caused Miss Haines to jump out of her chair. Standing over six feet tall, and with his large frame clothed from neck to knee in a dark, straight coat, he looks impressive, but it is the turban and the jet-black beard which give him the mark of authority. Having directed his mother to the chair beside Miss Haines' desk, he bows his head to a now completely speechless Miss Haines, who he obviously takes to be the person in charge, backs across the hall and stands by the open door, arms folded.

Gathering up my notes, I head for the weighing room where Mrs Burns, unfazed by the influx of new arrivals, has all in hand. Mats normally used for pregnant women to lie on in relaxation classes have been pulled from a corner. With the September sun bright through the windows behind them, and their shawls all the colours of precious jewels whirling around them, the women seem like a flight of bright butterflies. Sitting cross-legged on the floor, and with their babies on their laps, they chatter. Kuldip stands by his grandmother, who had insisted that the gas fire be turned up to its highest level, and now sits as close to it as the fireguard and her voluminous shawl will allow.

271

Mrs Burns and I have weighed each child. Well, at least we think that each has been weighed, and I am now trying to decide which weight to record on which set of notes, as all the children have been recorded as having the name Singh or Kaur, the address they live at being the only deciding factor.

Kuldip walks towards me. Bowing his head a little he speaks.

"My grandmother asks will the doctor be present?"

I am about to say that, in a moment he will be asked to accompany the women and children into the doctor's room, when the door before me opens, and Dr West enters. For a moment he stands, hands plunged into the pockets of his white coat, and then with a smile creasing his face he speaks in a loud voice. I do not understand his words, but the other occupants of the room do. For a moment there is silence, and then the level of noise rises to a high crescendo. With the notes, which I was about to take him, hanging in my hand, I follow him.

"Right you two," he says to me and Miss Haines. "I think we will see these ladies in here, don't want to cause anymore confusion, do we?"

Dr West, pulling a chair with him, seats himself before each woman who has a child. Baby Ranjit's grandmother lights up the scene as she stands behind each woman, eager to answer questions should the mother not be able. Dr West patiently smiles and listens. The chatter rises and falls and I feel completely useless as I stand and smile. Ably supported by Kuldip, who is keen to correct the doctor's words, the doctor

272

talks with each mother as she dresses her child. Appointments for immunisation clinics are made, and some order is restored.

I return some notes to give myself something to do and I look at the wall clock; it is six o'clock and the clinic should have ended an hour and a half ago, but the noise in the weighing room has not subsided. Dr West speaks as he and Kuldip walk into the hall and towards Mr Singh. The two older men talk; my young interpreter stands by them. Few of his services are required, but, as he wears his turban and his manhood is being put to the test, his grandma's cries go unheeded for once.

They had not arrived until 4.30 p.m., when the clinic should have ended; now, at 6.30 p.m. they climb back into the van which had bought them. Miss Haines had given Dr West a card with the clinic times written on it and had started to ask him to interpret it for Mr Singh senior, but when Mr Singh senior had turned and bowed to her she had retreated without completing her request.

Now we all sink on to chairs in the kitchen, cups in hand. Miss Haines sighs.

"Thank goodness you were there, Dr West, but how come you could understand them?" she asks as she gives him a second cup of tea.

Stretching out his legs and scratching the back of his neck he replies, "I was in India for some time before the war, in the Medical Corps, and we visited quite a few of the villages." Now he lifts his cup and raises it as if in a salute. "Here's to you and your persistence, Miss

Compton. The ladies all said that you had insisted that they came to the clinic, so well done."

Miss Haines gives me a belligerent stare. Dr West notices it, and in a voice sterner than I have yet heard, addresses her.

"Miss Haines, there are a great number of women in London who need our help. They do not leave their houses because they are afraid to do so, and we should be pleased that they have done so in our city. Here's to travel, and a little knowledge of others, hey Miss Haines?"

It took time for many of these families to venture out of their homes, but when their children's health was at stake, most parents would do their utmost to get to us.

Some two years after the events here, I remember another vital clinic that brought home to me just how keen most families were to give their children the best start in life.

It was in July 1962, after there had been a significant rise in the number of cases of children contracting polio in the previous year. Now a new vaccine, to be given by mouth on a lump of sugar, would be put into general use. All children of school age were to attend special clinics of which we would be in charge. The Polio Clinics, as the press named them, had been advertised in local papers and the importance of attending had been emphasised on the news.

I visited the local junior school and called on many of the families in my patch to tell them how important the vaccination was, and on the 28th July, opening uniquely on a Saturday, we began:

9.45a.m.
Although it is not due to open until ten, and it is now only a quarter to, people are already standing in front of the clinic.

Inside, the hall is being prepared. The cleaning women have pushed the chairs to the back of the room, and all the tables stand in line. They barricade off a section of the hall and stretch from halfway down, to curve at an angle towards the first door, which leads into the weighing room. The layout and functioning of the clinic have been discussed and now I know the part I must play. Armed with the large roll of thick red tape, which I have just retrieved from the kitchen, I march towards the two doors that lead to the outside world. Opening the inner of the doors, I start to tie the tape to the handle of the right-hand door, and I hear the piercing cry, "They're opening! Come on, Jeannie, don't start messing about."

Other voices join in.

"About time, it's enough to fry you standing on this corner."

"We'll need a blinkin' doctor ourselves if we stand here much longer."

A thump sounds on the outer door.

"It's not open yet," the first voice cries.

I have now backed away from the door and have tied the tape to the leg of the table which stands halfway down the hall, and at which Miss Haines will sit to enter each child's name on a card, and to get a signature before parent and child move on.

The duty allocated to me has been crowd-control. I am to direct the clients through the door and in orderly fashion send them beside the red tape. From there they are to proceed to the next tables, where Mrs Burns or Miss Winthrop will administer the vaccine, and will pop the lump of sugar into each child's mouth. And so to Miss Hampton for final check-and-card collection. Their exit is to be through the weighing room, where I am to direct them out. To make sure of it, there is a further strip of red tape, which I have attached to the second weighing room door and am now securing to the back of a chair which stands on the way to the outside door and will, I hope, separate those leaving from those entering.

The voices are now even more numerous and loud. I look at my watch; another quarter of an hour. I had better tell them to calm down. I lean close to the door and try to call out.

"There's somebody telling us something, will you shut up at the back there. What did you say, missus?"

"I'll never make them hear like this," I tell myself. "Better open the door a crack."

The door knocks me sideways as it swings open and I sit heavily on the red tape, which, having pulled Miss Haines' desk rapidly towards me, snaps. The throng presses on as I hear Miss Hampton's voice shouting somewhere in the distance.

276

10.15 a.m.

A little while later, order has been restored, even if the clinic started early and abruptly. Now the sugar lumps are being administered and I, between assisting Miss Haines with the mammoth task of recording each child's details, am directing people past the red-tape barrier. The journey is slow and I am working hard to keep everyone's tempers from fraying.

The ground in front of the clinic is still full, and more people are just climbing off a bus. With much arm waving, and calling as loud as I can, I direct the assembly, and in single file they press through the door.

"You don't have to push, madam, there will be enough vaccine for everyone, and there is no need to rush."

The older children take a lot of convincing that they will eat a lump of sugar, and not have to suffer a jab.

Still they arrive.

"Hello, miss." I look sideways at the voice and recognise Mrs Borough who has arrived with her son in tow. He's growing up strong. Smiling from ear to ear, and with voice as loud as I have ever heard, she calls, "Like you said, miss, we got to kill the bugs before they kill us."

I give Jimmy's head a ruffle, and say, "No arrowroot biscuits. I'm afraid, Jimmy, you'll have to be satisfied with a lump of sugar."

A dozen faces smile out behind mother and son, and I realise that at least two streets have arrived.

"Can't see how one lump of sugar can do much good." A grumpy voice sounds loud, but I leave its owner to the mercy of my Mrs Borough.

"Look, missus, if the Welfare tells you to take it . . ."

Then, carried on the breeze that has sprung up, I hear the voice of Mrs Watts long before I see her. The party march up Lancaster Street towards me: Mrs Watts, her two daughters and the women who had come to that first clinic with her. How many children they have with them I am not sure.

"Mrs Watts, we really need each child's parent to sign for the vaccine." I am trying to speak to her as she directs about a dozen children of assorted ages into a line.

"Oh! I'll do that, miss; don't think half that lot back at home can write."

It has taken a long time to see them through the process, and thankfully Miss Hampton has taken an executive decision, and allowed Mrs Watts to sign for children not hers.

"If they catch polio, no doubt it will be she who has to look after them, so she might as well sign for them," she says as she pushes her hair from her forehead.

As Mrs Watts rounds up her mob, I see Mrs Wilberforce hurrying towards her with Arnold in tow. Another child can be ticked off our list.

12.45p.m.
When I next look at my watch, it is almost one o'clock, and the clinic is due to end in a few minutes. One of the final women walks through the weighing room, two

young children in tow. She smiles at me and murmurs, "Thanks." I try to say, "That's OK," but I have said it so many times I've almost lost my voice, so I smile and walk out of the weighing room behind her. Miss Haines sits at her table and, for the first time since ten o'clock this morning, only she is at the table.

"How many do you think we have had?" I ask as I walk over to her.

She does not reply, but pushing the chair back she stands on weary legs.

"How many live in our area? That's how many we've had," she says as she walks off down the corridor. Turning, she calls, "Miss Compton, will you please go and see if there are any more children to come through."

Mercifully the space outside the clinic is empty and I hurry back to report. Miss Haines stands before the gas ring and the kettle has just started to boil. Mrs Burns is opening a large brown-paper packet and Miss Winthrop is putting out plates when Miss Hampton whirls into the kitchen.

"Miss Haines, the Medical Officer of Health will be sending down some more bottles of the vaccine, so be sure that these are recorded appropriately. Ah, tea, that is what I need."

With everyone exhausted from our morning's work, just the clink of china sounds, accompanied by the rustle of paper as sandwiches are selected and wolfed down.

Clearing my throat I speak, "Um, there are no more children waiting."

I get no further; Miss Hampton has seen Mrs Burns looking at her watch.

Miss Hampton's voice, stern and loud, silences all.

"Mrs Burns, if there are children whose parents wish them to be vaccinated, then we will do it. I will not have it said that we were given the opportunity to prevent an outbreak of this deadly disease in this area, and that we shirked our duty. If a child we turn away dies, then we will be responsible."

Mrs Burns, with face burning red, drinks her tea.

"Miss Compton, please recheck for new arrivals; if there are none we will close the outer doors until more vaccine arrives, then check again for more children." The voice does not ask for discussion, but for action.

With the sandwich behind my back and my mouth full I go back outside just as the bus arrives. A woman climbs off, pushing two children before her, and a lanky youth follows. Crossing the road and with a child on each hand, she heads towards me. Turning, she shouts in a voice loud enough to be heard across the city.

"Our George! You just come across here now."

The youth remains on the far pavement. Depositing the children on my side of the road she returns, and cuffs the boy across his shoulder. I suspect on previous occasions she had cuffed him around the head, but he has now outgrown her. Standing before me she announces: "Says he's too old, but I tell him the bugs don't know that he will be leaving school this summer, now do they?"

Smiling a smile I don't really feel, I have to agree with her. I had intended to ask her to wait outside but she is through the door before me. The last bottle of vaccine has been produced, and with face burning bright enough to light a room, the youth has opened his mouth to accept the sugar lump. The family leaves and this time I am determined to close the door, even if just for a few minutes, as soon as they are gone. My tea might have gone cold, but I would still like to drink it.

As my hand reaches for the doorknob, a white van draws up before me. For a moment I am unsure who it is, but it is only for a moment before Mr Singh senior steps down from the cab and disappears into the hall. The chatter of female voices fills the air as the rest of the van's passengers get out.

Miss Haines had thought the last few hours had been difficult — now they are just a distant memory as a whole new challenge faces her. Six women in tunics, baggy trousers and the now-familiar bright scarves thrown over their heads and shoulders, all talk at once. They bring with them a dozen children whose details must be entered on to cards. Mr Singh has left, we realise later, to fetch another vanload of patients. Miss Haines is overwhelmed and, fighting my way to her table, I struggle to help her.

From the crowd, a face smiles across at me, and I have never been so pleased to see a face before.

"Gupta, come over here and help us." Young Gupta Singh had come for his vaccine, but now he acts as interpreter; my usual helper, Kuldip, doesn't seem to be in this vanload, perhaps he's too grown up now. Miss Haines finds it hard to accept that there are no Christian names, as she knows them; but when Miss

Hampton suggests that Kaur or Singh, and the child's home address, will act as registration, and whatever the mother writes on the card will be a signature, all starts to settle down, and vaccines, which have just arrived, are administered. Mr Singh senior returns with more families and all is soon progressing well, if noisily.

1.55p.m.
As I stand in the weighing room, a group of boys between the ages of seven and ten come towards me. They laugh and push each other around and I watch them with care — so much energy can be dangerous in a confined space. I notice that one of the boys has a squint in one eye. I watch him pass.

"I must ask Mr Singh to tell his mother to get it seen to," I say to myself.

I look at my watch: only just two o'clock, I won't be too late home after all. Another group of boys approach and I notice another squint.

"Might be from the same family," I tell myself.

The boys pass and now, like a flash of light, the truth hits me: it is the same face that I have seen twice before. These boys have passed me three times. Jumping out into the hall I look for them. At first I don't see them and then I recognise them as once again they stand in the queue to be registered.

"Stop! Stop don't register them, Miss Haines." Putting my hand on one of the boy's shoulders, as if to stop him, I lean over towards her table. "Miss Haines, these boys have been round three times, they have had three lots of vaccine."

282

Mrs Burns looks across; the lump of sugar hangs inches from a child's mouth. Leaning forward the child snaps it up and disappears.

"What is it? What has happened?" Miss Hampton rises from her chair.

2.15p.m.
The situation has been explained; one of the boys has ducked under my arm and has shot out of the door. Mr Singh, who was standing by the door, brings him back and, with Gupta's help, the situation is explained. Now the boys sit with their mothers on mats in the corner of the weighing room. In fact, all children who have been vaccinated sit there. Mr Singh is telling them, in a very loud and forceful way, how foolish their behaviour has been. I have tried to explain that I am not sure if others have been for more than one sugar lump, but Mr Singh is making no exceptions. Miss Hampton walks into the room and makes the announcement.

"I have phoned the Health Department and they will ring the Ministry of Health and check what must be done — one of the Medical Officers will be down to see us."

Gupta translates and the room goes silent. Others, who have just received their vaccine, walk past, their eyes watching us curiously. One of the younger boys starts to cry and then everyone, including the mothers, joins him. Drinks of water are given to the boys and Mrs Burns makes very sweet tea — some of the unused sugar lumps are used — and the women are calmed.

283

Footsteps sound, and to everyone's delight Dr West arrives.

With Miss Hampton standing beside him he makes the announcement in Punjabi. The women are now silent and sit with heads bowed. It seems that an excess quantity of the vaccine will cause no lasting damage; it might, however, cause diarrhoea, and tonight a few of the boys might have to spend some time sitting on the loo.

"However," he finishes, "the excess today does not mean that they need not attend for the follow-up dose."

Mr Singh bows his head before the doctor and speaks to him in Punjabi; then, in silence, all the women and children exit. They wait at the front of the clinic, their children held close at hand, while Mr Singh ferries them back home. I remind myself that I must speak to them about the squint — what a good thing he had a distinctive face for me to notice! Or maybe I should have been more awake and not so eager to get home. Miss Hampton was right — our duty must always come first.

We later found that the city-wide vaccination programme had been declared to be a resounding success. Our clinic was one of the few that had required extra supplies of the vaccine, so we took the congratulations — but didn't mention that some of our clients had gone around three times!

CHAPTER
THIRTY-ONE

Tuesday, 6th October

The Indian summer seems to be lasting and walks in the park are very pleasant. Leaves are starting to fall; last year Alan and I had played games with them, but this year he seems to have grown very stern; maybe it's because last year he was a student; now he is a serious working man. The job is not all he had expected and even though his title is "doctor" he still feels that he is treated like the tea boy.

"Had to remind one of the secretaries that I'm not Mr Bunting, I am Dr Bunting, and then the silly cow got everybody asking me to cure their ailments."

He has not received any wages yet; they arrive a month in arrears, however we have already planned the spending of them. The new refrigerators, which can now be found in some of the larger shops, have attracted my attention. The summer past, with its flies and hot kitchen, had convinced me that fresh milk and meat are essential. We have been to a friend's flat; he presented us with ice cubes in our whisky and Alan was impressed.

9.30a.m.

"A man from the Public Health Department wants to speak to someone who visits Victoria Road."

Miss Winthrop, who is paying us one of her rare extended visits, pushes the phone towards me. Rising, I take the phone and, putting it to my ear, I speak.

"Miss Compton speaking, how may I help you?"

A man's voice asks, "Am I speaking to a Health Visitor?"

Putting on my best professional voice I reply, "Yes, and I visit on Victoria Road, well, at least on half of it."

There is a moment's silence and then he speaks again.

"I'm a Public Health Inspector and I have received a complaint about the state of some premises, namely number 200 Victoria Road. It seems that the elderly occupant has left her premises in such a condition that it is causing her neighbours concern."

The voice goes silent. I am left with nothing else to say other than, "I will visit and determine if there is a problem."

"Thank you." The voice is sharp and the line goes dead.

10.00a.m.

I walk along Victoria Road. This is the boundary of my patch and I have visited it little. The houses which line it on my right-hand side, the side where number 200 should be, stand behind small gardens. Holes punched into the sides of pathways which lead up to stone steps, and indeed on the edges of the stone steps themselves,

286

show that iron railings had once offered support to those climbing the steps, but the need for iron during the war has left only the holes remaining. Now only rubbish and an occasional weed line the steps. Number 200 has its number, just discernable, on its dusty front door. The house looks less used than some I have passed; adverts announcing rooms to let suggest that many on this road are multi-occupied, as are most of the large houses in this part of the city. The memory of Clifton Road is still with me, and I approach the house with caution. The front steps of number 200 are littered and the door does not look as though it has been opened for a considerable time. I knock; the door is firm and strong and my feeble tap seems not to travel far.

Descending the three steps to the pavement I take stock of the situation. A couple of houses along, an alleyway which is long, but not dark, runs between two of the houses. I walk beside a fence; many of its laths have been removed and behind it I can see sunlight. Apples, now starting to rot, squelch under foot and others, small but rosy, hang over the fence. The fence ends and I stand amazed. I had become accustomed to finding narrow and dank courtyards when passing through alleyways, but clear air and bright sun now hits me and I feel as stunned as I had been by my first sight of a back-to-back courtyard. A pathway, cobbled and firm, runs between gardens. Many of the gardens have, in part, been recently cultivated, but few of the fences which divide them remain; fuel has been short in recent years.

I had not counted how many houses I had passed after leaving number 200, but the rear of the premises I need to visit is easy to identify. Passing through what remains of a gate, I walk down a narrow path of stone slabs. Tall white daisies wave amongst yellow grass; overgrown stocks, still perfuming the air, lie almost blocking the path, and a wall, which faces me, and which forms the rear of an overgrown yard is covered by the large branches of a rose, whose few remaining white flowers exude a heady summery perfume. Before me a window lies in a wall made of strong, once-varnished, wood laths. To my right, the wood laths continue on and join the main wall of the house beside a window, which stands overhung by the rose. Further to my right, two tall wooden gates stand. They stand in a V shape, and as the hinged side of each gate is fastened to the wall of a house, I surmise that one gate leads to the back door of number 200, and the other to that of its next door neighbour. Lifting the latch on the gate to number 200, I push. It moves inwards a little, and then seems to become wedged. I push again; the top half of the gate moves, but the bottom does not. The gate looks frail; one of its laths has moved sideways and I try to peer through. A strange and unpleasant smell pushes me backwards. I have recently smelled some unpleasant, in fact awful, stinks, but this one is new to me.

This entrance cannot be used but to my delight I realise the window in the wooden construction is a door, and it opens quite readily. Knocking on the now-open door I call out.

288

"Hello, is anyone there?"

I get neither reply nor sign of life, so stepping in further I call a little louder.

"Hello, I'm the Health Visitor; I've called to see how you are."

I hear a rustling sound, and a voice, a little cracked, calls, "Oh, please do come in, I was just taking a nap."

I feel as though I am walking through a passageway, but now I realise that I walk past white curtains, which hang from ceiling to floor. They continue on before me, and in the breeze from the open door they seem to ripple, causing a very surreal effect.

The room I enter is light; the window, reasonably clear, lets in sunlight from beneath the rose, but the room is hot. Movement in the corner attracts my attention. On what must have once been an elegant chaise longue, a woman lies. My grandmother had owned such a piece of furniture; it had been covered in strawberry-coloured crushed velvet and, as a child, I was allowed to lie on it when ill, and it made illness more bearable. But, unlike my grandma's, this seat is piled high with blankets, coats, shawls and any number of covers, and as the diminutive figure rises, the coverings fall to the floor. Sitting upright, she looks at me with small, round, swollen eyes and in a broken voice speaks.

"I'm terribly sorry, I didn't hear you knock."

I, on my part, stand unsure of what I should do, or say, next. She is not a young woman, but then she does not look as though she is in her dotage. I introduce myself again, and again apologise for disturbing her rest. She shuffles amongst her coverings, tossing one to the floor, and then I realise why the room is so hot. A coal fire, which fills the whole of its large grate, glows red. One of the coals has broken free of the burning mass, and now rolls down on to the front of the fireplace; the shawl lies inches from it. Shouting out, I kick the burning coal backwards, only to realise that much of the grate, in which this bright fire burns, is filled with ash and there is little space for my burning coal, which rolls back to lie near to the shawl. Flicking the shawl sideways, she drops her feet to the floor and stands. As she rises, with her comes a sweet and not unpleasant smell. As if to remove hair from her eyes, she brushes her hand across her face, and steps forward with uncertain tread. I catch her before she falls, and seat her, leaning backwards against the couch.

"My goodness, that was a dizzy one!" She holds her hand to her head and presses her forehead.

Putting my bag down by a dresser, which supports china and glass, long-since neglected, I return in haste.

"Let me help you back into bed," I say as I attempt to lift her.

"No, no, I'll do it myself." The strength of her voice surprises me, and she turns and pulls herself back into the chaos from which she had climbed.

I found a glass in the dark but not too dirty kitchen, and gave the lady a drink of water. Having mumbled something about not being able to offer me tea, she fell asleep. I had seen letters on the top of the dresser and several pieces of correspondence addressed to a Mrs

Bourne, so I took this to be her name. Making sure that her blankets were well away from the fire, I left. She doesn't seem ill, exactly; nor does she seem to be quite right. I am bemused.

CHAPTER
THIRTY-TWO

Monday, 2nd November

Winter has arrived. We had been lulled into thinking that it would not come, but today an iced wind from the north leaves me in no doubt as to what will be coming very shortly. At least we are cheered by the fact that Alan should be receiving his first wages any day now. He has had to open a bank account, and is moaning that he would like to see some cash in his hand for a change. I don't think that he is enjoying this job.

The wind had carried me along Victoria Road; paper and grit had hit my legs as beer lorries rumbled past. I had walked up the alleyway, through the gardens, now bedraggled and windblown, and had called to see Mrs Bourne. The fire had been burning brightly once again and she had been sitting half asleep in her mound of covers. Having been unable to find any record of her, I had entered her surname on a fresh new card. I had attempted to elicit more information from her, but she was not forthcoming. The letters, which still rested on the dresser, had been addressed to Mrs V. Bourne, so I had entered the letter V in the appropriate place on the card.

A scuttle of coal stood by the fire, and in the kitchen, tins of soup rested on the cupboard top; someone was providing for this household. The sweet, unusual, essence still filled the air. On waking, and proclaiming that she would make tea for me, Mrs Bourne had climbed out of her coverings and disappeared into the other room. An icy wind, which made the fire blaze high and a piece of coal roll, had blown through the house, and I pulled the kitchen window closed, wondering why it had been opened in this weather. I did not find out, and the tea never arrived. When I went back into the main room, Mrs Bourne was sleeping softly once more.

11.00a.m.
I have just crossed the top of Upper Thomas Street. The grey, dark street where Baby Dean Broses had lived still remains uninviting. But I have looked for him and his mother on many occasions; in fact, I think that I always look for him. He should now be just over a year old, but somehow I don't think that he enjoys life.

I have in my bag cards for two children who, according to my records, have moved with their family into 226 Victoria Road. I climb the steps and bang on the door. A large lady in slippers answers. She had peered around a long, and rather tattered curtain, and had shaken her head at my enquiries about the family. Now, pulling the curtain across the door behind her, she steps out on to the first step.

"You Welfare?" she asks as she pulls the door closed, and continuing without waiting for my confirmation,

293

says, "There aren't any children here, miss, but I'm sure as there are some at 236; you might try there." Leaning forward to watch my progress she raises her hand as I arrive at the given number, and then she disappears.

My knock is answered abruptly, and I step down one step as the door is thrown open with some enthusiasm. A young woman, in a dress rather light for the present weather, stands above me. I am about to speak, but a voice, made coarse by much cigarette smoke, takes over.

"Shut that door. There's enough draught to freeze a body. Shut it, will you?"

Leaning forward the young woman grasps my sleeve, and I am pulled inside. In a whirl of red velour I pass the curtain and enter the room. A high, pale ceiling and peeling walls dominate, and damask curtains, open at ceiling level, but pinned shut at a lower level, cause the room to appear in a diffuse light. An ornate stone fireplace monopolises the far wall, and a woman of middle years, who had risen as I emerged from the curtain, stands before the yellow flames.

The croaky voice demands, "And who the hell are you?"

For a moment I stand, confused by the unexpected hostility, then my well-rehearsed speech comes to my rescue.

"Ah . . . Good morning, I'm sorry to disturb you, I'm a Health Visitor and I am looking for a woman with two small children, her name is —"

294

Before I can check, and speak her name, the woman steps forward, pulling her skirt straight and touching her bleached and highly dressed hair. Her voice croaks, "Nobody here got children."

She watches me under lowered lids as she retrieves a cigarette from a green onyx box which resides on a low table before the fire. The lighter flames and her eyes sparkle as she watches me.

A breeze stirs the air; a door has opened. I had not seen it open, but a young woman walks across the room, carrying something in her arms; having deposited her load, she turns. The walk, the movement . . . I recognise the face. For a moment I think that I must be dreaming. I had been thinking of Mrs Broses and her baby, and now she stands before me.

Stepping towards her and holding out a gloved hand I call her name. She turns, and with startled eyes looks across at me. The face is thin, as it had always been, and her frame, small in its loose clothes, looks fragile. Roses bedeck her cheeks and bright coloured rings surround the blue eyes, and now I see recognition cross her face, and for one moment she smiles, then the eyes drop and the face looks down.

"Mrs Broses, Mrs Broses, I've looked everywhere for you, have you been away? And how is Baby Dean? He must be quite a big boy by now."

In my delight at seeing her I have stepped forward and taken her arm. For a moment her fingertips touch the sleeve of my coat. Then, without looking at me she steps backwards and murmurs, "Hello, miss."

In my enthusiasm I continue. "So is Dean with you? I would love to see him."

Almost before my words are out she stops me. "No, miss, he's not here."

Her eyes meet mine, and pools of pale blue hold my gaze for but a moment. Turning away she mumbles, "He was poorly, went into hospital."

"When will he be out?"

I raise my hand towards her but she has reached the door through which she came and turning she shouts, "My Dean is dead, miss, never came out of hospital." Tears flood over the blue eyes, and then she is gone.

The woman smokes her cigarette; the girl who had let me in straightens some papers; I stand and watch the door. I had not seen him enter, but now a large man, wearing a high turban, stands and leans by the fireplace. His newspaper, written in words I don't recognise, rustles as he leans forward, his body directed towards me.

Gathering myself together I look again at the woman, who I am sure I recognise, and mumbling, "Thank you for your time and attention," I leave, hurriedly.

The man followed me to the door, and it had been closed behind me with force. I had no doubt that I was being thrown out, and for a moment I had felt real fear.

Now I stand on the pavement, cold wind blowing into my face. Anger and frustration have replaced fear. I need to know what happened to Dean: how had he died; *why* had he died. I want to know why Mrs Broses is in that house and who the man is. I need to talk with Mrs Broses.

Like an icicle down my spine I remember who the woman sitting by the fire is. In my midwifery days I had visited a brothel to deliver a young woman's baby. The woman by the fire was the Madam who had run that brothel.

The alleyway runs by the side of the house and I have no time to waste. Side windows of the house are covered, and at the rear there is a fence which Fort Knox would envy.

I stand and shout, "Mrs Broses, Mrs Broses, if you are able come to one of the windows, please do so, I would like to talk to you."

Nothing moves.

A woman comes out of one of the houses which back on to the large house; she wipes her hands on her apron as she walks towards me.

"Can you make less soddin' noise? My old man is trying to get some sleep."

I try to explain what has happened, but she is not interested and she becomes angry.

12.30p.m.

I stand in Miss Hampton's office; I have tried to keep control of myself, but I know that I have got carried away. She looks up from the paper, which seems to have held her attention for the last few minutes, and smiles at me.

"Miss Compton, I do see the issue, but I am unsure what I can do about it."

I take a breath so that I can explain what I feel should be done. I have something akin to a police invasion in mind, but she stops me.

"Didn't she say that the child had been in hospital? Did she ask for your help? Did she say that she was in danger? Did you see, or hear, children in the house?"

I look into her glasses; light reflects and there is nothing that I can say; she just does not understand. I turn to leave, anger burning.

"Miss Compton?"

I turn my head. Miss Hampton's glasses are removed, the eyes hold mine, and the voice is quiet.

"In this job we must learn not to become personally involved; if we take every problem as ours, there will be too much to carry. We must learn to make judgements on facts, not on suppositions. If we can do this, then maybe we can do something about those things that we are able to change. But we must also remember those issues, which at the time are not within our power to remedy. Maybe, just maybe, we might, at some time, be in a position to influence them. But the most difficult task of all, if we are to survive and be of any value, is to acquire the ability to know the difference between the two." Replacing her glasses, she returns her gaze to the papers on her desk, and mumbles, "Leave the address of the house on my desk, and I will take it to the council on my next visit."

CHAPTER
THIRTY-THREE

Tuesday, 1st December

10.00a.m.

On this cold and snowy morning it is a long trek up to Victoria Road, but Mrs Bourne, with her large, unruly fire, worried me. I had hesitated outside the house in which I had seen Mrs Broses, but with Miss Hampton's words still ringing in my ear I had lowered my head against the wind and carried on. The plants in the garden at the back of number 200, lie black and decayed; maybe a sprinkle of snow will improve their appearance. I skid on the remains of a plant and am just recovering my balance when I hear a voice call. I have seen few people at the back of these houses and I look up, searching for the owner of the voice.

"Um . . . Um! Are you the health people?" The voice is small, but now I see its owner; she peers at me from around the gate which is attached, in its V shape, to the house next to Mrs Bourne's.

"Yes! Good morning," I call as I step towards her.

I do not want to lose this contact, she may know something to help me to understand Mrs Bourne's situation.

A thin-faced woman in her middle years peers at me around the gate. She wrings her hands together in front of her apron and her face, beneath the turban scarf, looks pensive and extremely worried.

"Are you the Welfare?" She repeats the question as I stand before her.

"I am a Health Visitor, can I help you?"

Before I have time to say more she continues, "Only it's me what rang you. You see we don't know what to do next, the smell being so bad it's making my Jim and me feel really bad." Waving her hand towards Mrs Bourne's gate she heaves a sigh. I think that she is going to break into tears, but having turned back towards me, she continues. "We was good friends with Vi and Bert, played some wonderful music they did, but now . . ." She heaves a sigh and covers her face with her apron. "It was him dying like that, that's what did it. She's just gone to pieces, but I can't blame her." She nods her head and screws up her face; the tears seem near again.

"Did her husband die in the war?" I ask.

"Oh, no!" She shakes her head slowly. "He only died a couple of years ago; died in a bus crash, was on his way home from playing somewhere, the bus turned over, two of 'em on it died. She went mad and we didn't see much of her after, she just stormed around the house for a time and then seemed to go quiet. Wouldn't let nobody in."

"Who provides for her?" I ask.

She shakes her head slowly.

"Some young chap comes, but we don't see him often; I think he comes very late. Got no children, they haven't, so I don't know who he is. But something's got to be done." Suddenly leaping into action, she grabs my coat sleeve, pulls me forward, and in the strongest voice yet says, "Come and see what I mean."

We are through the gate, the twin to the one that I could not open, across a yard smelling strongly of disinfectant, in a door, through a kitchen that is scrubbed to perfection, and across a furnished room, which twins with the one Mrs Bourne rests in. We go into a hallway with highly-polished wood, up carpeted stairs, and into a small box room, all this in silence and at speed. Now the lady stands, and with hand held out, offers me the view from the window. In bemusement I step forward and look out of the window.

A small window looks at me across from Mrs Bourne's house, and a high wooden fence, recently mended, hides much of her kitchen window and door; there is little else to see.

Coming close behind me and speaking with some urgency she asks, "Can you see, can you see it?"

"Can I see what?" I ask, as I scan the scene again.

"Stand on your tiptoes, then you'll see it. No, wait I'll get a chair."

I stand bemused, what am I looking at? The chair arrives and I climb on. Now my view has changed. Up to the windowsill of the window next door, and all of that part of the door which I had not seen behind the fence, is buried in something. What it is exactly, I am not sure.

"What is it?" I ask as I gaze down.

"You may well ask! She regularly empties her teapot out of the window — we see her doing that — and as the toilet, which we don't think she can get to, is in the yard, we don't know what else comes out of the window."

Now the good lady's voice is quite loud, and now I know why the kitchen window had been open, and why there is such an unpleasant smell.

Climbing from the chair, I offer it to the lady, and giving her my most professional smile, I say, "Thank you for letting me know, I'll do what I can. Now I must visit Mrs Bourne."

"Her name's Violet, we call her Vi, give Vi my love."

12.00p.m.

"Miss Winthrop, did you get the name of that Public Health Inspector who rang me a couple of weeks ago?"

She is on her way to do the Tuesday clinic, and just manages a sharp "no" as she passes.

Mrs Burns' eyes watch her back as it disappears, then they rest on me.

"Just give them a ring and tell them the address; they visit different districts, the same as we do."

I am passed around for some little while until at last a voice says, "Bob Small here, what seems to be the problem?"

With a sigh of relief I state it.

"Have you been able to get into the yard?" he asks.

I have told him what I had seen from through the gate and from next door; I left out all the embellishments — next door were only guessing.

"Is the lady of sound mind, or will she think that we are coming to rob her?"

I am unsure of the answer, so we make arrangements to meet at the house, where he will decide what needs to be done.

The visit has been made. Mrs Bourne's neighbour had come in with us and explained to her that it was nothing to worry about and introduced Mr Small, before we left him to do his job.

Mr Small rang a couple of days later, while I was doing the Thursday clinic, and Miss Haines took the message. Apparently the yard had been emptied and the drains cleared. Miss Haines said that Mr Small had said that it had been quite a job, but Mrs Bourne had slept through the lot.

"Mr Small asked what medication she is on, he said it smelled powerful."

When I return to Mrs Bourne's house, everything now smells "powerful". The yard is clear and the toilet is accessible and flushes. This morning Mrs Bourne is awake; she sits on the side of the couch and watches me as I kick coals back into the fire.

"Mrs Bourne, we must get a fireguard for you, one of the coals has burnt a hole in the carpet and your house could catch on fire."

Ignoring me, she slips from the couch as she asks, "Who were those men who came?"

She hadn't been asleep after all, I think.

Heading towards the door, she mumbles, "I thought maybe they were part of the orchestra, I wondered if my Bert brought them?" The white curtain blows towards us; she lifts it and walks through as she calls, her voice louder than I have heard, "Albert, Albert, did you bring some of the boys back?"

The curtain blows, the wind is cold, but Albert is not there. The long narrow room lies in shadowy light; delicate furniture, overpowered by dust and cobwebs, seems to hide from human eyes. Music, piled high on a chair, slides to the floor and dust rises.

"Always leaving things around is Albert." She bends forward, and now I see her hands, twisted and deformed. She tries to stand, but can only make it with my help. Putting her hand on a violin case to steady herself, she almost sighs the words, "A beautiful player, my Bert. I used to play myself, too. Not the violin, though. I played this."

The gnarled hands rise, and to my surprise, hold a trombone. With a strength which I had not realised she had, she raises the instrument to her lips and plays. Yes, she can play and play well. I have got used to extraordinary things at this house.

It has taken time to return her to the couch, and finally I make the tea, which she has offered many times. With promises to find a fireguard, and to provide some sensible blankets, I leave, wondering if it is grief alone that has brought her to this state.

CHAPTER
THIRTY-FOUR

Monday, 7th December

11.00a.m.

The grant has been obtained, and the blankets have been ordered. I am planning my next visit to Mrs Bourne when the phone rings and I answer it.

"This is Aston Police Station, Sergeant Webb speaking. May I speak to the person who has visited a Mrs Bourne, who resides at 200 Victoria Road."

For a moment I stand and look at the phone, then pulling myself together I speak.

"This is Miss Compton. I am the Health Visitor who has visited Mrs Bourne, has something happened to her?"

Making a coughing sound in his throat he replies, "Mrs Bourne was arrested at three this morning for causing a disturbance by playing a musical instrument whilst in a public place, namely a public highway."

Unable to decide whether to laugh or sound serious I say, "My goodness, that must have given a few people an early call! She plays the trombone."

"A rather more serious crime than an early call, miss. Mrs Bourne is detained, and we would be obliged if you would go to her house now."

The line goes dead and I stand with my mouth open.

"What's happened?" Mrs Burns holds a cup of tea towards me.

"I don't know," I say as I grab my coat and head for the door. "Will you tell Miss Hampton that the police have asked me to go to Mrs Bourne's house? She has been arrested; she lives at 200 Victoria Road.

11.45a.m.

A constable stands by the gate, and even though it is cold and snow has started to fall again, there are more people around the houses than I have seen before. The constable steps towards me as I reach the gate. His voice is young, but he tries to make it gruff as he stops me.

"Not allowed in there, miss. Who do you want to see?"

Having stated who I am and that I have been asked to come to the house, I now wait for instructions.

"Step in will you, miss." The large man in a fawn overcoat looks down on me as we stand in the kitchen. It's the first time I have entered through this door. After answering questions relating to my qualifications, the man in the fawn coat asks if I know who looks after Mrs Bourne.

"I have no idea, sir, I just know that food and coal are provided regularly, but I have no idea who does this."

"What medication is the lady on?" Again the question about medication.

306

"I know nothing about her medication, and Mrs Bourne was difficult to communicate with."

He stops me there, and after disappearing into what I know was Mrs Bourne's room, he returns and tells me to go.

"We will be in touch if we need to speak again."

I think I'll let the woman next door tell them about the young man who does, or maybe doesn't, visit.

I think Miss Hampton is getting rather tired of my regular visits to her office; she lets out a long breath of air after I finish giving her all the information back at the clinic.

CHAPTER
THIRTY-FIVE

Monday, 14th December

It is a week later when Miss Hampton calls me to her office again. Mrs Bourne, it seems, was not arrested for disturbing the peace, but for being in possession of an illegal substance, namely pot. A reefer cigarette, apparently. When police had picked her up at three o'clock in the morning, she was walking down a main road, wearing her nightdress, dressing gown, high-heeled shoes and a straw hat. The music, whilst being reported as of good quality, had been the final thing to draw attention to her. Both she and the trombone were taken into custody.

I heard no more. It seems that whoever provided food also provided other things and I don't know if they found the person, but some of Alan's university friends told me that reefers were the answer to the sweet smell that had hung around, her sleepy manner and much else.

They also told me that you can become addicted by breathing in the fumes from others smoking. I thought back to my visits — I had enjoyed going to the house, maybe I was becoming addicted! I thought again — maybe it was the essence of sad music that had still hung in the air.

CHAPTER
THIRTY-SIX

Friday, 1st January 1960

No food parcels arrived from the nuns this year, but before Christmas I had done the rounds, just to make sure that all were surviving.

The Tates' house was silent and still — the younger children had not been returned from care. Jenny was sitting in front of a fire, which now had a bucket of coal standing beside it, and her mother was quietly sitting by the table which had a cloth on it. I wondered if Uncle Charlie would be part of their Christmas.

As I left the Tates' house, Mrs Roberts had slunk past. She had watched me, just her eyes moving sideways; and when I asked after Robert she had departed at speed; it was gossip she wanted, not health advice.

As usual, Mrs Watts had been busy. One of her children, and one of her eldest daughter's children, had started school in September. As arranged, they had attended the clinic, and had completed courses of immunisation and with promises that they would now be disease free, they had marched into school. Both children had acquired chickenpox as soon as they entered the establishment, and both now had very bad colds, which they were dutifully passing on to all the family. I was not very popular.

Mrs Parkin had been to the clinic with Baby Jean. She is doing great; at six months of age she crawls, has a surprising vocabulary of several words, is able to put a few words together, recognises colours and seems to be at the opposite end of the IQ scale to her brothers. What an amazing thing is nature. However, I am now unsure whether her older brother's assessment had been correct. Was it really his lack of ability, or his father's influence that had been measured? He had left school in July and had started in the hospital almost at once. As a porter he earns a wage, and is a regular and constant worker. Mrs Parkin is so proud of him, she now walks tall and even her boorish husband's behaviour can't dent her good spirits.

At the beginning of the winter my mother's heart condition had worsened; before Christmas I had taken a few days' leave, and had stayed with my family over the holiday period. Alan had been to his family home for the two days of Christmas, and although our families live only a few miles apart, we had not met. Alan had said he didn't want to put more pressure on me, as I was looking after the family.

We had managed to see in the New Year, or should I say the new decade, together. We had been to a party hosted by some of Alan's old university friends. A couple more of the mob had completed their PhD and much time had been spent looking at the job advertisements in academic journals.

CHAPTER
THIRTY-SEVEN

Friday, 8th January

January stretches out before me, long and cold. The sessions at the maternity hospital are still flourishing. At this present time, on Friday mornings, I run the advice sessions. This morning, at a tap on the door I call, "Come in."

A rather sober-looking woman in her early thirties enters the small room. Her dress is simple, but clean and smart, and she seems reticent to enter further than the doorway.

Standing, I hold my hand out towards her.

"Do come in Mrs . . . um . . ." I glance down at notes, which the staff nurse has just thrown in front of me. "Um, Mrs White, is it?"

"Yes, nurse," she says as she slides sideways into the chair, which stands by my table.

"White," I say to myself, "that rings a bell." I glance down at her address: 7 Stratford Avenue, Sutton Street.

"Do you live in Aston?" I ask.

She nods her reply.

For a moment I look at her and then ask, "Is your husband's name Bill?"

The eyes widen, the mouth drops open and for a moment her face is white, then jumping to her feet she almost shouts, "Has something happened to him?" Then half turning she heads back towards the door. "Is my Bill all right?"

Standing, I block her exit, and putting my hands out towards her I attempt to calm her.

"Mrs White, Mrs White, your husband is fine, it's just that I had told him that I would look out for you if you became pregnant. That's why I know the name — he's not here in hospital, nor is there anything for you to worry about."

Totally mystified, and now with face burning red, she returns to her seat. The story of her husband's kindness towards a lost, and rather frightened, newly established Health Visitor many months back, is told, and Mrs White smiles.

"That sounds like my Bill — never was a shy one about telling everyone our business, but he's right, we shouldn't have tried for another one. It was my mother going on about the boy being lonely, and now look what's happened."

Stopping speaking she places her hand on her lower abdomen and looks down at her blue woollen skirt. I smile, and remembering Bill's words, I speak.

"Not that bad is it? You might get a girl and then we can get you on the housing list."

"What do you mean a girl? Two girls, more like, I'm expecting twins." Now she is not sure whether to smile or frown.

"Well, congratulations." I say. "Two girls will certainly do the trick. You'll have a council house before you know it!"

"Hmm!" she mumbles "Knowing our luck, it's more likely to be two boys."

CHAPTER
THIRTY-EIGHT

Friday, 18th March

9.00a.m.
This morning Mrs Burns is engaged elsewhere and I am to do the antenatal clinic as well as the mothercraft class at the hospital.

10.00a.m.
At the hospital I stand and wait as women who are well advanced in their pregnancies pour through the doors into the class. When I do eventually enter the antenatal clinic, it is packed. I turn sideways and try to manoeuvre myself between the large bumps. One of the bumps, which is not huge, but is of some considerable size, blocks my way. I smile, and glancing up at the woman's face I start to make some courteous remark about the shortage of space. Then I realise that I am standing face-to-face with Mrs White, Bill's wife. My onward dash has been halted and I help her to find a seat.

"Goodness, Mrs White, I thought you weren't due until July," I say as I lower her into one of the chairs.

"Yes, it is supposed to be July; they think that the twins must both be quite large already."

"That's not bad news; you don't want tiny babies, do you?"

I smile down on her. The room is hot, and though the bodies, almost taken over by the life that grows within them, puff and blow as they struggle to sit or stand, no word of complaint sounds.

CHAPTER
THIRTY-NINE

Tuesday, 12th April

8.00a.m.

Alan is up before me, and now, finishing a piece of toast, he walks out of the kitchen, pulls on his coat and shouts, "See you this evening" as he slams the door. Over the last few weeks he has spent much of his spare time at the university, and two chaps, who have just completed their PhDs, along with Jude, who had obtained an MPhil, have sat in our sitting room on many evenings, and also on a couple of weekends. Academic journals, with pages open at job adverts, have been strewn across the table; some of the adverts had been underlined. I knew that Alan was unhappy in his present job. Maybe we will be moving to another part of the country, I told myself. Hopefully Health Visitor jobs won't be hard to find.

But today I must keep my mind on the present.

During my visit to Mrs Borough on Upper Sutton Street I had been delighted to see that a standpipe had been placed at the top of the street; fresh water, although still hard to carry, could now be readily obtained. When I walked into the courtyard, Mrs Short, still using her flower-patterned china jug, was delivering water to Mrs Long. I accepted my promised cup of tea, although it was Mrs Short who made it.

"She's not very well." Mrs Short made this announcement in a loud whisper as we left Mrs Long's house. "Her's got a bad heart, doctor says she is carrying too much water, in her legs not in the bucket." She had added the last comment with a smile.

Mrs Long's voice had boomed out behind us, "Her's not a bloke, you don't have to flirt." She stood by her door, the little glimmer of sun throwing only the weakest of shadow across her. Her legs, swollen to gigantic size, now seemed to complete the square. I turned to her and took her hand.

"You look after yourself for a change and do as the doctor tells you."

Still holding my hand she waved her other downwards to silence me and mumbled, "What's he know, he's just a lad?"

I'd waved as I left, the voice followed me.

"Bye, Welfare, look after yoursen."

7.30p.m.
I am very late. I call as I slam the front door and run up the stairs but Alan does not reply. Where can he be? Maybe he's gone to have a drink with a mate, I think to myself as I search around for a note. But no note is to be found. I set to and make a much needed cup of tea.

8.30p.m.
Alan has just come in.

318

"Where did you get to?" I ask.

"Have I got to tell you every time I go out?" His voice sounds clipped, but as I turn he drops his eyes down to papers which he holds in his hands. "If you must know we've sent off the application forms; I had to meet someone at the university because Walter had to get his last reference before we could post them."

I stand, a tin of peas in hand, completely lost; I do not know what he is talking about. With face now bright scarlet he puts the papers down, picks up the kettle and starts to fill it.

"What application forms? Are you applying for another job? Are we moving?"

He turns, kettle in hand.

"Well, if we get the jobs I hope you will be coming with us."

The gas pops on, the blue flame rises around the kettle, and he stands with his back to me.

"Alan, what jobs and who is we?"

"Walter, Peter and me. We have applied for jobs in a couple of American universities."

I stand, my mouth open and my eyelids blinking.

"Well, you've seen the adverts in the journals; they've been around the place for long enough. You can't say that you haven't seen them, Dot."

For the moment I am lost. I knew that they had been looking at journals, but these journals are nothing to do with me; I have my own work. I hadn't realised Alan had actually applied for anything.

"So when is this going to happen? I mean, when do you think that you will be going."

The kettle boils; he turns and pours water into the teapot and, without looking at me, puts the teapot on the table.

"What am I supposed to do?" I stand behind him waiting for an answer.

He spins around.

"Dot, we have to wait and see if the universities want us, but if they do, it will probably be the beginning of the next academic year, you know, October time." He puts beakers on the table and pours tea.

This all seems surreal, nothing to do with me.

"Do you have to go for an interview?" I ask the question almost for something to say.

Putting his beaker down he walks over and puts his arm around me.

"You'll be coming with us, won't you? Peter has asked his girlfriend if she wants to go and I assumed that you would want to come with us — it will be a great adventure."

"Do you have to go for an interview?" I repeat the question as I extricate myself from his grasp. The answer comes like a well-rehearsed part in a play.

"No, if they are interested in us we will be given an appointment to go to the American embassy in London."

These arrangements are well advanced and up to now I have not been included. Is this Alan's way of saying goodbye? Or am I supposed to run after him like a little lapdog?

CHAPTER
FORTY

Monday, 6th June

Interview dates for the American embassy have come through. The weekend has been a riot of noise and activity, from which I have felt excluded. Or maybe I have excluded myself. It is all too sudden; I have never thought about emigrating and working in another country has never entered my mind.

"You can come down to London with us and ask about nursing. We are going to the New World!" Alan had shouted as he whirled me and his interview papers around.

"Thanks for nothing," I thought as I tried to smile. I escaped to the bedroom to cry, and hearing Jude's voice in the living room kept me there.

The morning is bright and the pavement by the bus stop is now clear of building rubble. Where once the old red-brick warehouses had stood, high-storied, modern glass-fronted buildings now edge the road. A new world indeed, I think, as I head towards the old one.

"Are you all right? You look done in." Mrs Burns looks up into my face as she hands me the new birth cards that have just arrived.

"Yes, I'm fine, just a little difference of opinion between Alan and me."

I force a smile as I accept the small bundle of blue cards which she offers.

"Been quite a birth explosion," she says as she nods her head towards the cards in my hand. My mind had been elsewhere, but now I see three blue cards.

"Three premature babies born, all in one day?" I ask myself. The first card has the surname White printed in the appropriate place and I call out in delight, "Mrs White has had the twins."

The first child is a boy. Let's hope the second is a girl, my mind says. The second card announces another male child, who is of about the same size as his brother, just under five pounds. Oh, two boys, not much chance of a council house, unless we can pull a few strings, I tell myself. The third card rests in my hand, I glance down at it, mainly to reassure myself that whoever the other new infant is, is not of a very low weight. The weight recorded, as on the two cards before it, is just less than five pounds. And then my eyes rest on the surname, it is White, again, and it is another male infant. I look down at the other two cards and back to the one in my hands. The address given is 7 Stratford Ave, Sutton Street, the same as for the other infants. It takes a moment for the truth to sink in. Mrs White has given birth to triplets, and they are all boys.

322

10.30a.m.

I have visited Mrs White during her pregnancy so I know the house well. Approached through a long alleyway between two houses, the area opens out into a small square. A stone pathway runs between rows of narrow gardens, and each garden leads to a front door. Some of the gardens are cultivated, and this gives the area a feeling of space and care, which it otherwise would not have. The White family live on the right-hand side of the path; Mrs White's mother lives to their right, and an aunt of Mr White lives to their left. The gardens to the three houses lie side by side, and on this June morning, what should be a lawn stands covered by something resembling the rigging of a ship. Fighting my way through lines of flapping terry-towelling napkins, tiny vests and cotton dresses, I reach the door of number seven. Before I knock, the door is opened, and a dishevelled face looks out at me; the dark-ringed eyes seem hardly open, but then the voice calls out.

"Ha! Miss, miss, do come in; that is, if you can get in."

Bill White stands before me, a smile on his face and the door held wide. I know the house is small, but at least it has a kitchen and an outside toilet. On my last visit it had looked just large enough for a small family, but now as I step through the door my foot almost touches the first cot. Well, not a cot, exactly, but a wooden drawer. Mrs White rises from a chair at the far side of the room and, stepping between two small cribs and around the drawer, approaches me. Her face is pale and her eyes sunken as she attempts a smile and almost falls on me. Holding her shoulders I steady her and her husband produces a chair. Taking her hands from her face she waves them towards the sleeping infants.

"Look what we've gone and done, miss, not two but three and all boys!" Now she raises her hands again and starts to sob. Putting his arm around her Mr White pulls her to him.

"Come on, my love, come on. Nobody could have known this would happen; it's as much my fault as yours."

I stand amazed; three beautiful infants lie sleeping and their arrival is seen as a fault. Putting down the black bag, I step between the cots; each small head lies still and warm on its white cotton sheet, nothing but a murmur to say it lives.

I look back at Mr White who, still holding his wife looks across at me. His face says, "I find it hard to smile."

"They are beautiful, Mr White." Now I hesitate, it seems that something is wrong. "Are all your sons perfect?" I wave my hand towards them as I speak.

"Yes, miss, there's nowt wrong with um, all perfect, but you see, miss, they're all the same, and according to the hospital, allus will be."

Gazing across them I stand amazed, then looking back at Bill I ask, "Do you mean they are identical?"

Mr and Mrs White do indeed have identical triplet boys. I stand in the garden talking to Bill. Mrs White's mother has provided tea for all, and at everyone's suggestion Mrs White has returned to bed.

"You see, miss," says Bill, "the problem is that the hospital said they must not be separated, 'cause this could do them some damage, them being what you said."

"Identical," I remind him.

"Yes, that's what they said; said that they must always be together, we must not separate them."

His aunt replenishes the tea and gives her nephew a cigarette; she checks on the clothes which hang on the line across the garden, and then remains standing with us. Her nephew lights the cigarette and thanks his aunt.

"If they weren't that identical thing we could manage better, miss. My aunt here could have one at night and the mother-in-law said that she could have another one, just for the night, miss, cause they never stop crying."

Cigarette smoke rises between us and I understand what he is saying. Almost laughing, I reply,

"Mr White, they didn't mean that they couldn't be in different houses or rooms for a night or two here and there; they meant that they should be brought up together, and in the same way, like playing together and going to school together."

His aunt slaps Bill on the shoulder.

"There, told you as how it would be all right."

"Ring the changes," I say, "not the same baby with grandma all the time and the same one with you."

"A different one each night," his aunt finishes off the idea for me. Mrs White's mother returns, her daughter is having a sleep, and the arrangements for extended childcare are hatched over another cup of tea. A good thing I have a strong bladder, I think.

I really need to spend some time with Mrs White and to look at the infants, but as all are sleeping peacefully I make arrangements to visit later. Mr White walks with me to the end of the alley.

"Looks like we overdid it a bit, doesn't it, miss?"

"I think they are magic, Mr White; such a rare thing is a set of identical triplets."

He glances across at my face and for the first time I see a little look of pride.

"Yes, miss, but we only wanted one girl so that we could get on the housing, didn't we? Don't think three more boys will count."

"Yes, Bill, but think how great it will be to take four sons to see the Villa play."

Now he laughs out loud.

Punching his arm I leave, calling over my shoulder, "I'll ring the Housing Department and give them the news."

CHAPTER
FORTY-ONE

Wednesday, 22nd June

The interviews are to be held this week and I have decided not to go to London with the hopefuls. Alan has taken a week off work and he can talk of nothing else. I left for work early; I can't bear to go over events again.

The sun shines, but Park Lane looks in its usual grey state. However, this morning I have received good news; well, I think that it is good — three of the Tate children are to be returned home. Simon, who is now two and a half years old, will arrive back just after his older brothers and sister. Mr Tate sits by the table, his overalls now replaced by grey trousers and a polo-necked shirt; Mrs Tate is in the kitchen and the sound of running water fills the air.

"Her's been cleaning up since it got light."

Mr Tate looks down at his hands, cleans a couple of fingernails with his thumbnail and then pushes his hands into his pockets.

"What time will they be coming?" I ask as I lean on the table.

"They said this morning; didn't give a proper time. Her's had um home for a couple of weekends already, you know; got a bit upset first time they took um back, hope they don't take um again." He stands and walks over to the window which overlooks the road. "Look at me, started getting me upset, made our Jenny go to school, if there's too many in the house her'll get carried away again."

A car door slams. Mrs Tate runs from the kitchen, water running from her hands and Mr Tate catches her.

"Now, Pat, you promised, you said you would be calm."

Two boys enter holding the hands of a middle-aged woman. It is impossible to recognise them; they are well grown, quiet and neatly dressed. Neither leaves their guardian; their mother waits. The girl enters, holding the hand of a younger woman and I am delighted when she breaks away and heads towards her mother, but it is her father whom she clutches.

"Oh, look here, look here!" Mr Tate cries out as he lifts the child into his arms. The girl calls back to her brothers, and it is amazing to hear children talking in this house once again.

I walk to the younger woman and introduce myself.

"The girl and the older boy are at school now; we thought that we would give them a few weeks to become accustomed to their new school before the end of term."

"And Simon?" I ask.

She is looking for a paper in a briefcase and, glancing up, says, "If all goes well, and Mrs Tate does seem to be well controlled now, Simon should be with her in two weeks." Smiling up at me from her briefcase she says, "We'll try to keep you informed."

I feel dismissed; that I had better leave and visit again at a later date. As usual, I make my exit through the rear door. Mrs Roberts is slinking down the alley, and I do hope that she is not intending to pay her old friend a visit; somehow she does not fit well with the new Mrs Tate.

As I look back at the Tates' house, a voice that I recognise calls and I turn towards it. Mrs Watts is hurrying down the road towards me. I say hurrying; there is a lot of action on her part, but little progress, so I head towards her.

"Her's got the kids back, hey?" As she speaks, she wipes sweat from her forehead and struggles for breath.

I nod and murmur, "It would seem so," as I wait for her to get her breathing sorted out.

"I wanted to speak to you, miss, about my girls getting a council place." She takes a large breath, wipes her forehead with the back of her hand, and rearranges her corpulent breasts. I wait. "Only you see, last time we was up at your place, we went up and got their name put down on the list. Mrs Wilberforce showed us where to go."

"That was very kind of her," I say.

"Yes, it was. Only we haven't heard nothing from um, and I've heard as how they are building some new stuff up in town."

She stops for breath, I try to explain that the buildings are offices, not homes, but she is back in voice.

"Only I heard that they had started some council building and when someone said as how those were council places, I wondered if you had heard."

"Mrs Watts I don't think that the buildings in town are housing accommodation; I'm almost sure that they are offices."

"What sort of offices?" She pushes her face towards me, but before I have time to answer she continues, "How come they can spend money on building offices, and for who, not even you know, but they can't build a house for those as haven't a place to go?"

Just a minute, I think. Is this the proud Mrs Watts who doesn't need any help, who can always make it alone?

"I know that they are building a council estate somewhere near and I'm sure that they will let you know when you have to do something about moving, Mrs Watts."

"Whew! *I'm* not moving, you won't get me on some new council estate." Pushing her chest out even further, she turns to leave, then changing her mind she swings back to me. "Only get this straight: I'm not letting nobody put my girls as second best, OK?" With a poke at my arm and a final "whew" she turns and is gone.

CHAPTER
FORTY-TWO

Thursday, 23rd June

11.00a.m.

The Thursday clinic is busy and, to my surprise, well before it ends Mrs Watts walks in. Her youngest boy, a well built, firm young chap of two and a half years, walks beside her. I know that Mrs Watts will automatically have been sent an appointment for her son to attend for a routine toddler's appointment, but I am surprised to see her. I am even more surprised when, after her son has been seen by the doctor, as she starts to dress him, Mrs Wilberforce walks in through the doors. She does not have Arnold with her and Miss Haines exchanges glances with me as she passes through to the weighing room.

"Not pregnant is she?" she whispers as I return some completed notes.

I shrug. "Don't know."

But Mrs Wilberforce ignores all clinic staff and chats with Mrs Watts, and when all dressing is complete, leaves with her and her son. Many meaningful glances are given, but nothing is said.

CHAPTER
FORTY-THREE

Monday, 4th July

"It's here, it's here." Alan races up the stairs two at a time; he has waited in the hall for the postman to arrive for the last three days. Now the stiff white envelope with its formal heading is in his hand. I sit by the kitchen counter drinking coffee. He waves it around in the air in front of me.

"Well, open it if you are going to, I've got to go and catch a bus."

"Don't sound too excited," he says as he pushes the bread knife into its top.

The stiff sheet of paper comes out. I crunch my toast. Opening it with a still, white face, he reads and then, letting out a yell, he makes a grab for me. I swing sideways, away from him. I know the routine and this time I do not share his excitement; the ceiling can remain unblemished. So instead, he heads off to the bedroom to finish his dressing. There are phone calls to make before he can head to the factory and hand in his notice.

I had had no doubt from the beginning that all of them would be accepted for the posts, but now that it has happened and I have to make a final decision it feels very lonely, because I know what my decision will be. Marriage has not been discussed and I now know what my answer would be if it was.

The bus is less crowded than normal and I have a chance to ponder. We have been in that flat for two years, I think. And at the clinic for the same time, I remind myself. Maybe it is time for a change. You'll have to leave the flat, can't afford it on your own, my mind tells me. You didn't congratulate Alan, I tell myself, sternly. Never mind, I'm sure others will do it.

I have been to see Mrs Tate several times over the last couple of weeks and all seems to be going well. Last week Simon returned; a chap who has changed more I have never seen. He is a tall, thin two-and-a-half-year-old toddler and, as Mrs Tate had once predicted, one day he will probably be a big as his father. When the prediction had been made the possibility of it happening had seemed unlikely. But not now. Now he is blooming, sprightly and even chatty, and I am pleased to see his friend, the green rabbit, is still his constant companion. I must tell Dr West.

Today there is much activity at the Tates' house; the children are at home and, as I had walked down the road, to my displeasure I could not miss the large shiny car once again at the kerb. Uncle Charles stands in the main room handing out money to the smaller children. His perfume, redolent of expensive taste, fills the air. Mrs Tate walks around him. Somehow I have the feeling that he disturbs her; maybe she feels that he has power, power to separate her from her man and her children. Mr Tate sits alone. He has moved the small table over towards the bay window and now sits slowly counting some paper, his lips moving with every number he passes.

The stair-foot door opens and a vision appears. A year ago she had looked beautiful, but now she has matured and she has spent time with Uncle Charles. The clothes have been chosen with care, enough to emphasise her beauty but not to hide her youth. Now she knows how to use make-up, probably not to its greatest advantage, but near enough. All adult eyes are upon her, but it is her mother who crosses to her, a woman who had probably once been as beautiful.

"My darling Jenny, you will do your uncle proud."

But Jenny does not want her mother's greeting; she wants to be away from this house.

"Mother, you'll mess my hair. Uncle Charles, are you ready?"

Brushing all aside she steps towards him. Is Uncle Charles ready? He is almost drooling. Holding his long cigarette holder to one side he takes her hand, places it to his lips and murmurs, "You look divine."

Standing back to where she has been pushed, the quiescent, drugged, Mrs Tate, sees all with still eyes. I watch her and think: if only the old Mrs Tate could come back for just one moment. She would descend upon Uncle Charles, and take him to pieces. She would frighten him to death and ask her daughter what she was doing, and with boxed ears would send her to scrub her face and to look after the children.

But now, without a backward glance, Jenny leaves. For what she leaves and where she goes, who knows. The table now stands unattended and I see it is money that Mr Tate counts, a good deal of money.

"It's some of Mrs Tate's legacy; Charles found it for her."

He pulls on the perfumed cigarette, also a legacy from Uncle Charles and, seating himself behind the money, gives me a glance under his eyelids, and starts to count again.

"Will Jenny be returning?" I ask.

"Don't suppose so, left school now she has."

The perfumed smoke rises and Mrs Tate, Calverton or whoever she now is, returns, her young family following.

The cloud of smoke has gone, the crowd has dispersed, and Uncle Charles has won.

CHAPTER
FORTY-FOUR

Monday, 11th July

9.00a.m.
They will be leaving in four weeks.

"Just enough time to work my notice," Alan had said.

The three chaps and Judith are going, and on Sunday the flat had been a whirl of comings and goings as most of the university seemed to have been in, drinking beer and anything else that was brought along. It seemed that half the university's graduates were keen on emigrating.

"They are calling us the brain drain," one young man had shouted, as he knocked back his bottle of Bass beer.

I have become quite involved and the fever has started to get to me. Alan is going to write every day to let me know what is happening. I, for my part, have agreed to write to the American embassy; I have the address from Alan. I still haven't decided what I want to do, but I will at least ask about the availability of nursing posts in the city where they are to be established.

I feel quite exhausted and rather delicate as I climb off the bus on Monday morning and face the new office block. But something has happened. There is now a metal fence guarding the front entrances to the buildings, and yellow police tape, watched over by a constable, decorates each door. As I step off the bus and stand and look across, a man bumps into me.

"Move over, love," he says as he pushes past.

"What happened here?" I ask as he passes.

"Didn't you read the *Burlington Times?* Had a sit-in here on Saturday." He lifts his hand, smiles and is gone.

A copy of the *Burlington Times* covers my desk in the clinic. With astonishment, I notice that the likeness of Mrs Watts grimaces up at me, and is that Mrs Wilberforce I see behind her? Miss Haines had watched me under lowered lids as I passed her desk. Even Mrs Burns, hard at work, ignores me, and before I can look at the newspaper I hear the footfalls crossing the hall.

9.30 a.m.

I have been accused, by Miss Hampton, of inciting the women on my area to riot, and of causing Mrs Wilberforce, a respectable member of society, to become involved with riff-raff. I restrained myself from telling Miss Hampton that Mrs Wilberforce has always looked to me like a woman who only gets involved in that with which she wishes to be involved. Now, returning to my desk with a headache even more powerful than before, if that is possible, I turn my eyes to the newspaper once more.

Across the middle page it says "Women Cause Riot". It goes on to say that on Saturday morning a group of women, many with children in their arms, had forced entry into the office blocks which stand at the corner of Corporation Street. They had locked the doors from the inside, and when asked by the owners of the premises to leave, they had thrown water out of the upper windows and shouted abusive language. The police had been called and after a stand-off, lasting three hours, an entry had been forced, during which a police constable had had his hat knocked off when a forceful woman, surrounded by children, had attacked him with a metal chair.

I find it hard not to smile as I picture Mrs Watts, all four feet ten of her, swinging the chair at a six-foot constable.

"She must have been standing on a table," I tell myself.

Mrs Burns pushes a mug of tea into my hand.

"Looks like you need a drink," she murmurs as she presses her finger on the picture of Mrs Watts. "Did you know that they were going to do that?" She sits on her desk and sips her tea.

Looking down at Mrs Watts, I take the first welcome swallow.

"No, I didn't know they were going to do anything. I knew that Mrs Watts was very angry about the offices being built when her daughters couldn't get houses, and I knew that Mrs Wilberforce had been to the Housing Department with them. But who would have thought this, hey!" I lift the paper and drop it again. "If you read down the page you'll see that it is Mr Wilberforce who got them a lawyer."

338

With our heads over the paper we read on. After the incident with the constable's hat, Mrs Wilberforce and Mrs Watts had been arrested; they were accused of being the ringleaders and were charged with causing an affray. They were detained, and Mr Wilberforce, who is a lawyer and a lecturer at the university, had arranged legal representation for the two women, who will appear before magistrates today.

5.15p.m.
Leaving work later that day, at the corner of Park Lane and Sutton Street it looks like there is another riot. This time there are no police; in fact, I cannot see one man, just a large number of forceful and vocal ladies. I stand at the edge of the throng and wait for news to filter through.

Then the shout comes. "They've been let out, she's coming back!"

I have never seen Park Lane so alive. On every doorstep, women stand, hair in turbans, aprons folded over and children in arms. From the alleyways women are still emerging out on to the street, cheering and shouting. Mrs Watts' taxi passes. She sits high on her seat, her face red, and with a startled look she gazes past me, towards the waving crowd. The man beside her I assume is Mr Watts. I have never met him so I cannot be sure; however he holds her hand and I can not imagine anyone but Mr Watts being allowed, or daring, to do this. I turn away. No one needs me today, now they have a mission and a leader.

CHAPTER
FORTY-FIVE

Tuesday, 19th July

2.00p.m.

"There's a letter for you, Miss Compton." Miss Haines holds the envelope towards me, brightly decorated and perfumed, I can smell it from across the desk. "It came by hand; one of those women who once came up with that Mrs Watts brought it."

Miss Haines had not approved of Mrs Watts' behaviour, and it was a good thing that Mrs Wilberforce had no further need of our services; had she walked through the doors today she would have received an icy reception from Miss Haines.

The card within the envelope invites me to a wedding, and when I read on I realise it is a double wedding. However, it takes some time to work out to whose wedding I am being invited, because a Mrs Brown and Mr Watts invite me to the weddings of their daughters, Cecelia Jane and Elizabeth Mary. Then I realise: only the younger members of the family belong to Mr Watts, the older girls are from a previous marriage, and Mrs Brown had never married Mr Watts. After all this time calling her Mrs Watts, it turns out that's never been her official name. Still, she'll always be Mrs Watts to me — and, I suspect, to her loyal followers that celebrated her release from prison.

"Never got remarried, miss, didn't really know what happened to my first husband," she says when I ask her later that day. "I think he got killed in the war, like my Walter, but I never got a letter saying as how he was a good man or anything like I did with my boy, so he was probably drunk when a building fell on him or something like that." She looked up at the flowered picture; Wally looks back at her, and now she turns back to me, a broad half-toothed smile covering her round face. "So are you coming to the weddings then, miss? Will be quite a do because the newspaper people are coming, going to pay towards the party. Cor, we'll make the Jubilee look like nothing."

"Why the weddings all at once?" I ask.

"Oh! Haven't you heard, miss? The girls can each have a house on a new estate that they are building, but they must be married before they can have one." She throws her head back and laughs. "A sort of shotgun wedding, or as the old man says, a door-key wedding."

CHAPTER
FORTY-SIX

Saturday, 13th August

12.00p.m.
They have gone, the flat stands empty and I feel emotionally drained. Alan and his friends had left for Portsmouth from New Street Station. We had cried and kissed — well, *I* had cried — Alan had seemed a little preoccupied, I do not want to see them off on the ship; it would be exhausting and I would have to return alone, and anyway, I have the wedding to attend.

2.00p.m.
The day is fine and I stand outside the registry office, just a little confetti in hand.

"Hello, Miss Compton." A cultured voice startles me and a child takes my hand. I look down and Arnold smiles up at me.

"Look what I've got, miss." He holds a small bunch of flowers and a silver horseshoe towards me. Touching them and smiling I turn to his mother.

"Hello, Mrs Wilberforce I haven't seen you since —"

"I came out of prison." She finishes the sentence for me and we both laugh, a rather tight laugh on my part.

"Do you know, Miss Compton, I'm so proud of what I did. My husband never stops going on about it being a bad example for the children. I tell him, my grandma was a suffragette and if she were alive she would be so proud of me. If she hadn't stood up and been counted, we women would be still sitting in the kitchen, and we would have lost the war as well."

The brides come out into the sunshine, and the festivities begin. On Park Lane it looks like a Jubilee — a people's Jubilee. Half of Aston turns out to enjoy what the *Burlington Times* helps to provide.

I sit at a table well along the road, which is some distance from the bridal party.

"What a change to my first visit," I think as I look along the smiling throng and coloured bunting, "or will it all slide back to what it was, once this party is over?"

Maybe Mrs Wilberforce is right, I tell myself. If we don't make ourselves seen and stand up for what we believe, we will always stay in the kitchen . . . I glance along the road. Baby Broses smiles at me from my memory. Stay in the kitchen, or die in the slums, I finish my thought.

My shoulder bag hangs over the back of my seat and in it lies a piece of paper. The paper is headed CND and beneath it the words "Campaign for Nuclear Disarmament" tell me what the meeting will be about. Over the last few months I have read much on the dangers and expense of nuclear arms. I keep thinking how the money governments spend on these things could have bought fresh water for all the families on my patch, or new homes for those who live in houses beyond repair.

Looking towards the brides I know that I will not be missed if I slip away after the party. I have new friends to meet at the town hall. Only the other day I went to my first CND meeting and there the talk is of planning another big march next Easter. It's months away but I am keen to book my seat on the coach which will take me to Aldermaston and to the march in London.

As I scan the crowd and think of when I should slip away, all these people suddenly remind me how alone I am. I want Alan to be beside me; I want to hold his hand and have his arm around me. But by now he will be in Portsmouth and on his way to a new life. Tears well up. I look down at the table and pretend to blow my nose as I wipe my face. Then I feel eyes watching me and look across the trestle table. Sharp eyes in a thin face regard me and fair hair, newly permed, stands high on her head. She smiles at me and I realise it is Nelly; the same Nelly who had saved the day for the Watts family and turned curtains into clothes. She looks older than I remember, only the smile gives her away, but now I recall Mrs Watts had told me Nelly's husband had been killed in a factory accident. I feel ashamed for looking sad on such a day, when most people have had worse things to cope with than I. Raising my hand in greeting, I beam a smile at her.

"You all right, miss?" she calls.

I nod my yes above the noise and chatter.

She nods back then calls, "Going to get council houses, aren't they, the happy couples?" Before I can

344

reply she continues, "I certainly hope they do. And I hope they get bathrooms with them, too. Do you think they'll have hot water? I'd love to have a hot water tap and a bath. Imagine that!"

No reply is needed, other than my happy nod. Looking around at the crowd, I suddenly know that despite my momentary sadness, really I do not want to go to America. I want to stay here in England. These are my people; this is where I belong. And, maybe, just maybe, I can even do some good here.

Voices are shouting, "Shush!" and all gradually falls quiet.

Mr Watts is on his feet and though I can barely make out what he is saying, I can see Mrs Watts by his side. Beneath her wide-brimmed hat (no doubt a present from the *Burlington Times*) her face glows with pride as she watches her man.

It strikes me that good jobs and big houses, all the things that Alan is chasing, aren't essential after all. They might be desirable, but perhaps just two people, together through thick and thin, is enough. Is that what love is? As I try and work it out, the clinking of glass sounds and a little bottle of Babycham is passed to me.

"To the brides and grooms, may their new starts be good ones!" a voice calls out.

"To the brides and grooms!" we all echo as we wave our drinks and take a swig. As the bubbles tickle my nose, I laugh and raise my bottle to Nelly.